Today's knitter and crocheter is faced with a huge assortment of yarns—more than 2,000 varieties are currently on the market. This can be both a boon and a burden—a boon because the profusion of textures and styles opens up new vistas of creativity for the handicrafter and home knitter, a burden because no one person can keep track of the characteristics of the many yarns.

The Universal Yarn Finder™ makes all this information instantly available in an easy-to-use format. Yarns are divided into five classes, A to E, and are listed alphabetically by brand and yarn name. For each yarn, an at-a-glance chart conveys type, suggested needle and hook size, suggested gauge and tension, fiber content, weight, approximate yardage, care and cleaning tips, approximate number of skeins for an average garment for a man, woman, or child, and the manufacturer's suggested retail price.

You will be able to substitute yarns when those recommended for a pattern are not available as well as alter patterns creatively—to spice up a simple sweater or make a unique piece of wearable art. Universal Yarn Finder™ is an indispensable resource for every knitter or crocheter.

Maggie Righetti is a well-known designer, instructor, and writer for hand knitters.

Universal
Yarn Finder™

Universal Yarn Finder™

Maggie Righetti

PRENTICE HALL PRESS

New York   London   Toronto   Sydney   Tokyo

Published by Prentice Hall Press
A Division of Simon & Schuster, Inc.
Gulf+Western Building
One Gulf+Western Plaza
New York, NY 10023

PRENTICE HALL PRESS is a trademark of Simon & Schuster, Inc.

Library of Congress Cataloging-in-Publication Data

Righetti, Maggie.
  Universal yarn finder.

  1. Yarn—Tables.   2. Knitting.   3. Crocheting.
I. Title.
TT820.R56   1987   746.43'028   86-43108
ISBN   0-13-940065-6

Manufactured in the United States of America
10 9 8 7 6 5 4

Acknowledgments

The author wishes to acknowledge the help and assistance given her in compiling this volume. Betty Moore, her trusted secretary and treasured friend, helped with contacting yarn companies and gathering the information. Betty and Debbie Allen, another dear friend, worked long hard hours to correlate the data. Arthur Lulay of the textile division of DuPont made helpful additions and corrections to the glossary. Without their assistance this book would not have been possible.

Contents

Introduction

Knitting is a fine and ancient craft as old as history itself. Our early forebears discovered that fibers of animal fur twisted together could be looped over long slender animal bones to make a soft and pliable fabric that protected bodies and warded off the cold. Crocheting is not as old as knitting, but it too is a fine art-craft of thread and hook. Somewhere along the way, between then and now, people lost their understanding of knitting and crocheting and became afraid of these arts. That is where this book comes in. By giving back to knitters and crocheters the understanding of what they are doing and why, great new areas of creativity are being opened to handcrafters.

And that is what the *Universal Yarn Finder* is all about—the freedom to create and innovate—to "knit up a storm," or "weave a web," or "conjure up crochet" of different yarns and threads to make unique pieces of wearable art and articles of great beauty that are statements of individuality. I hope this book will open up new horizons of creativity and pride of workmanship.

Universal
Yarn Finder™

1 HOW TO USE THIS BOOK

No one can keep track of the characteristics of the thousands of yarns available in the marketplace today, or remember how much is needed for specific projects, what each yarn is made of, and how to care for it. The *Universal Yarn Finder* contains all of this information in easy-to-use charts in a convenient format. Under each separate class division, yarns are listed alphabetically, first by brand name, and then by yarn name. Across the page following the name of each individual yarn you will find columns containing the following information:

Type. A verbal description of the yarn to help you visualize its usage. If you need a smooth yarn, you'll know not to order one that is termed "fuzzy."

U.S. Needle and Hook Size. If you are working with British or metric-size needles you will find a conversion chart on page 177 to enable you to adjust to the correct size. Needle sizes are only *suggested* as a starting point for you to use to determine your gauge. No one cares what size needle you use—everyone cares what gauge you get. Use whatever size needle will give you the correct gauge for the directions you are following.

Gauge/Tension. The suggested number of stitches in one inch of worked fabric. This is not a hard and fast rule, but rather a guide. The manufacturer is saying, "You'll be happy with the fabric worked at this gauge, and your garment will hold its shape." But that doesn't mean that it cannot be worked at a different gauge. Most class C smooth classic worsted, good old standard 4-ply yarns, can be very successfully worked at either 4½ or 5 stitches to the inch. However, getting the gauge specified in the instructions is all-important. Knitting, crochet, and tatting patterns are made by multiplying the number of stitches in the gauge by the number of inches of desired finished width. If you do not get the correct gauge, you cannot get the desired size.

Fiber Content. The amounts of different fibers that compose the yarn are given in percentages. It is a handy column. If, for example, you have your heart set on making a pure cashmere lace shawl for a special person, you can run your fingers down this column, page after page, until you find a manufacturer that makes a 100 percent cashmere yarn. Then you can ask your favorite yarn supplier to

order it for you. Or, when you see a pretty sweater in a needlework magazine, you can look up the content of the recommended yarn to see if it is made of something you enjoy working with, or if it contains elements to which you are allergic.

Cleaning Care. Washability is a determining factor for many of us in the selection of a yarn because of convenience and time. This is particularly true of working women and mothers with small children. By looking at the chart, you can know before you buy.

Specialty products are available for use in washing textiles, and many companies specify a particular kind of cleaner such as Ivory®, Cot'nWash®, Sheep Shampoo®, or Woolite®. It is wise to follow the manufacturers' suggestions; they know what is the best care for their products.

Incidentally, the term "superwash" applies to sheep's wool that has been specially treated to be machine washable. Note that silk yarns usually call for dry cleaning, not because the silk fiber cannot tolerate water, but because the dyes used to color the fiber are not colorfast in water.

Skein, Hank, Ball, or Cone Weight. This is the quantity of yarn that the manufacturer packages into readily usable amounts. In the trade it is called a "put-up." By and large, the greater the amount, the less the yarn will cost per ounce or gram. Weavers and machine knitters often prefer to use coned yarns. Hand workers do not like the added problem of toting big heavy cones around.

Approximate Yardage. Yarn is almost always sold by weight; rarely by length or yardage. Unfortunately, no one uses yarn by weight, but rather by length as it runs through our fingers and looms. Two ounces of yarn can contain as little as 25 yards or as much as 250 yards, and the differences can be critical. Two skeins of the same type of yarn from different manufacturers may look exactly alike, but one may contain quite a bit more yardage than the other. If you were to try to substitute one for the other, skein for skein, you might run into the problem of not having sufficient yardage to finish your project.

Remember, "approximate" is not exact. Many factors can influence the amount of yardage in a skein. The dyes and bleaching agents that the manufacturer uses to produce the wonderful range of colors available will affect the weight of yarns. By and large, light colors will have more yards per skein, and dark colors will have fewer yards per skein because the dye will add weight to the yarn. If, for instance,

you are making an afghan of four tones of one color, you would be wise to purchase extra yarn of the darkest color so that you don't run out.

Approximate Retail Price. Before you fall head over heels in love with that marvelous color, you can tell how much a project will cost by multiplying cost per skein by the number of skeins needed. You'll know in an instant if a project will cost $4.95 or $49.50. Also, when you find things on sale, you'll know how much you are saving.

Approximate Number of Skeins for a Small-size Standard Knit Pullover Sweater with Long Sleeves and Crew Neck for a Man, Woman, Child, or Infant. This section is a life saver. From it you can estimate how much yarn will be needed for a project (*see* Guesstimating, p. 9). Crocheters will always need to purchase one-third more yarn than knitters, because crocheted stitches eat up more thread than knitted stitches. The charts in this section allow you to purchase the right amount of yarn *before* you select the pattern. Also, you can tell at a glance if there is enough yarn of one dye lot to make an article.

The information contained in the charts that begin on page 14 is as complete as I could make it. Not all yarn companies allowed information about their yarns to be published, and only the information supplied to us could be printed. Sometimes yarn manufacturers were unable to tell us vital facts about their products; therefore, some columns are left blank.

Substituting Yarn

If you have a pattern that you adore, but you do not choose to use the specified yarn, you can easily substitute a yarn that you prefer. All you need is a friendly pocket calculator and a few moments time.

1. From the instructions, read how many skeins (balls or hanks) are necessary to make the article.
2. Find the specified yarn on the chart. Read how many yards there are in each skein.
3. Multiply the number of skeins by the number of yards per skein to determine the total number of yards necessary to make the article.
4. Find the preferred yarn on the chart. Read how many yards there are in each skein. Divide this number into the total number of yards necessary.
5. Round the new figure off to the next whole number. This is the number of skeins of the preferred yarn that you will need to purchase.

For example, you might have a pattern for a gorgeous cardigan that calls for Heavenly, a wool and rabbit hair blend yarn. Unfortunately, you are allergic to both wool and rabbit hair. You'd love to make the sweater if you could find a similar-looking man-made fiber. And you do: It is called Fleece-Fuzz, but how do you know how much to purchase? The Heavenly pattern calls for 9 skeins in your size. The chart says that each skein of Heavenly contains approximately 210 yards.

$$9 \times 210 = 1890 \text{ total yards}$$

The chart says that there are 260 yards in each skein of Fleece-Fuzz.

$$1890 \div 260 = 7.269$$

Round the 7.269 off to the next whole number and you get 8. It will take only 8 skeins of Fleece-Fuzz to make the sweater. You can have your gorgeous sweater and wear it without itching and scratching.

Never be afraid to buy too much yarn. Most good yarn suppliers will accept returns of unopened skeins within a short period of time if the yarn was not on sale and you have kept the receipt.

There are myriad ways to use leftover yarn to good advantage. Why do you think our grandmothers invented the "Granny Square" afghan? Or the Norse and Fair Islanders their gorgeous patterns? To use up leftover yarn of course! My favorite way is to make a multicolored striped sweater in one piece from the neck down, changing colors whenever the fancy strikes me or when I use up the leftovers.

2 YARN: CARE AND CLASSIFICATION

Dividing Yarn into Classes

Yarns can be as fine as spider webs or as thick as the heavy cables that hold boats to docks. Technically either extreme—or anything in between—could be used for knitting, crocheting, weaving, tatting, and crafts. In reality both gossamer fine yarn and huge ropes can be difficult for handworkers to work with, and ordinarily we work with threads that are more of an ordinary size. It is those in-between sizes that this book is concerned with. There are thousands of yarns made by hundreds of spinners; so many, in fact, that a sizing system had to be devised to differentiate them. A class system was the result.

All commercially spun yarns have been arbitrarily divided into five basic classes, A, B, C, D, and E, according to usage and stitch gauge. Because the

divisions are arbitrary, not all yarns fit tidily into a class; some straddle the lines between classes and are therefore listed under two classes. Nonetheless, it is a handy system that enables us to understand what yarns can best be used for which purposes.

The following definitions and usages are those that are generally accepted for the classes of yarn.

Class A. Crochet thread, tatting thread, fingering, and lightweight yarns worked on small needles or tiny hooks to make baby clothes, socks, gloves, scarves, lace shawls, doilies, antimacassars, curtains, blouses, summer sweaters, and lightweight sweaters. Machine knitters, crocheters, and tatters use lots of class A threads. Weavers use them for warp. Usually they are worked at about 7 or more stitches per inch.

Class B. Sport and medium-weight yarns and threads worked on medium-size needles and hooks to make sweaters, dresses, skirts, suits, blouses, scarves, shawls, hats, mittens, baby clothes, leg warmers, and vests. Machine knitters, weavers, and crocheters use class B threads. Usually these yarns are worked at about 5 or 6 stitches per inch.

Class C. Heavy-weight yarns worked on large-size hooks and needles to make sweaters, mittens, vests, leg warmers, jackets, scarves, afghans, golf club covers, and other novelty items. They are also used doubled or combined to make coats, parkas, and handbags. The good old standby, standard 4-ply knitting worsted, falls in this class. Machine knitters require a bulky machine to work with class C. Usually these yarns are worked at about 4½ or 5 stitches per inch.

Class D. Very heavy, bulky, fleecy, or nubby yarns worked on huge needles or hooks to make coats, jackets, parkas, blankets, rugs, handbags, and specialty items such as craft projects, and doll's hair. Usually these yarns are worked at less than 4 stitches per inch.

Class E. Super-bulky and specialty yarns used to make rugs, craft items, coats, and jackets. Usually these yarns are worked at less than 3 stitches per inch.

One yarn can often be substituted for another if they are both in the same class and result in the same stitch gauge. Substituting a yarn from one class for one of a different class while trying to maintain the same stitch gauge can result in fabrics that are too firm or too flimsy.

Understanding Yarn Labels

Manufacturers often put a wealth of information on yarn labels. And since so much commerce is international today, they often do it with stylized symbols which require no language so that they can be understood in any country. It is to your advantage to be able to understand these markings. If any of the symbols on the label have a diagonal slash (/) through them or an X across them, it means *don't*—you may be courting disaster if you do.

A wash basin is a wash basin in any language. Oftentimes the basin will be empty, but sometimes there will be a hand in the water. Sometimes there will be a number which refers to the water temperature in Celsius degrees. It means that the completed item will be hand washable at that termperature. (See water temperature conversion chart on page 178.)

The squarish box is really intended to be a picture of a washing machine. Sometimes it too will have a number on it which refers to the water temperature in Celsius degrees. It means that the completed item will be machine washable.

A circle inscribed in a square refers to an automatic clothes dryer. These are available almost everywhere these days, and it may be a temptation to quickly fling the article in a dryer instead of laying it out flat on towels to dry. But if there is an X across the symbol, *don't do it!*

The drawing represents an iron, and indicates that the garment can be ironed, though why anyone would want to iron a sweater, I don't know. An X through the drawing indicates that the garment can't be ironed.

This iron with big black dots on the side of it is supposed to represent a steam iron. It tells you whether or not the article can be blocked with steam. Some synthetics will expand wildly if steam is applied. Mohair yarns will felt if they get near steam. Be sure to check for this symbol before you attempt to steam block any garment.

An isosceles triangle with or without the letters "cl" in it is the international symbol for chlorine bleach. (Why anyone would even think of putting chlorine bleach on a fine wool sweater, I do not know.) If there is an X across it, don't do it.

A hollow circle refers to dry cleaning. A letter A, F, or P describes the type of dry cleaning fluid that can be used. Your dry cleaner will understand which types are indicated.

7

This picture is supposed to represent the carriage of a knitting machine. It means that the yarn is recommended for machine knitting. There may also be a number on or underneath the symbol. This refers to the recommended tension setting. Obviously if it is a European yarn, the setting will be for European machines. If the yarn comes from the Orient, it will be for Japanese machines.

The following symbols are all worked into the symbol for the gauge swatch, though at other times they are separated.

American knitters and crocheters should be aware that Europeans prefer a much firmer and tighter knitted fabric than we do. By and large, they also make their individual stitches smaller. Therefore, the recommended gauge for European knitters and crocheters may not be either obtainable by or desirable for American handcrafters, and the needles recommended may seem too small to us. For instance, with class B yarn, a gauge of 6½ stitches per inch (26 m = 10 cm) on a 3¼ mm needle, recommended on a European yarn label, may not only be difficult to achieve but result in an undesirably firm fabric. Please don't hesitate to try the yarn at a larger gauge, say 6 or even 5½ stitches per inch. You may be very pleased with it worked at a looser gauge.

Metric
3½ — 4

Crossed knitting needles indicate the suggested size knitting needle to get the recommended gauge. However, this symbol doesn't tell you whether metric, United States, or British sizes are being recommended. If the yarn is European, metric is probably meant. If the yarn comes from England, Ireland, Australia, Canada, or New Zealand, it usually means British. There is a conversion chart on page 177 to allow interchanging.

A crochet hook indicates the suggested size crochet hook to get the recommended gauge. As with knitting needles, its not always clear what sizing system is being talked about. There is a conversion chart on page 000 to indicate how to change.

A square is a gauge swatch. The "10 × 10" at the top refers to centimeters; that is, 10 centimeters wide by 10 centimeters long. For Americans it will sometimes say 4 inches, which is almost the same size as 10 centimeters. Occasionally the gauge will be given in a smaller dimension, such as 1 or 2 inches. Sometimes there will be a left-facing arrow followed by a number. This is the recommended number of stitches in 10 centimeters or 4 inches. An arrow that points up is the number of rows in 10 centimeters or 4 inches. More often there will be a number followed by the letter m which means stitches. For example, 22 m means 22 stitches in 10 centimeters, or 4 inches of width.

Sometimes the international symbols for fibers are shown.

Wool

SUPERWASH

SuperWash Wool. Wool that is machine washable and dryable.

Cotton

The information on yarn labels allows us to be forewarned and forearmed as we go about indulging in creativity and exploration of the possibilities of mixing color and texture. I'm glad that the manufacturers give such information to us and that it is so easy to understand.

Guesstimating: An Inexact Science

I rarely ever follow a printed pattern in knitting and crocheting. I'm always changing, innovating, and creating, and because it has never been done before, I never know exactly how much yarn it will take to make a project. To give the experimenter some starting point, the last four columns on the right hand side of each chart indicates the amount of yarn needed for a standard long-sleeved crew-necked knitted pullover sweater for a man, woman, child, and infant.

For example, because I am a large woman I start with the amount necessary for a man's sweater in determining how much I need for myself. From there I assume that if I choose to make a cardigan instead of a pullover, it will take more yarn for the overlap at the front. If I add a turtleneck it will take a little more yarn. If I add a cowl

neck it will take a lot more yarn. Short sleeves will use less yarn. No sleeves will use considerably less yarn, about a third less than for long sleeves.

When making a multicolored sweater, I close my eyes and try to visualize the finished garment. I try to see what fractions are different from the main color—a little or a lot, or half-and-half. Then I go about my guesstimating from there.

Sometimes I think that knitting machines eat yarn. It always takes more yarn to knit the same sweater on a machine than by hand. This is because the yarn must be threaded through the carriage to begin with, and because it is almost impossible to add new yarn in the middle of a row. However, when you stop to consider the amount of time saved the wastage of yarn is negligible; machine knitters should just purchase an extra ball to start with.

An article made in single crochet stitch always uses approximately one-third more yarn than a similar item that is knitted. Beyond that, the rules for guesstimating get fuzzy. When you get into fancy crocheted pattern stitches such as 6 stitch shells or filet with picture patterns, or open work like lovers knots, you are on your own, or dependent on the recommendations of individual instructions which may or may not be correct.

Of course it *is* possible for both knitters and crocheters to make a 4-inch square swatch and then rip it out to determine how many yards per square inch are used. This is easy, but the next step, trying to figure out how many square inches there are in a multi-piece project, is very complex. I prefer to guesstimate.

Weavers are in better shape for guesstimating than crocheters are, because the process features formulas to help them figure out square inches of fabric from yards of yarn.

Always guesstimate on the long side. Never cut corners and tell yourself, "Oh, I won't need *that* much!" You may, and there may be no more left when you need it if you don't plan in advance. Here is where a good relationship with your local friendly yarn supplier comes in. The retailer may be willing to hold yarn for you for a short period of time, or may be perfectly agreeable to exchanging unopened skeins for credit within a reasonable period of time if you have kept your receipt. I always buy what I think I will need *plus* an extra skein.

The closets of handworkers all over the world are full of projects that couldn't be completed because there wasn't enough yarn to finish them. My closet is full enough already.

Dye Lots: Paying the Piper

The spectrum of color that is available to us today from spinners and dyers is truly wondrous and spectacular. Can you imagine having to go back to the limited colors that were available only a century ago? Or to the scant number of hues that were available to pioneers—walnut husk brown, onion skin yellow, and tea stain ecru? I, for one, am glad that we can have regal purples, brilliant reds, and stunning blues, clear yellows and bright biting greens, at inexpensive prices. But alas, as with everything in life we must pay the piper. The piper demands that we purchase, all at one time, sufficient yarn of the same dye lot or batch number to make the entire project.

Dyeing is an art, not a perfect science that gives identical results time after time. There are so many variables of time and temperature in the dye bath—humidity and pressure, porousness and consistency of the fiber—that it is almost impossible to guarantee that today's batch of yarn will be absolutely the same as last month's. For this reason, manufacturers label each batch of yarn with a number called "dye lot number" or "batch number" to let us know that all the yarn in a group was dyed at the same time and so that we won't accidentally confuse one batch with another. The price we will pay for not paying the piper can be unintended stripes and color change.

It is possible to have identical dye lots, called "ever match," but it makes the dyeing process and hence the cost of the yarn more expensive. Few of us who use yarns in any quantity are willing to pay the added price.

The responsibility for purchasing sufficient yarn of the same dye lot is yours. After all, the project is yours. Always check the labels yourself even if someone else says, "I'm sure they are all the same." Then the pride and pleasure will be yours when you complete a perfectly colored article.

3 YARN CHARTS

In the following pages you will find the yarn charts that make up the main body of this book. The charts begin with class A, lightweight fingering yarns, and continues through class B, medium-weight sport yarns; class C, heavy-weight yarns; class D, bulky yarns; and class E, superheavy specialty yarns. Under each class, yarns are listed alphabetically by brand name, followed by the names of the yarns of that brand.

The name of the country in which each yarn is sold is found in the second column. Across the page, columns list for each yarn: the suggested U.S. needle size, the suggested gauge or tension per inch, the fiber content of the yarn, cleaning care, skein or other package weight, the yardage approximate to the skein, and the approximate retail price. The last three columns are "guesstimate" columns: the approximate number of skeins needed for making a small-size, standard knit pullover sweater with long sleeves and a crew neck for a man, a woman, a child, or an infant.

International standard country codes are used to indicate the countries in which each yarn is sold. The countries and codes included in the charts are as follows:

AU   Australia
CA   Canada
DE   Federal Republic of Germany (west Germany)
dis.   discontinued
DK   Denmark
ES   Spain
FR   France
GB   United Kingdom (Great Britain)
HK   Hong Kong
IT   Italy
JP   Japan
MX   Mexico
NL   Netherlands
NO   Norway
SW   Sweden
USA   United States

Fingering Weight Yarns

CLASS A

Brand and Yarn Name	Where Sold	Type	US Needle Size	Gauge/Tension per Inch	Fiber Content	Cleaning Care	Skein, Hank, Ball, or Cone Weight	Approx. Yardage	Approx. Price	Approx. No. of Skeins for a Small-size Standard Knit Pullover Sweater with Long Sleeves and Crew Neck			
										Man	Woman	Child	Infant
Aarlan Arwetta	USA	smooth	2-4	8-7	75% wool 25% nylon	hand wash	50 gm	210	3.40	8-10	5-7	5-6	4-5
Baby Subera	USA	classic	2-3	7	100% wool	hand wash	50 gm	230	5.00	8-10	4-6	3-5	2-4
Braumwolle Cotton 8/4	dis.	mercerized	3-4	7	100% mercerized cotton	warm water wash	50 gm	185	2.80	—	5-6	—	—
Etoile	USA	classic	2-4	8	55% viscose 30% polyester 15% polyamide	hand wash	20 gm	120	5.50	—	12-14	8-10	6-8
Andean Yarns Alpaquita	USA CA	3-ply natural	4	7	100% alpaca	hand wash	50 gm	200	4.50	8	7	6	4
Alpaquita	USA CA	3-ply dyed	4	7	100% alpaca	hand wash	50 gm	200	5.00	8	7	6	4
Anny Blatt Alpag	USA CA AU GB	natural brushed	3-5	6	100% alpaca	hand wash dry clean	50 gm	215	10.50	9	7	4	2
Alpag	USA CA AU GB	natural dyed & brushed	3-5	6	100% alpaca	hand wash dry clean	50 gm	215	11.00	9	7	4	2
Baby	USA CA AU GB	smooth fingering	3-4	6	100% wool	superwash	50 gm	195	5.75	9	7	4	2
Gyps	USA CA AU GB	soft Lurex	0-1	9	65% viscose 35% polyester	hand wash dry clean	20 gm	150	6.95	—	10	—	—
Gyps "Cocktail"	USA CA AU GB	soft Lurex	0-1	9	65% viscose 35% polyester	hand wash dry clean	20 gm	150	7.25	—	10	—	—
Lady	dis.	dress crepe	3	7	100% wool	hand wash dry clean	50 gm	315	5.95	9	7	4	2

A

	Country	Type	Needle	7	Fiber	Care	Unit	Yardage	Price	9	7	4	2
No. 3	USA CA AU GB	smooth fingering	0-1	7	100% wool	superwash	50 gm	195	5.60	9	7	4	2
Argyll Ltd. Cotton	CA USA	smooth approx. 4-ply	knitting machine	—	100% cotton	hand wash	340 gm cone / 12 oz	1,753 m / 1,849 y	22.75 (CA $)	—	—	—	—
Ferndale	CA USA	smooth approx. 4-ply	knitting machine	—	85% Courtelle 15% wool	hand wash	340 gm cone / 12 oz	1,707 m / 1,849 y	19.50 (CA $)	—	—	—	—
Laser	CA USA	smooth 4-ply	knitting machine	—	100% high bulk acrylic	machine wash	340 gm cone / 12 oz	1,707 m / 1,849 y	16.50 (CA $)	—	—	—	—
Starlite	CA USA	sparkle approx. 4-ply	knitting machine	—	80% Courtelle 20% nylon	machine wash	340 gm cone / 12 oz	1,707 m / 1,849 y	21.00 (CA $)	—	—	—	—
Tica	CA USA	poodle type	knitting machine	—	90% acrylic 10% polyester	machine wash	340 gm cone / 12 oz	1,818 m / 1,969 y	20.00 (CA $)	—	—	—	—
Ziggy	CA USA	sparkle	knitting machine	—	80% acrylic 20% nylon	machine wash	340 gm cone / 12 oz	1,776 m / 1,925 y	22.00 (CA $)	—	—	—	—
Astra Yarns 3/2 Astra Mercerized Cotton	USA	mercerized	—	—	100% cotton	gentle wash block dry	1¼ lb.	1,260	26.00 c	1	¾	½	½
5/2 Astra Mercerized Cotton	USA	mercerized	—	—	100% cotton	gentle wash block dry	¾ lb.	2,100	18.00 c	1½	1¼	1	1
10/2 Astra Mercerized Cotton	USA	mercerized	—	—	100% cotton	gentle wash block dry	¾ lb.	4,200	18.00 c	1½	1¼	1	1
20/2 Astra Mercerized Cotton	USA	mercerized	—	—	100% cotton	gentle wash block dry	¼ lb.	8,400	26.00 c	1	¾	½	½
6½/3 Astra Ray	USA	—	—	—	100% rayon	gentle wash block dry	1¼ lb.	1,820	16.50 lb.	1	¾	½	½
2/20 Classic Worsted wool	USA	worsted	—	—	100% wool	gentle wash block dry	1¼ lb.	5,600	22.00 lb.	1	¾	½	½
8/2 Fast Cotton	USA	karded	—	—	100% cotton	gentle wash block dry	1¼ lb.	3,360	10.00 lb.	1	¾	½	½
4/8 Orspun	USA	worsted	—	—	100% acrylic	gentle wash block dry	2½ lb.	950	12.00 lb.	½	¼-½	¼	¼
Au Ver a Soie Noppee	—	satin luster single ply	4	7	100% silk	dry clean	100 gm	400	—	—	4	—	—
Perlee	—	smooth lustrous	2	9	100% silk	dry clean	100 gm	800	—	—	2½	—	—
Aurora Wellscroft Nub	USA	single ply rich tweed with nubs	3-4	7	100% wool	hand wash	100 gm	380	6.00	3-4	3	2	1
Balger® Balger	—	metallic 1-ply	knitting machine	—	polyester viscose	hand wash dry clean	500 m reels	550	—	run-along	—	—	—
Balger	—	metallic 8-ply	knitting machine	—	polyester viscose	hand wash dry clean	250 gm	2,300	—	run-along	—	—	—

Brand and Yarn Name	Where Sold	Type	US Needle Size	Gauge/Tension per Inch	Fiber Content	Cleaning Care	Skein, Hank, Ball, or Cone Weight	Approx. Yardage	Approx. Price	Approx. No. of Skeins for a Small-size Standard Knit Pullover Sweater with Long Sleeves and Crew Neck			
										Man	Woman	Child	Infant
Bartlettyarns Fisherman	USA	softspun, (1-ply singles)	2C	7	100% wool	hand wash dry clean	1 lb.	1,800	15.50	1 lb.	1 lb.	½ lb.	½ lb.
Glen Tweed	USA	softspun (1-ply singles)	2C	7	100% wool	hand wash dry clean	1 lb.	1,800	15.50	1 lb.	1 lb.	½ lb.	½ lb.
Berger du Nord Moon Light	USA	—	3	7¾	55% viscose 15% polyester 30% metal	—	20 gm	120	6.50	run-along			
Transpararence	USA	—	6	7¼	100% viscose	—	50 gm	160	6.95	run-along			
Bernat Berella Sock and Fingering	USA	smooth classic worsted	3	8	60% blended acrylic 40% nylon	machine wash	40 gm	205	1.99	9	7	4	3
Berroco Aurora	USA	metallic/slub run along	3	7	20% metallic 46% acetate 34% rayon	—	40 gm 1 lb tube 2 lb cone	155 1,755 3,510	5.12	NR	—	—	NR
Bouquet Lollipop	USA CA	baby	3-4	7	100% acrylic	machine wash & dry	50 gm	300	2.05	—	—	4	2
Piccadilly	USA CA	shrink treated	3-4	7	80% wool 20% nylon	machine wash & dry	50 gm	275	2.65	8	6	4	—
Sparkletwist	USA CA	rayon wrap	3-4	7	80% acrylic 20% rayon	machine wash & dry	50 gm	245	2.25	—	—	5	2
Brentwood Yarns America	USA	multi/bump	3	7/1	acrylic & rayon	hand wash	skein/cone	160/1,600	4.50/43.00	12	10	7	4
Brenetta	USA	dress	3	7/1	wool & rayon	hand wash	skein/cone	300/2,400	4.00/30.00	8	6	5	3
Floss	USA	shiny/fill	2	8/1	rayon	hand wash	tube/cone	300/2,400	3.50/27.00	8	6	5	3
Germaine	USA	bumpy/fill	2	8/1	rayon	hand wash	tube/cone	220/2,200	3.20/30.00	12	10	7	5
Monti Carlo	USA	twist/cotton	3	7/1	cotton	hand wash	tube/cone	160/1,600	3.60/34.00	12	10	7	5
Moondust	USA	dress/metal	3	7/1	wool & metal	hand wash	skein/cone	220/2,200	5.00/48.00	12	10	7	5
Rayco	USA	shiny/cotton	3	7/1	cotton & rayon	hand wash	skein/cone	206/1,600	5.60/34.00	12	10	7	5
Brunswick Baby Sparkeltwist	USA CA AU	metallic	3	7	80% acrylic 20% rayon	machine wash & dry	1 oz.	175	—	13	10	5	3
Bambini	USA CA AU	smooth	3	7	100% Civona acrylic	machine wash & dry	40 gm	200	—	10	8	4	3
Delf Baby	USA CA AU	smooth	3	7	100% acrylic	machine wash & dry	1 oz.	175	—	13	10	5	3

Yarn	Source	Texture	Gauge	Needle	Fiber Content	Care	Weight	Yds	Price				
Fairhaven	USA CA AU	smooth	3	7	100% wool	dry clean only	1 oz.	175	—	13	10	5	NR
Nylamb	USA CA AU	smooth	3	7	80% wool 20% nylon	dry clean only	40 gm	200	—	10	8	4	NR
Picnic	USA CA AU	smooth	4	7	100% mercerized cotton	hand wash, machine wash	50 gm	225	—	8	6	3	2
Windspun	USA CA AU	smooth	3	7	100% acrylic	machine wash & dry	1 oz.	175	—	13	10	5	3
Bucilla Lollipop	USA	space dyed	3	8	100% DuPont Orlon	machine wash & dry	1 oz.	175	1.60	12	8	5	3
Winfant	USA	baby & fingering	3	8	100% DuPont Orlon	machine wash & dry	1 oz.	175	1.50	12	8	5	3
Wondersheer	USA	mercerized cotton	6	5 (double strand)	100% cotton	machine wash & dry	400 yds.	400	3.15	6	4	3	2
Caron Cuddlesoft	USA	cuddly worsted solid baby soft	4	7	100% DuPont Orlon	machine wash & dry	2 oz.	360	1.39	8	6	4	2
Petite Dazzleaire	USA	brushed fuzzy	5	6	60% acrylic 40% nylon	machine wash & dry	1.5 oz.	168	1.18	15	11	6	4
Chanteleine Chausette	dis.	smooth worsted	3–4	7	70% wool 30% nylon	hand wash machine wash	50 gm	175	2.95	8	6	3	1–2
Glenan (same as Chausette)	USA	classic sock yarn	2–3	6–7	70% wool 30% nylon	machine wash	50 gm	175	3.60	8	6	3	1–2
Layette	USA	classic soft baby yarn	2–4	6½–7½	52% lambswool 48% Dralon	machine wash	50 gm	275	4.75	5–6	4–5	2–3	1–2
Siamoise	dis.	fuzzy, brushed Angora	3–5	6–7	50% Angora 30% lambswool 20% nylon	hand wash dry clean	20 gm	110	6.50	NR	10	6	2
Shetfine	dis.	Shetland slightly fuzzy	4–5	6–7	100% wool Woolmark	hand wash	50 gm	220	3.25	8	6	3	1
Zephyr	USA	very soft brushed	3–4	6–7	70% acrylic 30% wool	hand wash	50 gm	370	3.40	6	5	3	1
Chat Botte Angora Bouclé	USA CA AU	bouclé	4	4½	40% Angora 35% rayon 15% nylon	hand wash dry clean	10 gm	52	6.00	NR	30	NR	NR
Atours	USA CA AU	metallic thread	—	—	100% metallic	hand wash dry clean	10 gm	770	4.00	—	—	—	—

Brand and Yarn Name	Where Sold	Type	US Needle Size	Gauge/Tension per Inch	Fiber Content	Cleaning Care	Skein, Hank, Ball, or Cone Weight	Approx. Yardage	Approx. Price	Approx. No. of Skeins for a Small-size Standard Knit Pullover Sweater with Long Sleeves and Crew Neck			
										Man	Woman	Child	Infant
Chamaree	USA CA AU	metallic	1	8	92% rayon 8% polyester	hand wash dry clean	30 gm	109	5.50	NR	12	NR	NR
Chat D'Acier	USA CA AU	smooth	3	7	51% nylon 49% wool	hand wash hand stain removal	50 gm	219	4.00	9	8	6	5
Loto	USA CA AU	smooth	2	9	100% cotton	machine wash colorfast	50 gm	180	5.00	12	10	6	4
Milady	USA CA AU	smooth	3	7	55% wool 45% acrylic	hand wash dry clean	50 gm	187	3.80	11	9	7	5
Nenuphar	USA CA AU	classic	3	6½	100% wool	hand wash dry clean	50 gm	205	4.50	10	9	6	4
Porto Fino	USA CA AU	smooth	0–1	9	100% cotton	hand wash dry clean	50 gm	383	4.50	10	7	4	3
Relax	USA CA AU	fleecy/fluffy	4	7½	60% mohair 40% acrylic	hand wash dry clean	50 gm	300	9.60	12	8	5	NR
Shetland	USA CA AU	classic	3	6½	100% wool	hand wash dry clean	50 gm	191	5.00	13	10	6	4
Super Baby	USA CA AU	smooth	1	7½	100% wool	machine wash	50 gm	225	5.80	13	10	5	4
Sylphide	USA CA AU	smooth	1	7½	100% acrylic	machine wash	50 gm	265	3.90	12	10	7	5
China Silk Co., Inc. Han (Also sold as Ping Ling Silks, Han 6-ply, distributed by Kreinik Mfg. Co.)	USA CA AU GB	continuous filament tram	2 (double strand)	7	100% silk	dry clean	125 gm 1 lb.	1,000 3,600	45.00	5	4	2	1
Heron	USA CA AU GB	cultivated mulberry smooth	3	6	100% silk	dry clean	100 gm 1 lb.	445 2,000	21.20	6	5	3	2
Ibis	USA CA AU GB	Schappe spun silk blend	3	6.5	50% silk 50% wool	dry clean	100 gm 1 lb.	445 2,000	14.40	6	5	3	2

Yarn	Country	Type	Needle	Gauge	Fiber	Care	Weight	Yardage	Price				
Ming	USA CA AU GB	continuous filament Douppioni/shantung	4	7	100% silk	dry clean	120 gm / 1 lb.	480 / 1,800	30.00	2	3	5	6
Pagoda #1	USA CA AU GB	spun cord pearlized	2 (double strand)	7	100% silk	dry clean	100 gm / 1 lb.	835 / 3,720	19.20	1	2	4	5
Classic Elite Yarns, Inc. — Dazzle	USA	novelty metallic	used as runner	—	45% rayon 35% polyester 20% Lurex	dry clean	40 gm	265	7.50	run-along			
Creative — Cinderella	USA	novelty velveen	—	—	70% wool 30% rayon	dry clean	1½ lb.	2,400	22.00	—	—	—	—
Confetti	USA	smooth speckled	—	—	100% acrylic	machine wash	1 lb.	6,000	10.20	—	—	—	—
Crystal Palace Yarns — Allegro	USA	bouclé	3–4	6½–7	100% silk	hand wash / dry clean	50 gm	200	6.90	NR	NR	5	6
Sparkle Plenty	USA	metallic to knit in combination	—	—	acetate Lurex	hand wash	2 oz.	1,200	10.40	1	1	1	1
Xian	USA	lustrous classic	4–6	6–6½	100% combed silk	hand wash / dry clean	50 gm	135	10.20	NR	NR	6–7	NR
DMC — Brilliant Crochet/ Knitting Cotton	USA	smooth twisted	2	7	100% cotton	hand wash, warm water, mild soap	50 gm	218	1.99	—	—	—	—
Cebelia Cotton Size 10	USA	smooth twisted	3	8	100% cotton	hand wash, warm water, mild soap	50 gm	282	3.25	—	—	7	—
Ecossia Size 5	USA	smooth twisted	3	6.5	100% cotton	hand wash, warm water, mild soap	50 gm	184	3.75	—	—	7	—
Splendida Size 4	USA	high sheen lustrous soft twist	2	8	100% cotton	hand wash, warm water, mild soap	50 gm	223	4.15	—	—	—	—
Drop Spindle — Home Dyed	USA	tussah silk-2-ply	6–7	6	100% silk	hand wash / dry clean	8 oz.	125	—	—	—	1	—
Home Dyed	dis.	5/2 cotton	7 (2 strands)	5–6	100% cotton	hand wash	1 lb.	1,950	—	—	—	1 skein	—
Erdal Yarns — Glitter	USA	2-ply	2	9	70% rayon 30% Lurex	—	2 oz. / 1 lb.	334 / 3,040	4.30 / 30.00	run-along			
Glowette	USA	4-ply	4	8	70% rayon 30% Lurex	—	2 oz. / 1 lb.	250 / 2,000	4.00 / 27.50	run-along			

A

Brand and Yarn Name	Where Sold	Type	US Needle Size	Gauge/Tension per Inch	Fiber Content	Cleaning Care	Skein, Hank, Ball, or Cone Weight	Approx. Yardage	Approx. Price	Approx. No. of Skeins for a Small-size Standard Knit Pullover Sweater with Long Sleeves and Crew Neck			
										Man	Woman	Child	Infant
Esslinger Angora Princess	USA	fluffy 2-ply	5	6	20% lambswool 80% Angora	hand wash, cold dry flat	20 gm	104	9.98 white 13.28 colors	—	11	8	—
Baby Cornelia	USA	baby	4	6	100% acrylic	machine wash	50 gm	213	2.65	—	—	3-4 layette	—
Cornelia Pompadour	USA	baby	4	6	86% acrylic 14% viscose	machine wash	50 gm	213	2.75	—	—	3-4 layette	—
Saphir	USA	dressy 2-ply	3	7	40% silk 30% super kid mohair 30% acrylic	hand wash, cold	20 gm	68	5.95	—	13	10	—
Flere Trader, USA Flere Trader (single strand)	USA	basic	knitting machine	7-10	100% acrylic	hand wash machine wash	1 lb.	5,200	—	—	—	—	—
Froehlich Wolle Camel	USA	smooth	4-5	7	70% wool 30% camel hair	hand wash, warm	50 gm	220	5.00	—	—	—	—
Sonnenwolle	USA	smooth	4	7	60% wool 20% silk 20% ramie	hand wash, warm	50 gm	220	5.00	—	—	—	—
Grandor Fine Knop	USA	textured	3	7	100% cotton	hand wash	1 oz.	140	1.75	—	—	—	—
Heavy slub	USA	thick & thin	3	7	100% cotton	hand wash	1 oz.	100	1.50	—	—	—	—
Mercerized 10/4	USA	smooth	3	7	100% cotton	hand wash	½ lb.	900	10.90	—	—	—	—
Grignasco Gricable	USA	cable twist	3	7	65% acrylic 35% wool	warm wash	50 gm	246	2.49	7	5	3	2
Grijohnny	USA	classic	3	7.5	50% wool 50% acrylic	warm wash	50 gm	274	2.35	6	5	3	2
Griparty	USA	metallic twist	3	7.5	60% Cupro 40% —	warm wash	20 gm	153	3.50	11	7	5	4
Halcyon Yarn 5/2 Pearl Cotton	—	smooth mercerized	2-3	7-8	100% cotton	cool wash strong contrast prewash yarn dry clean	2.4 oz. cone 12 oz.	300 yd approx. 1,500	—	2,100 yd.	1,500 yd.	1,150 yd.	750 yd.
Newport Linen	—	16/2 linen dry spunline	2-3	7-8	100% linen	wash	approx. 2 oz. cone approx. 1 lb.	300 yd 2,400 yd	—	2,000 yd.	1,500 yd.	1,150 yd.	750 yd.
Harrisville Designs Shetland Style	USA	Shetland weight solid heather	4	6½	100% virgin wool	hand wash dry clean	100 gm 8 oz.	440 1,000	5.00 8.40	5-6	4	2-3	1-2

A

Name	Origin	Description			Fiber	Care	Weight	Yardage	Price				
Hayfield of England Pretty Pastels 3-ply	USA CA GB	3-ply baby	3	7½	50% acrylic 50% bri-nylon	machine wash	40 gm	222	2.25	—	—	—	2
Pretty Whites 3-ply	USA CA GB	3-ply baby	3	7½	50% acrylic 50% bri-nylon	machine wash	40 gm	222	2.25	—	—	—	2
Heirloom Carasoft	USA CA	super soft	5	6	100% Creslan acrylic	machine wash & dry	1 lb.	2,750	8.95	—	—	—	—
Carmel	USA CA	tone on tone dress	6 hand knit 8–10 machine knit	5 hand knit 7¼ machine knit	65% rayon 35% pure virgin wool	hand wash dry clean	1 lb.	1,200	22.95	—	—	—	—
Erin	USA CA	solids & heathers	5	7	80% Orlon 20% virgin wool	machine wash & dry	1 lb.	3,200	10.95	—	—	—	—
Hyannis	USA CA	smooth dress	3 hand knit 5–7 machine knit	6 hand knit 8½ machine knit	70% pure virgin wool 30% rayon	hand wash dry clean	1 lb.	2,500	21.95	—	—	—	—
Nicole	USA CA	solids & heathers	9 machine knit	0/4	65% Orlon 35% wool	machine wash & dry	1 lb.	5,300	12.50	—	—	—	—
Parade	USA CA	smooth	9–10 9–12 machine knit	1/3	100% Orlon	machine wash & dry	1 lb.	5,700	8.95	—	—	—	—
Savannah	USA CA	smooth dress	6 hand knit 8–10 machine knit	6 hand knit 6¾ machine knit	82% Orlon 18% nylon	machine wash dry clean	1 lb.	1,300	16.95	—	—	—	—
Hovland Annie	NO	smooth	5	5	10% mohair 10% wool 13% polyamide 67% acrylic	hand wash dry flat	50 gm	164	2.45	—	8	—	—
Annie with Lurex	NO	smooth	5	5	67% acrylic 13% polyamide 10% mohair 10% wool	hand wash dry flat	50 gm	164	3.00	—	8	—	—
Cascade	—	fluffy light twist	10–11	3½	78% wool 22% viscose	hand wash dry flat	50 gm	108	3.70	—	—	—	—
Conny	NL	variegated mixture of colors & types of yarn	10–11	3½	15% mohair 32% cotton 53% acrylic	hand wash flat dry	50 gm	47	3.60	—	10	—	—
Etnic	DE	nubby	4	5½	100% cotton	hand wash dry flat	50 gm	135	2.80	—	9	5	—
Modern	DE	nubby	4	5½	46% cotton 54% viscose	hand wash dry flat	50 gm	146	3.20	—	9	5	—

Brand and Yarn Name	Where Sold	Type	US Needle Size	Gauge/Tension per Inch	Fiber Content	Cleaning Care	Skein, Hank, Ball, or Cone Weight	Approx. Yardage	Approx. Price	Approx. No. of Skeins for a Small-size Standard Knit Pullover Sweater with Long Sleeves and Crew Neck			
										Man	Woman	Child	Infant
Rose	NO	fluffy	10–11	3½	10% mohair 10% wool 13% polyamide 67% acrylic	hand wash dry flat	50 gm	102	3.25	11	9	7	—
Soft	NL	slightly fluffy	8	4½	100% cotton	hand wash dry flat	100 gm	222	6.30	7	6	3	—
Jack Frost Fashion Pompadour	—	—	3	7	85% DuPont Wintuk Orlon 15% rayon	machine wash & dry	1½ oz.	—	—	—	—	—	—
Omni	—	smooth baby fingering & sport purpose yarn (3-ply)	3 5	7 6	100% DuPont Wintuk Orlon	machine wash & dry	2 oz.	—	—	—	—	—	—
Omni-Multi	—	smooth	3 5	7 6	100% DuPont Wintuk Orlon	machine wash & dry	1½ oz.	—	—	—	—	—	2
Jaeger Jaeger Alpaca	dis.	classic	3	7	100% alpaca	hand wash dry flat	50 gm	198	—	8	6	4	2
Jagger Spun Highland Heather 2/20	USA	classic worsted heather	machine tension 5–6	8–9 (double strand)	100% wool	hand wash dry clean	1 lb. cone	5,600	14.75	14 oz.	11 oz.	5 oz.	3 oz.
Highland Heather 2/8	USA	classic worsted heather	machine tension 5–6 1–3	7–8 (machine) 6–7	100% wool	hand wash dry clean	1 lb. cone 4 oz. skein	2,240 580	14.75 4.95	15 oz. 4	12 oz. 3	6 oz. 2	4 oz. 1
Maine Line 2/20	USA	smooth classic worsted	machine tension 5–6	8–9 (double strand)	100% wool	hand wash dry clean	1 lb. cone	5,600	14.25	14 oz.	11 oz.	5 oz.	3 oz.
Maine Line 2/8	USA	smooth classic worsted	machine tension 8 1–3	7–8 (machine) 6–7	100% wool	hand wash dry clean	1 lb. cone 4 oz. skein	2,240 580	14.25 4.75	15 oz. 4	12 oz. 3	6 oz. 2	4 oz. 1
Superfine Merino	USA	supersoft smooth classic worsted	machine tension 5–7 (double strand)	8 (double strand)	100% wool	hand wash dry clean	1 lb. cone ½ lb. cone 2 oz. skein	5,040 2,520 630	23.50 13.75 4.50	15 oz. 8	12 oz. 6	6 oz. 3	4 oz. 2
Zephyr Wool-Silk	USA	soft smooth classic worsted	machine tension 5–6 (double strand)	7.5–8.5 (double strand)	50% merino wool 50% tussah silk	dry clean	1 lb. cone ½ lb. cone 2 oz. skein	5,040 2,520 630	32.50 18.25 5.60	15 oz. 8	12 oz. 6	6 oz. 3	4 oz. 2
Joseph Galler, Inc Alouette	USA	bright pastels baby yarn	4–5	7	100% Courtelle acrylic	machine wash	1 oz.	145	1.30	12	10	6	3–4
Baby Lang Cotton	USA	soft baby cotton	5–6	—	100% combed cotton	machine wash	50 gm	212	4.00	10	8	4	2–3

A

Name	Origin	Type	Needle	Needle	Fiber	Care	Put-up	Yards	Price				
Baby Lang Wool	USA	soft baby wool	5-6	6½	100% superwash wool	machine wash	50 gm	223	4.80	8	8	4	2-3
Cashmere Swiss	USA	classic soft	5-6	7-6½	40% cashmere 30% lambswool 30% wool	hand wash	20 gm	110	5.20	12-13	6	8	4
Cinderella	USA	soft brushed	5-6	7-6½	80% acrylic 20% mohair	hand wash, machine wash	1 oz.	100	1.40	12-14	10-12	8	4
La-Se-Ta	USA SW	high luster silk	5-6	7	100% silk	hand wash, dry clean	50 gm	158	14.00	10	10	—	—
Lino-Fino	USA SW	thick & thin	5-6	7½-7	62% cotton 38% linen	hand wash, machine wash	50 gm	170	4.70	8	7	6	3
Marisa	USA SW	smooth high sheen	5-6	7½	100% Egyptian cotton	hand wash, machine wash	50 gm	230	4.80	12	8	8	4
Parisian Cotton	USA	sunfast cotton	5-6	7½-7	100% mercerized cotton	hand wash, machine wash	1 oz.	105	1.90	14	10	10	5
Soiree	USA	glitter	5-6	6½	94% acrylic 6% metallic	hand wash, machine wash	40 gm	220	2.40	—	12	—	—
Swiss Linen	USA	classic cool	5-6	6½	100% linen	hand wash, machine wash	50 gm	198	4.80	14	12	—	—
Knitting Fever Versatile	USA	—	2	8½	100% wool		50 gm	360	6.00	—	6	—	—
Lanas Margarita Astrakan	dis.	bouclé	3-4	7	56% acrylic 37% wool 7% nylon	hand wash	50 gm	222	4.50	—	—	—	—
Mohair X	USA	specialty	—	—	100% mohair	hand wash	25 gm	218	4.60	—	—	—	—
Perle Dos	USA	acrylic	2	7	100% acrylic	machine wash	50 gm	254	3.40	—	—	—	—
Yucatan	USA	novelty	5	6	100% nylon	hand wash	50 gm	164	4.70	—	—	—	—
Lane Borgosesia Boy	USA	basic	3	7	100% wool superwash	machine wash	50 gm	267	4.30	—	—	—	2
Lily Art. 950 Sugar 'n Cream Baby & Fashion	USA CA	3 ply classic	3	7	100% cotton	hand wash, machine wash	1.25 oz.	150	1.55	15	12	7	5
Lion Brand Aree	USA	fine bouclé with a sheen	—	—	96% acrylic 4% polyimide	machine wash & dry	1.4 oz. 40 gm	177	—	—	—	—	—
Finelon	USA	3-ply soft baby	3	6½	100% DuPont Wintuk Orlon	machine wash & dry	1 oz.	160	—	—	—	—	—
Jasmine	USA	2-ply	3, C hook	5 dc, 7	100% acrylic	machine wash & dry	1.4 oz. 40 gm	245	—	—	—	—	—

Brand and Yarn Name	Where Sold	Type	US Needle Size	Gauge/Tension per Inch	Fiber Content	Cleaning Care	Skein, Hank, Ball, or Cone Weight	Approx. Yardage	Approx. Price	Approx. No. of Skeins for a Small-size Standard Knit Pullover Sweater with Long Sleeves and Crew Neck			
										Man	Woman	Child	Infant
Lisle Playgirl	USA	basic	3	8	60% rayon 40% cotton	handwash cold water	4, 8 & 16 oz. skeins 5 lb. cones in natural only	1,200 lb.	12.50 hand dyed 5.00 natural 18.00 lb. cones in natural only	4	4	2-3	2
Lynn Ellen Yarns 5/2 Pearl Cotton	USA	mercerized	—	—	100% cotton	gentle wash block dry	4 oz.	525	5.50	4-5	3-4	2-3	2
Macauslan Shetland	USA GB	basic	4-5	7	100% Shetland wool	wool wash dry clean	1 oz.– 1 lb. 2½–3 lbs	145 2,300	2.50-3.25	12	10	7	3-4
Mary Lou Duette 2/24 (double strand)	USA	novelty machine	—	—	100% Turbo acrylic	machine wash	1 lb.	4,500	8.80	1	1	½	—
Kiss 2/24	USA	stretch machine	—	—	60% acrylic 40% spandex	machine wash	1 lb.	—	8.00		run-along		
Lyric 2/24 (double strand)	USA	novelty machine	—	—	100% Turbo acrylic	machine wash	1½ lb.	6,700	13.20	1	1	½	—
Melody 3/15	USA	novelty machine	—	—	100% DuPont acrylic	machine wash	1.1 lb.	2,800	12.00	1	1	½	—
Wool-Eze 2/11	USA	novelty machine	—	—	70% wool 30% acrylic	machine wash	1 lb.	—	10.80	1	1	½	—
Mayflower Mayflower Cotton 8	USA GB CA	basic flat	3	7	100% cotton	machine wash hot iron do not bleach	50 gm	187	2.00	13	10	4	2
Melrose Babs	USA	novelty	3	7½	54% cotton 46% rayon	—	40 gm	150	3.75	—	—	—	—
Bouclette	USA	—	2-3	7½	65% wool 25% rayon 10% nylon	hand wash dry clean	2 oz.	300	5.00	—	—	—	—
Cottonella	USA	—	2-3	8	35% cotton 65% rayon	—	2 oz.	350	4.65	—	—	—	—
Cravalaine	USA	—	2-3	7.5	64% wool 28% rayon 8% Lurex	—	2 oz.	300	7.25	—	—	—	—
Cravalaine Print	USA	—	2-3	7.5	—	—	2 oz.	300	8.00	—	—	—	—
Cravenella	USA	—	2-3	7.5	70% wool 30% rayon	hand wash dry clean	2 oz.	300	5.00	—	—	—	—
Cravenella Print	USA	—	2-3	7.5	70% wool 30% rayon	hand wash dry clean	2 oz.	300	5.65	—	—	—	—

A

Name	Origin	Texture	Needle	Needle	Fiber	Care	Unit	Yards	Price					
Craynella	USA	—	6 (2 strands)	6.5	55% wool 45% rayon	—	2 oz	150	5.99	—	—	—	—	—
Darella (metallic)	USA	—	2–3	8	40% lamé 60% rayon	—	25 gm	200	7.20	—	—	—	—	—
Fashionella	USA	—	9–10½	9	55% wool 45% rayon	—	2 oz.	200	5.75	—	—	—	—	—
Frill	USA	—	5	5½	100% rayon	—	1.5 oz.	100	4.80	—	—	—	—	—
Lacella	USA	bouclé novelty	3	7	100% rayon	—	2–2½ lb.	2,100 lb.	32.00	—	—	—	—	—
Lurex	USA	metallic	—	—	50% Lurex 50% nylon	—	20 gm	200	6.50	—	—	—	—	—
Match Mate	USA	—	—	—	100% rayon	—	50 gm	300	5.00	—	—	—	—	—
Metallic Match Mate	USA	—	—	—	27% metallic 61% acetate 12% nylon	—	30 gm	200	5.00	—	—	—	—	—
Painted Prints	USA	—	2–3	7.5	70% wool 30% rayon	—	2 oz.	300	5.99	—	—	—	—	—
Thinette	USA	—	—	—	100% rayon	—	1 oz.	150	5.00	—	—	—	—	—
Merino Madiera "10"	USA	metallic	—	—	55% metalized polyester 45% nylon	—	—	22	2.25	—	—	run-along	—	—
Zig	USA	matte-shiny thick-thin	3	7	75% rayon 25% cotton	—	50 gm	145	5.50	—	—	—	—	—
Millor Andino	USA	smooth	—	7	75% acrylic 25% nylon	machine wash & dry	9 oz.	1,154	—	3	2	—	—	—
Carioca	USA	bouclé	—	7	40% cotton 47% acrylic 13% nylon	machine wash & dry	9 oz.	1,504	—	3	2	—	—	—
Gloria	USA	crepe	—	7–8	60% acrylic 40% nylon	machine wash & dry	9 oz.	1,415	—	3	1¼	—	—	—
Infanta 2/25	USA	smooth	—	9	90% acrylic 10% nylon	machine wash & dry	9 oz.	2,546	—	—	1	—	—	—
Metalico	USA	metallic wrapped	—	7	55% acrylic 35% nylon 10% polyester	machine wash & dry	9 oz.	1,080	—	—	2	—	—	—
Naturel	USA	thick & thin	—	7	85% cotton 15% nylon	machine wash & dry	9 oz.	1,189	—	2	2	—	—	—
Tepeyac	USA	bouclé	—	7–8	65% acrylic 35% rayon	machine wash & dry	9 oz.	1,221	—	—	2–3	—	—	—
Trenzado	USA	smooth cabled	—	7	90% acrylic 10% nylon	machine wash & dry	9 oz.	1,251	—	3	2	1	1	1

Brand and Yarn Name	Where Sold	Type	US Needle Size	Gauge/Tension per Inch	Fiber Content	Cleaning Care	Skein, Hank, Ball, or Cone Weight	Approx. Yardage	Approx. Price	Approx. No. of Skeins for a Small-size Standard Knit Pullover Sweater with Long Sleeves and Crew Neck			
										Man	Woman	Child	Infant
Vellon	USA	mohair-like	—	7	100% acrylic	machine wash & dry	9 oz.	—	—	—	—	—	—
Natura Baby & Sport	USA	smooth classic worsted	3	7	100% Wintuck acrylic	machine wash & dry	2 oz.	—	—	—	—	—	—
Baby & Sport Pompador	USA	Pompador	3	7	84% Wintuck 16% rayon	machine wash & dry	50 gm	—	—	—	—	—	—
Nature Spun Yarns Nature Spun 3/15	USA	worsted	3	7	100% wool	hand wash dry clean	1 lb.	2,800	18.95	—	—	—	—
Nomis Angel's Hair Thread	USA	smooth thread	run-along for shimmer	—	60% polyester 40% nylon	machine wash & dry	900 yd. or 450 yd. spool	450-900	450-5.50 900-9.00	1	1	1	1
Excellence Baby	USA	smooth	3	7	100% DuPont acrylic	machine wash & dry	1 oz.	200	—	13	10	5	3
Heel & Toe Yarn	USA	smooth thread	use with yarn to reinforce socks	—	100% nylon	machine wash & dry	—	200	3.00	run-along			
Magic Yarn	USA	clear elastic thread	use with yarn to eliminate stretching	—	100% spandex	machine wash & dry	spool	330	—	—	—	—	—
Nomis Cotton	USA	perled	3	7	100% mercerized cotton	machine wash & dry on low (delicate) settings	¾ lb. cone	1,575	—	2	1	partial	partial
Together Thread	USA	smooth thread		run-along	55% polyester 45% nylon	machine wash & dry	—	450-900	450-5.50 900-9.00	1	1	1	1
Patons Baby Yarn	USA CA	smooth classic	3	8	100% acrylic	machine wash & dry	50 gm	305	—	8	6	4	2
Crystal Baby Yarn	USA CA	smooth Pompadour	3	8	77% acrylic 23% viscose	machine wash & dry	50 gm	305	—	8	6	4	2
Pernelle Baby	USA	smooth	3-4	8	100% acrylic	machine wash	50 gm	265	3.50	—	5-6	—	—
Fil D'Ecosse	USA	mercerized	2-3	7½	100% cotton	hand wash dry clean	50 gm	175	4.50	—	8-9	—	—
Footing	USA	smooth	2-3	7	73% wool 27% polyamide	hand wash dry clean	50 gm	200	3.50	—	6-7	—	—
Phentex Galleria Fingering	USA CA	2-ply	1	8st:11 R =1po.	100% acrylic	machine wash cold machine dry gentle	50 gm	315	1.39	—	—	—	—

A

				8st-11R =1po.							
Machine Knit Fingering	USA CA	2-ply	1		100% acrylic	machine wash cold machine dry gentle	1 lb.	2,860	10.95	—	—
Phildar Anouchka	USA	mohair blend soft	4	7	80% acrylic 15% mohair 5% wool	hand wash machine wash	50 gm	257	3.25	6	—
Loisirs	USA	perle	3	7.5	85% acrylic 15% wool	hand wash machine wash	50 gm	255	2.75	6	—
Look Phil	USA	ribbon	—	—	100% viscose	hand wash	25 gm spool	68	4.00	—	—
Luxe	USA	classic	3	7.5	85% acrylic 15% wool	hand wash machine wash	50 gm	268	2.45	6	—
Menottes	USA	fancy	4	7	58% acrylic 28% viscose 14% wool	hand wash machine wash	50 gm	174	3.10	—	2
Midship	dis.	linen blend	3	7.5	73% acrylic 17% cotton 10% linen	machine wash	50 gm	219	2.95	9	—
Option Soleil	dis.	cotton/ acrylic	3	7.5	50% acrylic 50% cotton	hand wash	100 gm	292	3.75	5	—
Perle 5	USA	crochet cotton	3	7	100% cotton	hand wash	40 gm	152	2.95	12	—
Perle 8	USA	crochet cotton	2	7	100% cotton	hand wash	40 gm	283	3.10	9	—
Relais 5	USA	crochet cotton	3	7	100% cotton	hand wash	50 gm	174	3.20	9	—
Shindig	USA	fancy	3	7.5	77% acrylic 14% wool 9% polyester	hand wash	50 gm	267	4.95	7	—
Sunset	USA	fancy	3	7.5	65% acetate 35% polyester	hand wash	20 gm	163	3.95	10	—
Ping Ling Ping-Ling 112 colors	USA CA	smooth lustrous filament silk	1	10	100% silk	dry clean	100 gm	700 yd.	—	2½	—
Pingouin Alpaga et Laine	dis.	—	3	27/4	52% alpaca 48% wool	—	50 gm	165	—	—	—
Baby Pingouin	dis.	3-ply	3	30/4	75% acrylic 25% wool	machine wash dry clean	50 gm	245	2.45	—	—
Barcarolle	dis.	4-ply shiny	3	29/4	100% polyamide	hand wash dry clean	50 gm	195	4.75	12*	—
Concerto	dis.	2-ply with metallic strand	2	32/4	82.5% acrylic 12.5% polyester	machine wash dry clean	50 gm	340	3.95	6*	—
Comfortable Fin	USA FR	heather 2-ply	3	27/4	55% acrylic 45% wool	machine wash dry clean	50 gm	200	2.45	7*	—

Brand and Yarn Name	Where Sold	Type	US Needle Size	Gauge/Tension per Inch	Fiber Content	Cleaning Care	Skein, Hank, Ball, or Cone Weight	Approx. Yardage	Approx. Price	Approx. No. of Skeins for a Small-size Standard Knit Pullover Sweater with Long Sleeves and Crew Neck			
										Man	Woman	Child	Infant
Corrida 4	USA FR	smooth 4-ply	3	28/4	60% cotton 40% acrylic	machine wash dry clean	50 gm	120	—	—	6*	—	—
Corrida 3	USA FR	smooth 4-ply	3	28/4	60% cotton 40% acrylic	machine wash dry clean	50 gm	230	2.95	—	6*	—	—
Cotton Naturel	dis.	smooth 4-ply	3	30/4	100% cotton	machine wash dry clean	50 gm	220	—	—	7*	—	—
Cotton Naturel #5	dis.	2-ply beaded	2	30/4	100% cotton	dry clean	100 gm	440	3.95	—	—	—	—
Coton Perle #5	USA FR	2-ply	2	33/4	100% cotton	machine wash dry clean	50 gm	220	3.75	—	10*	—	—
Fil d'Ecosse #12	dis.	—	—	—	100% cotton	—	50 gm	525	—	—	—	—	—
Fil d'Ecosse #5	USA FR	—	2	33/4	100% cotton	—	50 gm	175	—	—	—	—	—
Fil d'Ecosse Fin	dis.	—	1	39/4	100% cotton	—	50 gm	310	—	—	—	—	—
Laine et Nylon	dis.	smooth 4-ply	3	30/4	73% wool 27% polyamide	machine wash dry clean	50 gm	200	—	—	8*	—	—
Mohair 50	USA FR	fuzzy	4	22/4	50% mohair 50% acrylic	hand wash dry clean	50 gm	170	—	—	7*	—	—
Mohair 70	USA FR	fuzzy	4	22/4	70% mohair 30% acrylic	hand wash dry clean	50 gm	170	5.95	—	7*	—	—
Oued	USA FR	fuzzy mohair	3	27/4	80% acrylic 10% wool 10% mohair	hand wash dry clean	50 gm	240	2.95	—	5*	—	—
Perle Fin	dis.	beaded 2-ply	3	30/4	100% acrylic	machine wash dry clean	50 gm	300	—	—	7*	—	—
Pescadou	dis.	curly 2-ply	3	28/4	60% acrylic 40% polyamide	machine wash dry clean	50 gm	165	—	—	8*	—	—
Pingofine	USA FR	beaded 3-ply	3	30/4	75% acrylic 25% wool	machine wash dry clean	50 gm	220	1.99	—	7*	—	—
Pingolaine	USA FR	smooth 4-ply	3	30/4	100% wool	machine wash dry clean	50 gm	220	2.95	—	8*	—	—
Pingoperle	dis.	2-ply, beaded surface	3	28/4	75% acrylic 25% wool	machine wash dry clean	50 gm	265	1.99	—	7*	—	—
Pingorex Baby	USA FR	3-ply	3	30/4	100% acrylic	machine wash dry clean	50 gm	265	2.45	—	6*	—	—

A

Place Vendome	USA FR	metallic	2	34/4	60% viscose	hand wash dry clean	20 gm	175	3.95	—	—	11*	—	—
Rainbow Mills Paint Box	USA	hand-dyed	1	7	60% cotton 40% rayon	hand wash dry clean	100 gm	275	9.75—variegated 9.00—solids	—	5	4	2-3	1-2
Red Heart® Red Heart Baby Yarn	USA	3-ply smooth	3	7½	100% Wintuk Orlon acrylic	machine wash & dry	2 oz.	300	1.29	—	—	—	—	2
Red Heart Pompadour Yarn	USA	3-ply smooth Pompadour	3	7½	84% Wintuk Orlon acrylic 16% rayon	machine wash & dry	2 oz.	250	1.35	—	—	—	—	3
Red Heart Sock & Sweater Yarn	USA	3-ply smooth	3	7½	100% Wintuk Orlon acrylic	machine wash & dry	2 oz.	300	1.29	—	—	—	—	2
Red Heart Sofspun Baby Yarn	USA	3-ply smooth	3	7½	100% Orlon acrylic	machine wash & dry	3 oz.	450	1.65	—	—	—	—	2
Red Heart Sofspun Pompadour Yarn	USA	smooth Pompadour	3	7	84% Orlon acrylic 16% Olefin	machine wash & dry	3 oz.	410	1.49	—	—	—	—	2
Reynolds Baby Reyelle	USA	baby	3	8	100% Orlon	wash	1 oz.	180	—	—	—	—	—	—
Parfait Plus	USA	—	4 single 8 double	3½–5½ 4½–6	75% acrylic 25% nylon	wash	30 gm	130	—	—	—	7 single** 13 double**	—	—
Richard Poppleton Guernsey 5-ply	USA CA GB AU	fisherman	½–2	7	100% wool	hand wash	100 gm	245	4.95	—	10	9	7	—
Santa Fe Yarn Cashmere/Silk	USA	fingering	4	7	70% cashmere 30% silk	dry clean	20 gm	111	11.00	—	15	13	—	2
Schaffhauser Cashmere Bijou	USA	classic	3-4	7	50% cashmere 50% lambswool	hand wash	20 gm	109	6.75	—	—	12	—	—
Jeunesse	USA	smooth	3-4	7	100% acrylic	machine wash	—	1,433	14.90	—	—	—	—	—
Lambswool	USA	classic	3-4	7	100% lambswool	hand wash	50 gm	273	4.95	—	—	6	—	—
Mon Amour	USA	classic baby wool	3-4	7	100% virgin wool	machine wash	50 gm	246	5.75	—	—	6	—	2
Noella	USA	multicolored and solid classic sock yarn	3-4	7	75% wool 25% polyamide	machine wash	50 gm	204	4.30	—	—	—	—	—
Perfina	USA	multicolored and solid classic sock yarn	3-4	7	75% wool 25% polyamide	machine wash	—	1,225	19.50	—	—	—	—	—

*Size 14
**Short sleeved

Brand and Yarn Name	Where Sold	Type	US Needle Size	Gauge/Tension per Inch	Fiber Content	Cleaning Care	Skein, Hank, Ball, or Cone Weight	Approx. Yardage	Approx. Price	Approx. No. of Skeins for a Small-size Standard Knit Pullover Sweater with Long Sleeves and Crew Neck			
										Man	Woman	Child	Infant
Revue	USA	metallic	2-3	7	58% acrylic 42% metallic	machine wash	—	182	4.95	—	8	—	—
Soiree	USA	variegated and solid colored classic	3-4	7	70% wool 30% silk	hand wash	50 gm	263	5.60	—	6	—	—
Scheepjeswol Invicta Extra	USA CA GB	flat sock yarn	3	7	75% new wool 25% nylon	machine wash, 40°C shrink resistant cool iron do not bleach	50 gm	230	3.00	14	9	—	—
Superwash Extra	USA GB HK	classic flat	3	7	100% new wool	machine wash & dry, 30°C do not bleach do not iron	50 gm	160	3.50	—	9	—	—
Vril	USA CA GB	fashionable summer	2	11¼	50% cotton 40% viscose 10% nylon	machine wash, 40°C do not bleach do not iron	50 gm	187	5.00	15	11	—	—
Vril Fine	USA CA GB	fashionable summer	4	7½	39% cotton 35% polyester 26% linen	machine wash 40°C do not bleach do not iron	50 gm	121	5.00	14	12	—	—
Schoeller Illustra	USA	metallic run-along	4	7	68% viscose 32% metalized fibers	machine wash	20 gm	87	5.89	—	15	—	—
Scotts Woolen Mill Afrique	USA	slubbed	2-4	6-8	100% cotton	solids, hand wash cold mixed colors, dry clean	2 oz. skein ½ or 1 lb. cone	260 2,100 lb.	2.35 17.00	8	6	4	2
Serenity	USA	bouclé	2-4	6-8	74% cotton 26% nylon	hand wash cool	2 oz. skein ½ or 1 lb. cone	335 2,700 lb.	3.40 25.00	8	6	4	2
6/2 Cotton	USA	2-ply classic	2-4	6-8	100% cotton	solids, hand or machine wash cold water mixed colors, dry clean	2 oz. skein ½ or 1 lb. cone	315 2,520 lb.	2.10 14.60	8	6	4	2
10/2 Rayon	USA	smooth (complements Milan)	(use 3 strands to obtain sportweight)		100% spun rayon	dry clean only	2 oz. skein 1 or ½ lb cone	525 4,200 lb.	2.25 16.00	6	4	2	1
Serendipity Skeins Bouquet	USA	airy, fine, soft 3-ply hand-dyed	3-4	7-7½	100% wool	hand wash dry clean	4 oz.	840	—	2	2	1	1

Yarn	Origin	Texture	Needle	Needle	Fiber	Care	Put-up	Yards	Price				
Shasha Yarn Baby Yarn	USA	smooth	5	5½	acrylic	wash	50 gm	183	2.00	—	8–10	—	—
4-ply	USA	smooth	2–3	7	wool	dry clean	50 gm	218	2.00	—	6–8	—	—
Flamme Rustique	USA	knubby	2–5	5½	cotton	wash	50 gm	160	3.40	—	5–6	—	—
Mohair	USA	smooth	5–6	6½	mohair wool acrylic	dry clean	50 gm	220	3.60	—	—	—	—
Mirage	USA	smooth	6	5	wool acrylic	dry clean	50 gm	137	2.60	—	5–6	—	—
Sirdar 4-Ply	USA	—	3	7½	45% acrylic 15% wool 40% bri-nylon	—	50 gm	260	3.60	—	—	—	—
4-Ply	USA	wash and wear	3	7½	55% bri-nylon 45% acrylic	—	40 gm	210	3.50	—	—	—	—
Snuggly 2-ply	USA	baby	3	8	55% bri-nylon 45% acrylic	—	40 gm	387	2.00	—	—	—	—
Snuggly 3-ply	USA	baby	3	8	55% bri-nylon 45% acrylic	—	40 gm	264	2.00	—	—	—	—
Snuggly 4-ply	USA	baby	3	7½	55% bri-nylon 45% acrylic	—	40 gm	198	2.00	—	—	—	—
Soie et Soie Silk Lace	USA JP	lustrous lacy smooth dressy	4	8½–9	100% filament silk	dry clean	plastic bubble hank 25 gm	200 m	—	—	—	—	—
Solberg Yarns Fiol	USA	classic mercerized	2–6	6	100% cotton	machine wash	50 gm	185	3.49	—	12	7	4
Stardust Stardust Lame	—	2-ply	—	—	—	wash dry clean	tube	75	2.40	—	trim	—	—
Stardust Lame	—	3-ply	—	—	—	wash dry clean	tube	75	2.70	—	trim	—	—
Sunbeam 2-ply Pure New Wool	CA	—	2	9	100% wool	machine wash	25 gm	169 m	2.75 (CA $)	—	6	—	—
Susan Bates Softura Baby Yarn	dis.	basic	3	7½	100% Orlon	machine wash & dry	50 gm	260	—	8	6	4	2
Softura Pompadour	dis.	Pompadour	3	7½	84% Orlon 16% rayon	machine wash & dry	50 gm	230	—	8	6	4	2
Tamm Yarns Estilo Tamm	USA CA AU MX	2-ply thin	—	14/2 3-4	60% acrylic 40% poly-nylon	machine wash dry flat	454 gm	3,670	16.60	—	1 cone	—	—
Tandorri 1-ply Tussah	USA	smooth natural soft luster spun wild silk	3	8	100% silk	hand wash dry clean	1 lb.	2,100	—	1	1	—	—

Brand and Yarn Name	Where Sold	Type	US Needle Size	Gauge/Tension per Inch	Fiber Content	Cleaning Care	Skein, Hank, Ball, or Cone Weight	Approx. Yardage	Approx. Price	Approx. No. of Skeins for a Small-size Standard Knit Pullover Sweater with Long Sleeves and Crew Neck			
										Man	Woman	Child	Infant
Raw Silk	USA	dull twisted homespun sunscoured single 1-ply silk	3	8	100% silk	hand wash dry clean	1 lb.	5,000	—	1	1	—	—
Unger Yarn Allure	USA CA	—	3	7	79% wool 21% rayon	hand wash dry clean	1.75 oz.	250	4.50	—	6	—	—
Precious	USA CA	—	4	7	50% camel hair 50% lambs-wool	hand wash dry clean	1.6 oz	220	10.40	—	7	—	—
Welcomme Alpaga	USA	smooth	3-4	7½	100% alpaga	hand wash dry clean	50 gm	200	8.00	—	6-7	—	—
Esquisse	USA	smooth	3-4	8	65% viscose 35% polyester	hand wash dry clean	20 gm	155	5.75	—	11-12	—	—
Escarboucles	dis.	smooth	2-3	7½	87.5% acrylic 12.5% polyester	hand wash dry clean	50 gm	340	4.50	—	4-5	—	—
Lambswool	USA	smooth	3-4	7½	100% lambs-wool	superwash dry clean	50 gm	220	6.25	—	6-7	—	—
London Metallic	dis.	shiny	3-4	7	60% rayon 40% metalized polyester	hand wash dry clean	20 gm	170	6.80	—	8-9	—	—
Poil de Chameau	dis.	smooth	3-4	7	50% camel hair 50% wool	hand wash dry clean	50 gm	230	10.00	—	6-7	—	—
Wendy Ascot 4-ply	USA CA GB AU	—	1-3	7.0	80% wool 20% bri-nylon	machine wash	50 gm	185	2.99	7	7	5	3
Darling 4-ply	USA CA GB AU	baby	1-3	7.0	55% Courtelle acrylic 45% bri-nylon	machine wash	20 gm	93	1.20	—	—	—	3-5
Pampas	USA CA GB AU	—	2-4	6.5	65% cotton 35% linen	hand wash	50 gm	219	4.20	3-5	3-5	3	—
The Linen Look	USA CA GB AU	suit type excellent for knitting machines	2-4	6.5	65% cotton 35% linen	hand wash	200 gm	876	15.95	1	1	1	—
Yarn Country/ Newton Knits Candle lite	USA	soft metallic	—	—	65% rayon 35% polyester	dry clean	2 oz. tube	495	—	—	10 oz.	—	—

A

Ecstasy	USA	dress knubby	4 or machine	6½	75% acetate 25% nylon	1-color wash, & dry dry clean	1 lb. cone	1,550	—	22 oz.	18 oz.	15 oz.	12 oz.
Newlite	USA	dressy	2 or machine	8	80% DuPont acrylic 20% nylon	machine wash & dry	1 lb. cone	3,000	—	14 oz.	12 oz.	10 oz.	8 oz.
Sunday Angora	USA	brushed	4 or machine	8	10% wool 90% acrylic	machine wash & dry	app. 1 lb. cone	3,500	—	16 oz.	13 oz.	10 oz.	9 oz.
Thread of lite	USA	metallic 1-ply	—	—	70% acetate 30% metallic	hand wash	2 oz. cone	10,000	—		run-a-long		
Thread of lite	USA	metallic 3-ply	—	—	70% acetate 30% metallic	hand wash	2 oz. cone	3,000	—		run-a-long		
Twinkle	USA	acrylic with metallic twist	2 or machine	7	100% acrylic	machine wash & dry	1 lb. cone	3,000	—	19 oz.	16 oz.	14 oz.	12 oz.
2/12 Orlon	USA	smooth, dull	2–3 or machine	7	80% acrylic 20% nylon	machine wash & dry	1 lb. cone / 1 lb. cone	2,000 / 2,800	—	16 oz. / 18 oz.	14 oz. / 16 oz.	12 oz. / 14 oz.	10 oz. / 12 oz.
2/12 S.D	USA	space-dye	2 or machine	7	100% Orlon	machine wash & dry	1 lb. cone	2,800	—	16 oz.	14 oz.	12 oz.	10 oz.
Venesian	USA	dressy	2 or machine	8	80% wool 20% rayon	dry clean	1 lb. cone	2,300	—	20 oz.	16 oz.	14 oz.	12 oz.

Sport Weight Yarns

CLASS B

Brand and Yarn Name	Where Sold	Type	US Needle Size	Gauge/ Tension per Inch	Fiber Content	Cleaning Care	Skein, Hank, Ball, or Cone Weight	Approx. Yardage	Approx. Price	Approx. No. of Skeins for a Small-size Standard Knit Pullover Sweater with Long Sleeves and Crew Neck			
										Man	Woman	Child	Infant
Aarlan Alpaca & Silk	USA	tweed	6-7	5½	55% wool 25% silk 20% alpaca	hand wash warm water	50 gm.	120	5.00	—	7-9	—	—
Angora Silk	dis.	fluffy	5-7	6-5½	40% Angora 40% silk 20% lambs-wool	dry clean	20 gm.	99	6.00	—	9-12	—	—
Brillanta	USA	sport	5-7	6-5½	60% cotton 40% viscose	hand wash	50 gm	100	4.00	12-14	10-12	8-10	6-8
City	USA	sport	4-6	6	100% merino wool	hand wash	50 gm	160	5.00	8-10	5-7	4-6	3-5
Cotolana	USA	sport	4-6	6-5½	50% wool 50% cotton	hand wash delicate	50 gm	155	5.00	8-10	5-7	4-6	3-5
Derby	USA	sport	3-6	6-5½	100% Shetland wool	hand wash	50 gm	145	4.00	12-14	10-12	6-8	5-7
Dynasty Silk	dis.	smooth shiny	6	6	100% silk	dry clean	50 gm	125	10.80	—	7-10	—	—
Elle	USA	sport	4-6	5½	65% acrylic 15% wool 10% polyamide 10% viscose	hand wash	50 gm	130	3.50	10-12	8-10	6-8	5-7
Fashion	USA	sport	3-5	5½	50% wool 50% viscose	hand wash	50 gm	140	4.50	12-14	10-12	8-10	6-8
Glamour	USA	sport	5-7	5½	50% viscose 45% cotton 5% polyamide	hand wash	50 gm	100	4.00	12-14	10-12	8-10	6-8
Marmora	USA	sport	6-8	5½	35% wool 30% cotton 22% silk 13% acrylic	hand wash	50 gm	140	5.50	9-12	7-9	5-7	4-6
Perla	USA	sport	5-7	5½	75% viscose 25% nylon	hand wash	50 gm	110	3.30	12-14	10-12	7-9	5-7

Brand	Country	Description	US Needle	Metric Needle	Fiber	Care	Ball	Yds	Price				
Royal	USA	sport	4–6	5½	40% wool 40% acrylic 20% mohair	hand wash	50 gm	135	3.80	10–12	8–10	6–8	5–7
Royal Color	USA	sport	4–6	5½	40% wool 40% acrylic 20% mohair	hand wash	50 gm	110	3.80	10–12	8–10	6–8	5–7
Royal Tweed	USA	sport	4–6	5½	70% wool 30% acrylic	hand wash	50 gm	135	3.80	10–12	8–10	6–8	5–7
Shetland	dis.	tweed	6–5	6	100% Shetland wool	warm water wash	50 gm	140	3.60	—	6–7	—	—
Soie/Silk	USA	sport	3–5	6	50% wool 50% silk	hand wash	20 gm	81	4.00	14–16	12–14	9–11	7–9
Andean Yarns Alpaquita	USA CA	natural 3-ply	5	6	100% alpaca	hand wash dry flat	50 gm	200	4.50	8	7	6	4
Alpaquita	USA CA	dyed 3-ply	5	6	100% alpaca	hand wash dry flat	50 gm	200	5.00	8	7	6	4
Anny Blatt Alpag	—	natural & dyed & brushed	4–6	6	100% alpaca	hand wash dry clean	50 gm	218	7.50 natural 8.75 dyed	9	7	4	2
Angor	USA CA AU GB	fluffy	5–7	5	70% angora 30% wool	hand wash dry clean	20 gm	95	10.95	15	12	8	4
Antique	USA CA AU GB	metallic ribbon	6–8	5	72% viscose 28% polyester-metallise	hand wash dry clean	20 gm	40	6.50	—	24	—	—
Bora Bora	USA CA AU GB	smooth sport	6	4½	100% cotton	hand wash dry clean	50 gm	90	4.25	16	13	8	4
Ecoss	USA CA AU GB	4-ply smooth mercerized	7–8	4½	100% Egyptian cotton	hand wash dry clean	50 gm	90	5.50	16	12	8	4
Folie	USA CA AU GB	fluffy mohair blend	6–9	4½	53% mohair 34% wool 13% acrylic	hand wash dry clean	40 gm	118	5.75	14	10	5	3
Gardenia	USA CA AU GB	plyed cotton, viscose	4–7	5	75% cotton 25% viscose	hand wash dry clean	50 gm	95	6.25	16	12	8	4
Honey-Moon	USA CA AU GB	soft brushed	5–6	4½	80% mohair 20% silk	hand wash dry clean	20 gm	50	6.50	28	22	10	5

Brand and Yarn Name	Where Sold	Type	US Needle Size	Gauge/Tension per Inch	Fiber Content	Cleaning Care	Skein, Hank, Ball, or Cone Weight	Approx. Yardage	Approx. Price	Approx. No. of Skeins for a Small-size Standard Knit Pullover Sweater with Long Sleeves and Crew Neck			
										Man	Woman	Child	Infant
Kid	USA CA AU GB	soft kid mohair blend	6-9	4½	80% kid mohair 20% chlorofibres	hand wash dry clean	50 gm	110	10.50	14	10	6	3
Luciole	USA CA AU GB	novelty ply, metallic & smooth	6-7	5	55% viscose 23% wool 10% polyamide 12% polyester	hand wash dry clean	20 gm	48	7.50	—	48	—	—
Mango	USA CA AU GB	cotton, viscose ply	2-4	5	57% viscose 43% cotton	hand wash dry clean	50 gm	90	6.50	20	16	7	4
No. 4	USA CA AU GB	smooth superwash	4-6	6	100% wool	superwash	50 gm	130	4.75	14	10	5	3
No. 5	USA CA AU GB	smooth superwash	4-5	5	100% wool	superwash	50 gm	100	4.50	17	12	5	3
100% Mohair	dis.	soft kid mohair	5-7	5-6	100% kid mohair	hand wash dry clean	20 gm.	50	6.95	23	19	11	4
Pearl	dis.	mercerized shiny	5	6	100% cotton	hand wash dry clean	50 gm	160	4.10	12	9	5	2
Seringa	USA CA AU GB	smooth & shiny ply	3-6	5	71% cotton 29% viscose	hand wash dry clean	50 gm	85	8.95	19	13	6	3
Seringa-Multico	USA CA AU GB	smooth & shiny ply	3-6	5	71% cotton 29% viscose	hand wash dry clean	50 gm	85	10.50	19	13	6	3
Soft	USA CA AU GB	kid mohair blend	5-7	5	80% kid mohair 20% chlorofibres	hand wash dry clean	50 gm	170	10.50	9	7	4	2
Super Kid	USA CA AU GB	kid mohair	6-8	4	80% kid mohair 20% Courtelle	hand wash dry clean	50 gm	119	9.95	14	10	6	3
Tahiti	USA CA AU GB	2-ply twist	2-5	5	65% viscose 35% cotton	hand wash dry clean	50 gm	98	5.50	18	14	8	4

B

Brand / Yarn	Country	Description	Needle	Needle	Fiber Content	Care	Ball	Length	Price				
Argyll Ltd. Cocktail Fizz	CA	mohair weight	9	4	69% acrylic 31% nylon	machine wash	25 gm	51 m	—	—	—	—	—
Fluffy	CA USA	fluffy	machine	—	75% acrylic 25% nylon	machine wash	340 gm cone 12 oz.	1,790 m 1,940 yd.	—	—	—	—	—
Fluffy Chunky	CA	chunky	9	3½	80% acrylic 20% nylon	machine wash	100 gm	185 m	6.50 (CA $)	—	—	—	—
Fluffy One DK	CA	DK	6	6	80% acrylic 20% Angora type nylon	machine wash	100 gm	350 m	5.80 (CA $)	—	3	—	—
Laser DK	CA	DK	6	6	100% acrylic	machine wash	100 gm	304	4.50 (CA $)	—	5	—	—
Mistral DK	CA	DK	6	6	51% viscose 19% polyester 15% wool 15% acrylic	hand wash	50 gm	109 m	5.80 (CA $)	—	7	—	—
Picasso DK	CA	DK	6	6	97% acrylic 3% nylon	machine wash	50 gm	146 m	3.99 (CA $)	—	5	—	—
Aurora Wellscroft Nub	USA	single ply rich tweed with nubs	5–6	6	100% wool	hand wash	100 gm	380	6.00	3–4	3	2	1
Avocet Yarns Albany DK	USA CA	classic	6	6	80% wool 20% alpaca	hand wash	50 gm	120 m	6.99	—	—	—	—
Chic DK	USA CA	brushed	6	6	90% Courtelle 10% wool	hand wash	50 gm	174 m	4.99	—	—	—	—
Mother of Pearl	USA CA	dressy crimped look	6	5½	97.5% viscose 2.5% Irise	hand wash	50 gm	95 m	8.99	—	—	—	—
Soiree	USA CA	silky tubular ribbon	9	5½	88% viscose 12% nylon	hand wash	50 gm	94 m	6.00	—	—	—	—
Soiree Lurex	USA CA	silky metallic tubular ribbon	8	5½	65% viscose 19% Lurex 16% nylon	hand wash	50 gm	94 m	8.99	—	—	—	—
Tweed DK	USA CA	tweed	6	6	46% acrylic 45% wool	hand wash	50 gm	120 m	4.00	—	—	—	—
Bartlettyarns Fisherman	USA	2-ply sport	3B	6	100% wool	hand wash dry clean	1 lb.	1,750	17.00	1 lb.	1 lb.	½ lb.	½ lb.
Glen Tweed	USA	2-ply sport	3B	6	100% wool	hand wash dry clean	1 lb.	1,750	17.00	1 lb.	1 lb.	½ lb.	½ lb.
Homespun	USA	2-ply sport	3B	6	100% wool	hand wash dry clean	1 lb.	1,750	18.00	1 lb.	1 lb.	½ lb.	½ lb.
Baruffa Vespucci	USA	blended tweed effect	5	5	100% cotton	hand wash	50 gm	110	4.75	—	8	—	—
Berger du Nord Angora 70	USA	soft	4	5½	70% Angora 30% wool	—	20 gm	95	9.50	—	—	—	—

Brand and Yarn Name	Where Sold	Type	US Needle Size	Gauge/ Tension per Inch	Fiber Content	Cleaning Care	Skein, Hank, Ball, or Cone Weight	Approx. Yardage	Approx. Price	Approx. No. of Skeins for a Small-size Standard Knit Pullover Sweater with Long Sleeves and Crew Neck			
										Man	Woman	Child	Infant
Douceur 4	USA	—	6	5¼	85% wool 15% kid mohair	—	50 gm	135	4.50	—	—	—	—
Island Light	USA	—	5	5¼	100% wool	—	50 gm	120	3.95	—	—	—	—
No. 4	USA	—	5	5¾	100% wool	—	50 gm	135	3.75	—	—	—	—
Bernat Acacia	USA	novelty slub	5	5½	60% viscose 40% cotton	hand wash	50 gm	95	3.95	14	12	6	3
Berella Sportspun	USA	smooth classic worsted	6	5½	100% blended acrylic	machine wash	50 gm	150	1.95	9	8	4	3
Cassino	USA	fashion basic	6	5½	100% cotton	hand wash	50 gm	110	3.95	12	11	5	—
Chloe	USA	fashion basic	6	5½	100% cotton	hand wash	50 gm	90	3.95	14	12	7	—
Frosting	USA	variegated roving	6	5½	70% wool 30% bright	hand wash	40 gm	110	3.95	12	10	5	—
Panama	USA	tweed blend	5	5½	46% cotton 30% acrylic 24% linen	hand wash	50 gm	90	3.50	14	15	7	—
Saluki	USA	cable twist	6	5½	60% acrylic 40% nylon	machine wash	50 gm	150	2.75	9	7	4	3
Sorbetto	USA	novelty vrille	5	5½	30% cotton 25% acrylic 20% linen 20% viscose 5% nylon	hand wash	50 gm	110	4.95	14	10	7	—
Soufflé	USA	ribbon	8	5½	100% nylon	hand wash	200 yd.	200	3.25	12	10	6 (double strand)	—
Sweety	USA	brushed	5	5½	80% acrylic 10% mohair 10% wool	machine wash	50 gm	250	2.95	6	5	3	—
Berroco Pixie	USA	—	8	4½	33% cotton 32% rayon 25% polyester 10% nylon	hand wash	50 gm 1 lb. 2–4 lb.	90	4.65	—	11	—	—
Poppy	USA	—	6	5	54% linen 23% viscose 18% cotton 5% acrylic	hand wash	50 gm 1 lb. 3–5 lb.	90	5.75	—	11	—	—
Stretch Yarn	USA	elastic bouclé run-along	—	—	42% cotton 30% rayon 28% spandex	—	25 gm 1 lb. tube 2 lb. cone	100 1,800 3,600	3.55	—	—	—	—

B

Bouquet Yarns Candy	USA CA	classic	6	6	100% acrylic	machine wash & dry	50 gm	155	1.75	—	12	7	4
Capriccio	USA CA	brushed	6	5½	70% acrylic 30% mohair	machine wash & dry	50 gm	215	2.85	10	9	6	—
Opera	USA CA	metallic overwrap	6	6	94% acrylic 6% metallic	dry clean	50 gm	225	2.30	—	6	4	—
Polo	USA CA	classic	6	6	100% acrylic	machine wash & dry	50 gm	155	1.75	14	12	7	4
Sparklette	USA CA	rayon overwrap	6	6	90% acrylic 10% rayon	machine wash & dry	50 gm	140	1.85	—	14	8	5
Sportivo	USA CA	classic	6	5½	60% acrylic 20% mohair 20% wool	machine wash & dry	50 gm	160	2.45	12	10	7	—
Style	dis.	classic	6	6	30% wool 70% acrylic	machine wash & dry	50 gm	155	1.95	14	12	7	4
Twilight	USA CA	rayon wrap	6	5½	90% acrylic 10% rayon	machine wash & dry	50 gm	190	1.85	—	6	3	2
Viva	USA CA	specialty	6.	6	60% acrylic 40% nylon	machine wash & dry	50 gm	255	2.60	—	6	4	2
Brentwood Yarns Blackstone	USA	textured acrylic	4	6/1	acrylic	hand wash	skein/cone	160/1,600	2.40/22.00	15	11	8	5
Glamourette	USA	bumpy cotton	4	6/1	cotton/rayon	hand wash	skein/cone	160/1,600	3.00/28.00	15	11	8	5
Starlite	USA	flat/shine	4	6/1	wool/rayon	hand wash	skein/cone	150/1,200	5.00/40.00	15	11	8	5
Brown Sheep Co. Brown Sheep Co.	USA CA	worsted	5	6	100% wool	hand wash	4 oz. 2 lb.	600 2,400	3.50 29.60	6	5	2–3	2
Brown Sheep Co.	USA CA	worsted #2 sports 4-ply	4	6	100% wool	hand wash	4 oz. 2 lb.	420 3,360	4.00 32.00	5	4	2	1
Brunswick Ballybrae Sport	USA CA AU	natural tweed	5	6	100% virgin wool with natural oil	hand wash	50 gm	210	—	7	6	5	3
Casablanca	USA CA AU	knobby	5	6	50% cotton 25% linen 25% acrylic	machine wash & dry	40 gm	130	—	8	7	6	—
Fore'N Aft	USA CA AU	smooth	5	6	100% acrylic	machine wash & dry	50 gm	175	—	7	6	5	3
Heatherblend Sport	USA CA AU	smooth	5	6	80% acrylic 20% wool	machine wash & dry, delicate	50 gm	175	—	7	6	5	NR
Pomfret	USA CA AU	smooth	5	6	100% wool	dry clean only	50 gm	175	—	7	6	5	NR

Brand and Yarn Name	Where Sold	Type	US Needle Size	Gauge/Tension per Inch	Fiber Content	Cleaning Care	Skein, Hank, Ball, or Cone Weight	Approx. Yardage	Approx. Price	Approx. No. of Skeins for a Small-size Standard Knit Pullover Sweater with Long Sleeves and Crew Neck			
										Man	Woman	Child	Infant
Shetland Sport	USA CA AU	smooth	5	6	100% wool	machine wash & dry	50 gm	160	—	7	6	5	NR
Sparkle-twist	USA CA AU	metallic	5	6	85% acrylic 15% rayon	machine wash & dry	50 gm	175	—	7	6	5	3
Wil O'Wisp	USA CA AU	smooth	5	6	100% Civona acrylic	machine wash & dry	50 gm	220	—	7	6	5	3
Bucilla Glamour	USA	ribbon	6	5	50% cotton 50% viscose	hand Wash	1¾ oz.	93	6.00	NR	10	NR	NR
Perlette	USA	perle twist	5	6	100% DuPont Orlon fiber	machine wash & dry	1¾ oz	200	2.70	9	6	4	2
Sahara	USA	tweed-like	6	5	66% DuPont Orlon 34% cotton	hand wash	1¾ oz	77	2.90	6	5	3	2
Sport	USA	classic sports yarn	5	6	100% Orlon fiber	machine wash & dry	1¾ oz	170	1.95	9	6	4	2
Spotlight	USA	metallic	5	6	87% polyester 13% nylon	hand wash	20 gm	130	5.30	NR	14	NR	NR
Spotlight II	USA	metallic	6	5	85% polyester 15% nylon	hand wash	—	50	3.50	NR	14	NR	NR
Tempo	USA	looks like mercerized cotton	D crochet hook	6	100% Creslan acrylic	machine wash & dry	1¾ oz	158	2.10	NR	9	4	3
Busse Dandy	USA	tweedy sport with small contrasting flecks	4	6	70% new wool 30% viscose	hand wash	1¾oz. (50 gm)	220	4.75	9	8	4	—
Onyx	USA	slub texture, worked with 2 strands	4–5	6–7	60% rayon 40% cotton	hand wash, cold	50 gm (1¼ oz.)	164	4.00	12	10	—	—
Squash-Sporty	USA	classic sport weight	4	6	75% new wool 25% nylon	machine wash	1¾oz. (50 gm)	180	4.50	10	8	4	2
Candide Candide Lightweight	USA	homespun Shetland type	5	6	100% wool	hand wash	2 oz. 57 gm	275 yd 251 m	2.50	7	5	3	2
Caron Comfort 12®	USA	sport weight	8	4	100% Comfort 12	machine wash & dry, gentle cycle do not bleach	50 gm (1.75 oz.)	84	1.59	15	12	9	6

B

Name	Origin	Texture	Needle	Needle	Fiber	Care	Ball Size	Yards	Price				
Cotton Clouds	USA	thick & thin novelty	8	4	67% cotton 33% rayon	hand wash, cool do not bleach dry flat do not iron	50 gm (1.75 oz.)	90	1.99	16	13	9	7
Cotton Tweed	USA	novelty	7	4.5	58% cotton 25% acrylic 12% polyester 5% rayon	hand wash cool do not bleach dry flat do not iron	50 gm (1.75 oz.)	144	1.99	10	8	6	3
Dawn Wintuk Sports	USA	classic sports	5	6	100% orlon	machine wash & dry	2 oz.	218	1.19	9	7	4	2
Dazzle Sports	USA	dressy	6	5	60% acrylic 40% nylon	machine wash & dry	2 oz.	224	1.40	8	5	4	2
Fashion Right Sweater & Vest	USA	sport weight	6	5	100% acrylic	machine wash, warm, delicate setting tumble dry, low heat	2 oz.	240	1.19	9	7	4	2
Glimmer	USA	sparkling novelty	7	4	40% acrylic 30% rayon 13% polyester 11% wool 6% nylon	machine wash, cold dry flat do not bleach do not iron	40 gm (1.6 oz.)	109	2.29	11	9	4	3
Jewel	USA	cotton novelty	7	5	100% mercerized cotton	machine wash & dry, gentle, low heat or dry flat do not bleach do not iron	50 gm (1.75 oz.)	98	1.89	13	11	6	4
Chanteleine Evelyne	USA	tweedy slub	6	6	46% cotton 31% acrylic 23% linen	hand wash	50 gm	148	3.60	9-10	7-8	4-5	3
Frehel	USA	heather classic	6	5¼-5½	100% wool	superwash	50 gm	137	4.50	10-11	7-8	4-5	2-3
Glenan	USA	classic sock yarn	2-3	6-7	70% wool 30% nylon	machine wash	50 gm	175	3.60	8-9	7	4-5	2-3
Miss Acryl	USA	smooth classic	6	5½-6	100% Courtelle acrylic	hand wash machine wash	50 gm	165	2.40	9	7	4	2
Rumba	USA	slub cotton tweed & solid colors	6	6	54% acrylic 46% cotton	hand wash machine wash	50 gm	122	3.00	10	8	5	3
Shetfine	dis.	Shetland slight fuzz	6	6	100% wool Woolmark	hand wash	50 gm	220	3.25	8	6	3	1
Shetwool	dis.	sport Shetland, slight fuzz	5	5½-6	100% wool Woolmark	hand wash	50 gm	148	3.25	9	7	4	2

Brand and Yarn Name	Where Sold	Type	US Needle Size	Gauge/Tension per Inch	Fiber Content	Cleaning Care	Skein, Hank, Ball, or Cone Weight	Approx. Yardage	Approx. Price	Approx. No. of Skeins for a Small-size Standard Knit Pullover Sweater with Long Sleeves and Crew Neck			
										Man	Woman	Child	Infant
Siamoise	dis.	brushed Angora	6	5–6	50% Angora 30% lambs-wool 20% nylon	hand wash dry clean	20 gm	110	6.50	NR	10	6	2
Sonia	USA	classic	6	5–5½	100% wool	hand wash	50 gm	148	4.00	10–11	7–8	4–5	2–3
Charity Hill Farm USA Charity Hill Sport	USA	classic woolon-spun 2-ply	5	6	100% wool	hand wash	2 oz. 1 lb.	210 1,680	3.10 21.90	8 1	6 1	4 —	2–3 —
Chat Botte Alpaga Superfin	USA CA AU	fleecy	3	7	100% alpaca	hand wash dry clean	30 gm	120	7.00	12	10	6	3
Campanule	USA CA AU	smooth	4	5¼	80% acrylic 20% wool	hand wash dry clean	50 gm	136	2.00	12	10	7	4
Caraibes	dis.	bouclé	5	4¼	83% cotton 17% polyester	hand wash dry clean	50 gm	88	5.50	18	15	9	5
Caucase	USA CA AU	smooth	6	5	80% acrylic 20% wool	hand wash dry clean	50 gm	145	3.60	10	8	5	3
Dallas	USA CA AU	novelty	4	5½	52% rayon 48% cotton	hand wash dry clean	50 gm	131	5.00	12	10	7	4
Dolce Vita	USA CA AU	fleecy	4	6	60% acrylic 40% mohair	hand wash dry clean	40 gm	118	6.20	14	12	7	4
Mohair Kid	USA CA AU	fleecy	3	6	80% mohair 20% Vinyon	hand wash hand stain removal	50 gm	57	10.00	13	10	6	5
Orchidee	USA CA AU	fluffy	6	4	68% acrylic 22% mohair 10% wool	hand wash dry clean	50 gm	137	4.60	10	8	5	3
Petrouchka	USA CA AU	classic	4	6	90% wool 10% Vinyon	hand wash dry clean	50 gm	145	4.40	12	10	6	5
Sole Mio	USA CA AU	smooth	4	5½	100% cotton	machine wash	50 gm	95	5.00	14	12	8	4
Starlight	USA CA AU	bouclé	4	6	70% cotton 27% acrylic 3% polyester	hand wash dry clean	50 gm	98	5.50	15	13	NR	NR

B

Company / Yarn	Source	Texture		Fiber	Care	Weight	Yardage	Price				
China Silk Co., Inc. — Canton	USA CA AU GB	blended fibers, lustrous	4 / 6	65% silk 35% linen	dry clean	100 gm / 1 lb.	265 / 1,200	16.80	6	5	3	2
Classic Peony	USA CA AU GB	cultivated mulberry, bouclé, fancy with loops	5 / 5	100% silk	dry clean	100 gm / 1 lb.	310 / 1,380	21.20	6	5	3	2
Egret	USA CA AU GB	soft, thick/thin	6 / 5	50% silk 50% cotton	dry clean	100 gm / 1 lb.	265 / 1,200	12.80	6	5	3	2
Flying Crane	USA CA AU GB	cultivated mulberry smooth, single ply	6 / 4.5	100% silk	dry clean	100 gm / 1 lb.	265 / 1,200	20.00	6	5	3	2
Imari	USA CA AU GB	cultivated mulberry classic, smooth	4 / 6	100% silk	dry clean	100 gm / 1 lb.	265 / 1,200	21.20	6	5	3	2
Medallion	dis.	slubby silk noil	4 / 6	100% silk	dry clean	100 gm	335	8.80	5	4	2	1
Pagoda #2	USA CA AU GB	spun cord pearlized	5 / 7	100% silk	dry clean	100 gm / 1 lb.	410 / 1,860	19.20	6	5	3	2
Christopher Farms — Fisherman Yarn	USA	smooth single ply	5 / 6	100% wool	hand wash	4 oz.	400	3.80	5	4	2	—
Classic Elite Yarns — Cashmere #1	dis.	smooth sportweight	5 / 6	100% cashmere	dry clean	20 gm	56	8.75	—	20	—	—
Graffiti	USA CA	nubby	7 / 4½	54% cotton 46% rayon	hand wash	50 gm	80	3.50	—	13	—	—
Heather	dis.	smooth sportweight	4 / 6	100% wool	dry clean	40 gm	150	2.95	—	7	—	—
L.A.	USA CA	slub	7 / 4½	50% cotton 50% rayon	hand wash	50 gm	85	3.50	—	13	—	—
La Swa 3-ply	USA	smooth	5 / 6	60% wool 40% silk	dry clean	40 gm	150	5.95	—	7	—	—
Manhattan	USA	brushed	5 / 6	63% mohair 18½% wool 18½% nylon	dry clean	1½ oz.	193	—	—	6	—	—
Soie 2-ply	dis.	lustrous	5 / 6	100% silk	dry clean	50 gm	137	—	—	11	—	—
Soie Bouclé	dis.	bouclé	5 / 6	100% silk	dry clean	50 gm	137	—	—	11	—	—

Brand and Yarn Name	Where Sold	Type	US Needle Size	Gauge/Tension per Inch	Fiber Content	Cleaning Care	Skein, Hank, Ball, or Cone Weight	Approx. Yardage	Approx. Price	Approx. No. of Skeins for a Small-size Standard Knit Pullover Sweater with Long Sleeves and Crew Neck			
										Man	Woman	Child	Infant
Columbia-Minerva Sassy	USA	novelty	5 F	5½ 5	85% So-lara acrylic 15% Memorelle nylon	machine wash & dry	50 gm	215	1.49	11	9	4	3
Condon's Yarns Sport	USA	100% wool	4	5¼	100% wool	hand wash	4 oz.	275	2.10	5	4	3	—
Copley Camargue DK	USA GB	fashion basic	6	5½	58% acrylic 25% nylon 17% wool	hand wash, gentle machine wash dry flat dry clean	50 gm	162	2.59	9	7	4	2
Light 'n Bright®	USA GB	lustrous double knitting classic	6	5½	66% viscose 34% acrylic	hand wash, luke warm water dry flat dry clean	50 gm	118	4.95	12	9	6	3
Cotton Cloud Aurora Earth	USA	on mercerized 8/2	4 (use double)	6	100% cotton	machine wash & dry	20 oz.	4,000	12.00	2	1	½	¼
Autumn Leaves	USA	6-ply cable mercerized	8	5	100% cotton	machine wash & dry	50 gm	121	3.25	10	8	5	3
Baby Pearly Perle	USA	mercerized perle 5/2	6 (use double)	5½	100% cotton	machine wash & dry	4 oz.	525	5.50	6	3	2	2
Pearly Perle	USA	mercerized perle 5/2	6 (use double)	5½	100% cotton	machine wash & dry	12 oz.	1,500	14.00	2	2	½	¼
Pearly Perle	USA	mercerized perle 3/2	5	5	100% cotton	machine wash & dry	18 oz.	1,500	22.00	2	1	½	¼
Rainbow Ribbons	USA	woven ribbon mercerized	8	5	100% cotton	machine wash & dry	50 gm	87	5.00	15	12	6	3
Snowflake	USA	thick & thin mercerized	9	4	100% cotton	machine wash & dry	8.8 oz.	825	10.00	4	3	2	1
Snowflake	USA	thick & thin mercerized	9	4	100% cotton	machine wash & dry	100 gm	328	4.50	10	7	4	2
Spring Rain	USA	smooth 6-ply mercerized	2-3	7	100% cotton	machine wash & dry	50 gm	90	4.00	15	12	6	3
Summer Breeze	USA	thick & thin 4-ply mercerized	8	5	100% cotton	machine wash & dry	50 gm	90	3.50	12	10	5	2

B

Name	Origin	Texture		Needle	Fiber	Care	Weight	Yards	Price				
Winter Wind	USA	6-ply cable mercerized	8	4½	100% cotton	machine wash & dry	50 gm	77	3.25	15	12	6	3
Country Spun™ Country Spun Sport	USA	woolen spun	5–7	5–6	100% wool	machine wash, delicate dry flat	4 oz. 1 lb.	420 1,700	5.50 21.00	5	4	3	2
Crystal Palace Yarns Allegro	USA	bouclé	6	5–6	100% silk	hand wash dry clean	50 gm	200	6.90	—	—	—	—
Country Silk	USA CA	shantung classic	5–7	5–5½	100% silk	hand wash	50 gm	185	6.20	8	6	NR	NR
Creme	USA CA	classic soft lustrous	6–7	5–5½	50/50 merino wool/ silk	dry clean	50 gm	135	8.80	8–10	6–7	NR	NR
Sikiang	USA	high sheen filament	5–6	5½–6	100% reeled filament silk	hand wash dry clean	50 gm	165	15.00	11–13	9–10	—	—
Di.Vé Blitz	USA	tweed	6	5.5	60% acrylic 40% wool	hand wash	50 gm	165	2.49	—	7	—	—
Bolivia	USA	smooth cotton	6	5.5	100% cotton	hand wash	50 gm	128	2.99	—	8	—	—
Melanite	USA	slubbed blend	5	6	50% cotton 30% linen 20% viscose	hand wash	50 gm	115	3.25	—	8	—	—
Topazio	USA	matte finish	5	5.5	50% linen 20% linen 30% acrylic	hand wash	50 gm	132	2.99	—	8	—	—
DMC Brilliant Crochet/Knitting Cotton (Double strand)	USA	smooth twisted	5	6	100% cotton	hand wash, warm water, mild soap	50 gm	218	1.99	—	12	—	—
Cebelia Cotton (Size 5)	USA	smooth	4	6	100% cotton	hand wash, warm water, mild soap	50 gm	141	3.25	—	8	—	—
Cebelia Cotton Size 10 (Double strand)	USA	smooth	4	6	100% cotton	hand wash, warm water, mild soap	50 gm	282	3.25	—	8	—	—
Cotonia Size 2	USA	matte, soft	7	5.5	100% cotton	hand wash, warm water, mild soap	50 gm	109 yds./ ball	3.25	—	—	—	—
Cotonia Size 4	USA	matte	5	5.5	100% cotton	hand wash, warm water, mild soap	50 gm	175	3.25	—	8	—	—

Brand and Yarn Name	Where Sold	Type	US Needle Size	Gauge/Tension per Inch	Fiber Content	Cleaning Care	Skein, Hank, Ball, or Cone Weight	Approx. Yardage	Approx. Price	Approx. No. of Skeins for a Small-size Standard Knit Pullover Sweater with Long Sleeves and Crew Neck			
										Man	Woman	Child	Infant
Ecossia Size 5 (Double strand)	USA	smooth twisted	7	5.5	100% cotton	hand wash, warm water, mild soap	50 gm	184	3.75	—	13	—	—
Lumina	USA	nubby, lustrous	4	5.25	56% cotton 44% viscose	hand wash, warm water, mild soap	50 gm.	137	4.20	—	—	—	—
Matelia	USA	matte, soft, cable twist	6	5	100% cotton	hand wash, warm water, mild soap	50 gm.	102	4.00	—	—	—	—
Pearl Cotton Size 3	USA	pearl, lustrous twisted	3	6.5	100% cotton	hand wash, warm water, mild soap	50 gm	147	4.95	—	8	—	—
Splendida Size 2	USA	high sheen, lustrous, soft twist	6	5	100% cotton	hand wash warm water, mild soap	50 gm	93	4.15	—	—	—	—
Splendida Size 4 (Double strand)	USA	high sheen, lustrous, soft twist	5	5.5	100% cotton	hand wash warm water, mild soap	50 gm	223	4.15	—	—	—	—
Starlia	USA	matte & brilliant blend, multistrands	6	5	54% cotton 46% viscose	hand wash warm water, mild soap	50 gm	87	3.60	—	—	—	—
Subtila	USA	matte & satin blend, cable twist	6	5.25	65% cotton 35% viscose	hand wash warm water, mild soap	50 gm	87	3.50	—	—	—	—
Dorothee Bis Minouche	USA	—	6	6	100% alpaca	—	50 gm	200	8.50	—	6	—	—
Pharaon	USA	—	6	5½	76% rayon 24% cotton	—	50 gm	151	6.00	—	8-10	—	—
Drop Spindle Home-dyed Super White	USA	cultivated silk-smooth	3-4	5-6	100% silk	hand wash dry clean	3.5 oz.	252	—	—	7	—	—
Dyed in the Wool Pure Cultivated Silk	USA	hand painted	4	6	100% silk	dry clean	500 gm	1,875	160.00	1	1	—	—
Erdal Yarns Beatnik	USA	cream	8	5	100% cotton	—	50 gm 1½ lb.	115 1,050	2.00 10.50	—	11 —	—	—
Beatnik	USA	variegated	8	5	100% cotton	—	50 gm 1½ lb.	115 1,050	2.30 15.00	—	11 —	—	—
Chainette	USA	—	6	6½	100% rayon	—	100 yd.	100	1.30	—	14 tubes	—	—

B

Name	Origin	Texture	Gauge	Needle	Fiber Content	Care	Put-up	Yards	Price	Colors	
Harlequin	USA	ribbon	6	6½	100% rayon	—	50 gm / 1 lb.	165 / 1,550	3.50 / 28.00	10 minicones	—
Illusion	USA	—	9	5	50% Angora 25% lambswool 10% nylon 15% acrylic	—	20 gm	100	3.00	16	—
Jungle	USA	—	8	5	78% silk 22% rayon	—	50 gm / 1 lb.	115 / 1,050	4.10 / 30.00	10	—
Kaleidoscope	USA	variegated	8	5	100% cotton	—	50 gm / 1½ lb.	90 / 840	2.25 / 16.50	13	—
Kaleidoscope	USA	solid	8	5	100% cotton	—	50 gm / 1½ lb.	90 / 840	1.75 / 14.00	13	—
Luna	USA	—	8	5	75% rayon 25% cotton	—	50 gm / 1½ lb.	100 / 950	2.35 / 16.00	10	—
Magic	USA	variegated	8	5	75% rayon 25% cotton	—	50 gm / 1½ lb.	100 / 950	2.10 / 14.50	10	—
Magic	USA	solid	8	5	75% rayon 25% cotton	—	50 gm / 1½ lb.	100 / 950	2.10 / 14.50	10	—
Pistachio	USA	—	8	5	70% rayon 30% acetate	—	50 gm / 1½ lb.	130 / 1,170	3.00 / 23.00	12 minicones	—
Peri	USA	—	9	5	45% linen 33% cotton 22% rayon	—	50 gm / 1 lb.	98 / 900	2.50 / 20.00	12	—
Rainbow	USA	—	9	4	100% rayon	—	50 gm / 1½ lb.	85 / 780	1.95 / 13.50	12	—
Esslinger Angora Princess	USA	fluffy 2-ply	5	6	20% lambswool 80% Angora	hand wash, cold dry flat	20 gm	104	9.98 white 13.28 colors	11	8
Caring	USA	textured	6	5½	65% cotton 35% acrylic	hand wash	50 gm	119	4.29	14	—
Geisha	USA	mohair, medium	5	6	85% acrylic 15% mohair	machine wash moth proof	50 gm	192	3.79	8	4
Sabina	USA	silky bouclé	5	5	46% acrylic 29% viscose 25% linen	hand wash	50 gm	108	4.95	10	—
Flere Troder/USA Flere Troder/USA (Double strand)	USA	basic	5	6½–5	100% acrylic	hand wash machine wash	1 lb.	5,200	—	—	—
Froehlich Wolle Camel	USA	smooth	4–5	7	70% wool 30% camel hair	hand wash warm water	50 gm	220	5.00	—	—
Coton-Swiss Holiday	USA	3-ply novelty	4–6	6	75% cotton 25% viscose	wash 100° F max.	50 gm	120	4.00	—	—
Coton-Weekend	USA	3-ply flake	4–6	6	100% Egyptian cotton	wash 100° F max.	50 gm	120	2.60	—	—

Brand and Yarn Name	Where Sold	Type	US Needle Size	Gauge/Tension per Inch	Fiber Content	Cleaning Care	Skein, Hank, Ball, or Cone Weight	Approx. Yardage	Approx. Price	Approx. No. of Skeins for a Small-size Standard Knit Pullover Sweater with Long Sleeves and Crew Neck			
										Man	Woman	Child	Infant
Dietolle Wolle	USA	smooth classic	4-5	5-6	100% wool	hand wash machine wash, gentle, warm	50 gm	176	4.25	—	—	—	—
Gemini Brio	dis.	shiny ribbon multicolor	4	6	100% rayon	dry clean	—	100	7.00	—	10 12	—	—
Goldfingering	USA	metallic	6	6	20% polyester 80% viscose	dry clean	25 gm	110	4.50	—	—	—	—
Goldfingering Multi	USA	metallic	6	6	20% polyester 80% viscose	dry clean	20 gm	88	4.00	—	—	—	—
Goldfingering Double Gold	USA	metallic	6	6	20% polyester 80% viscose	dry clean	50 gm	110	8.00	—	—	—	—
Silkworm	USA	silky, shiny	5	6	100% rayon	dry clean	—	150	5.00	—	12 14	—	—
Grandor Catalan	dis.	knubby	3	6	59% cotton 33% acrylic 4% linen 4% polyester	machine wash	50 gm	120	2.50	—	8	—	—
Shantung	dis.	smooth	3	6	65% natural silk 35% pure wool	hand wash	25 gm	100	3.00	15	12	—	—
Sumatra	USA	hairy, brushed	8	5	67% acrylic 33% nylon	machine wash	25 gm	54	1.75	14	12	—	—
Sunbeam Mohair	USA	hairy, brushed	8	5	67% mohair 28% wool 5% nylon	hand wash	25 gm	54	3.25	14	12	7	—
Tussah Z	USA	smooth	3	6	100% tussah silk	dry clean	1 oz.	95	1.80	—	—	—	—
Tussah Z1	USA	smooth	4	5	100% tussah silk	dry clean	1 oz.	60	1.80	—	—	—	—
Tussah Z2	USA	smooth	4	5	100% tussah silk	dry clean	1 oz.	60	1.80	—	—	—	—
Susanna	dis.	smooth ribbony	5	4½	100% cotton	machine wash	50 gm	125	3.90	—	11	8	—
Grignasco Gricable	USA	cable twist yarn	5	6	65% acrylic 35% wool	machine wash, warm	50 gm	246	2.49	7	5	3	2
Grifox	USA	Shetland-type classic & heathers	5	6	50% wool 50% acrylic	machine wash, warm	50 gm	191	2.15	8	6	3	2

B

Yarn	Country	Texture	Needle	Needle	Fiber content	Care	Weight	Yardage	Price				
Grirudy	USA	mohair-type fuzzy-broad subtle color changes	5	6	50% acrylic 40% mohair 10% wool	hand wash, warm	50 gm	219	5.29	7	5	3	2
Halcyon Yarn 3/2 Pearl Cotton	—	smooth perle twist mercerized	4-7	5½-6½	100% cotton	cool wash, machine dry damp, dry flat, strong contrast: dry clean	2.4 oz / approx. 16-18 oz	180 / 1,200-1,350	—	22 oz	16 oz	11 oz	7 oz
Gemstone Silk	—	smooth shiny	3-5	5-6	100% spun silk	cool wash, dry clean	3.5 oz	275	—	—	15 oz	—	—
Victorian	—	smooth 2-ply	4-5	5-6	100% wool	handwash, dry clean	approx. 4 oz	approx. 350	—	20 oz	16 oz	12 oz	8 oz
Harrisville Designs HD Tweed 2-ply	USA	2-ply with nubs	7	5	100% virgin wool	hand wash, dry clean	100 gm / 8 oz	220 / 500	5.40 / 9.25	6	5	3-4	2
Hayfield of England Brushed (double knitting)	USA CA GB	brushed doubleknit	6	5½	50% acrylic 50% nylon	machine wash	100 gm	361	4.95	3	3	2	—
Caribbean	USA CA GB	knubby shimmer	6	5½	50% viscose 18½% Casmillion 18% nylon 13½% cotton	machine wash	50 gm	91	3.95	—	8	—	—
Hawaii (Double knitting)	USA CA GB	nubby	6	5½	50% acrylic 50% nylon	machine wash	50 gm	154	3.95	9	8	—	—
Memories	USA CA GB	satin sheen doubleknit	6	5½	50% viscose 30% acrylic 20% nylon	machine wash	50 gm	128	2.95	12	10	—	—
Papillon	USA CA GB	angora-like and feel	6	5½	50% brushed acrylic 50% nylon	hand wash; machine wash	40 gm	105	2.95	12	11	—	—
Premier Brushed (Double knitting)	USA CA GB	brushed shimmer	6	5½	50% acrylic 50% nylon	machine wash	100 gm	361	5.75	3	3	—	—
Pretty Cotton	USA CA GB	smooth	6	5½	52% cotton 24% acrylic 24% nylon	machine wash	40 gm	136	2.50	6	5	3	—
Pretty Pastels (Double knitting)	USA CA GB	baby	6	5½	50% acrylic 50% nylon	machine wash	40 gm	136	1.95	8	7	4	2
Pretty Whites (Double knitting)	USA CA GB	baby	6	5½	50% acrylic 50% bri-nylon	machine wash	40 gm	136	1.95	8	7	4	2
Pretty Whites Lustre	USA CA GB	smooth shimmer	6	5½	42% acrylic 42% bri-nylon 16% viscose	machine wash	40 gm	128	2.25	9	8	5	2

Brand and Yarn Name	Where Sold	Type	US Needle Size	Gauge/Tension per Inch	Fiber Content	Cleaning Care	Skein, Hank, Ball, or Cone Weight	Approx. Yardage	Approx. Price	Approx. No. of Skeins for a Small-size Standard Knit Pullover Sweater with Long Sleeves and Crew Neck			
										Man	Woman	Child	Infant
Raw Cotton	USA CA GB	smooth	6	5½	100% cotton	hand wash	50 gm	121	2.50	9	8	5	2
Safari	USA CA GB	ribbon-type doubleknit	6	5½	50% nylon 50% acrylic	machine wash	50 gm	167	6.50	7	6	3	—
Surfer	USA CA GB	—	6	5½	47% polyester 42.5% acrylic 10.5% nylon	machine wash	50 gm	142	4.50	7	6	3	—
Top Nop (Double knitting)	USA CA GB	nubby double-knit	6	5½	50% acrylic 50% nylon	machine wash	100 gm	296	5.75	6	5	3	—
Heirloom Century	USA CA	solids & heathers	5	6	100% virgin wool	dry clean hand wash	1 lb.	2,000	12.50	—	—	—	—
Erin	USA CA	solids & heathers	6	5 (2 strands)	80% Orlon 20% virgin wool	machine wash, dry clean	1 lb.	3,200	10.95	—	—	—	—
Foxfire	USA CA	smooth & sparkle	6	5	60% acrylic 40% nylon	machine wash dry clean	1 lb.	1,750	8.20	—	—	—	—
Olympic	USA CA	smooth	6	5	100% Wintuk Orlon	machine wash & dry	1 lb.	1,750	8.20	—	·	—	—
Oceanside	USA CA	smooth	3 machine knit 8–10	6 7	100% mercerized cotton	hand wash dry clean	1 lb.	1,600	18.95	—	—	—	—
Hovland Aase	GB	smooth	4	6	100% wool	careful hand wash	100 gm	198	5.80	10	8	7	—
Aran	NO	smooth	7	4½	80% acrylic 20% wool	hand wash dry flat	400 gm	744	7.75	2	2	1	—
Aran	NO	smooth	7	4½	80% acrylic 20% wool	hand wash dry flat	50 gm	93	2.30	12	10	7	—
Pingorina	NO	2-ply Angora blend heather	4	27/4	65% wool 25% Angora 10% polyamide	hand wash dry clean	20 gm	119	1.95	—	14	—	—
Ironstone Flake	USA	mercerized	—	6	100% cotton	hand wash	100 gm	328	4.50	6	5	4	—
3/2 Pearle	dis.	—	—	6	100% cotton		100 gm	275	3.50	—	4	—	—
Spiral	dis.	—	—	6	100% cotton		100 gm	438	3.50	—	4	—	—
Jaeger Jaeger Cotton Flammé	USA CA GB	fancy thick & thin	6	5½	55% cotton 45% rayon	hand wash dry flat	50 gm	126	—	12	9	7	3

B

Name	Country	Type	Needle	Needle	Fiber	Wash	Put-up	Yards	Price	18 oz	15 oz	9 oz	6 oz
Jagger Spun Highland Heather 3/8	USA	waxed classic worsted	5–6	7	100% wool	hand wash dry clean	1 lb. cone / 4 oz. skein	1,490 / 370	14.75 / 4.95	5	4	3	2
Jagge Ragg	USA	waxed classic worsted tweeds & heathers	5–6	7	100% wool	hand wash dry clean	1 lb. cone / 4 oz. skein	1,400 / 360	12.00 / 4.25	5	4	3	2
Joseph Galler, Inc. Deauville	USA SW	bright classic	6–7	5	53% linen 47% rayon	hand wash dry clean	50 gm	129	4.90	14	12	6	—
Fantasia	USA	thick & thin	6–7	5½	60% wool 20% linen 20% silk	hand wash	50 gm	150	5.80	14	10	8	4
Fiorina	USA SW	fine cable cotton	7	5	100% Egyptian cotton	hand wash machine wash	50 gm	126	4.90	15	13	7	4
Flamme	USA FR	thick & thin	7	5	100% cotton	hand wash machine wash	40 gm	105	2.25	16	12	10	5
Frivolous	USA	bouclé	6–7	5½–5	100% wool	hand wash dry clean	50 gm	153	5.20	14	10	8	—
Fun & Sport	USA	classic	7	6–5½	100% Courtelle acrylic	hand wash machine wash	50 gm	200	1.90	10	8	4	2–3
Galler's 100% Silk	USA	classic	6–7	6–5	100% silk	hand wash dry clean	50 gm	265	20.00	—	4	—	—
Ice Cream	USA SW	bright sporty	5–6	6–5½	62% cotton 38% rayon	hand wash dry clean	50 gm	140	3.50	—	12	8	—
Pony	USA SW	classic sport	6–7	6–5½	100% wool	hand wash machine wash	50 gm	154	3.50	14	12	8	4
Sea-Breeze	dis.	novelty dressy	6	5½	68% rayon 21% acrylic 11% wool	hand wash	50 gm	150	3.70	—	10	7	—
Troubadour	USA	soft silky baby yarn	7	5½–6	88% acrylic 12% rayon	hand wash machine wash	50 gm	180	2.70	—	10	8	3
Katia Alpaca	USA	—	7	5	68% acrylic 32% alpaca	—	50 gm	150	4.60	—	7	—	—
Astola	USA	—	6	5½	60% acrylic 40% mohair	—	50 gm	206	4.80	—	6	—	—
Bolero	USA	—	5	5¾	100% rayon	—	50 gm	115	6.00	—	9–11	—	—
Creppi	USA	—	5	5½	87% acrylic 13% nylon	—	100 gm	302	5.85	—	3–5	—	—
Fete	USA	—	5	7	65% acrylic 35% metallic	—	25 gm	137	5.40	—	—	—	—

Brand and Yarn Name	Where Sold	Type	US Needle Size	Gauge/Tension per Inch	Fiber Content	Cleaning Care	Skein, Hank, Ball, or Cone Weight	Approx. Yardage	Approx. Price	Approx. No. of Skeins for a Small-size Standard Knit Pullover Sweater with Long Sleeves and Crew Neck			
										Man	Woman	Child	Infant
Tornasol	USA	—	6	6	55% rayon 45% acrylic	—	50 gm	126	3.75	—	8	—	—
Knitting Fever Dynasty	USA	—	7	5	47% silk 43% acrylic 10% nylon	—	40 gm	143	4.50	—	8	—	—
Lanas Margarita Chispa	dis.	novelty	3	6	42% acrylic 58% cotton	hand wash	50 gm	185	4.10	—	—	—	—
Delfos	USA ES FR IT DE GB	novelty	6	5	65% acrylic 35% nylon	hand wash	50 gm	136	3.60	—	10	—	—
Delicata	USA DE ES FR GB IT	superkid mohair	6	5	90% mohair 10% nyon	hand wash	25 gm	122	7.20	—	12	—	—
Egeo	USA ES FR IT DE GB	tweed	5	6	50% cotton 50% acrylic	machine wash	50 gm	142	3.50	7	6	4	2
Liquen	USA ES FR IT DE GB	coconut or mustache	5	6	42% cotton 42% acrylic 16% nylon	machine wash	50 gm	142	4.50	7	6	4	2
Margarita 75	USA ES FR IT DE GB	fuzzy	4	6	50% acrylic 50% mohair	hand wash	50 gm	186	4.40	—	5	—	—
Margarita Tres	USA ES FR IT DE GB	classic	5	6	100% acrylic	machine wash	100 gm	295	5.60	3	3	2	1
Rustik Lin	USA ES FR IT DE GB	thick & thin	5	5	60% cotton 40% linen	hand wash	100 gm	260	6.50	—	4	—	—
Lane Borgosesia Bimbi	USA	shrink resistant anti-allergic	4	6	100% virgin wool	hand wash	50 gm	210	4.50	—	—	—	3
Hilton	USA	basic	5	6	100% merino wool	hand wash	50 gm	213	3.50	—	6	—	—
Hilton Tweed	USA	multi-colored fleck	5	6	100% merino wool	hand wash	50 gm	213	3.99	—	6	—	—
Lana del Borgo	USA	Shetland	6	5.5	60% wool 40% cotton	hand wash	50 gm	133	4.99	—	7	—	—
Lee Wards Sport	USA	basic	5	6	100% Orlon	hand wash machine wash	2 oz.	250	—	—	6-8	—	—
Lily Art 925 Sugar 'n Cream Sporty	USA	2-ply pear twist sportweight	4	6	100% cotton	hand wash machine wash	1.75 oz.	161	2.00	14	11	8	6

B

Yarn	Origin	Description	Needle	Gauge	Fiber Content	Care	Put-up	Yds/lb	Price				
Lion Brand Charmette	USA	cable twist sport yarn	6 / G	6	100% acrylic	machine wash	40 gm	153	—	—	—	—	—
Debyshire Solids & Prints	USA	3-ply sport or baby yarn	Hook E / 5	4½ / 5	100% DuPont Wintuk	machine wash & dry	solid 2 oz. ombré 1½ oz.	224 / 178	—	—	—	—	—
Glitter Knit	USA	3-ply sport-metallic look	4	6	95% Orlon Wintuk 5% metallic thread	machine wash & dry	40 gm	—	—	—	—	—	—
Jamie (solids & prints)	USA	baby 3-ply, pompadour	E & G / 6	4 / 5½	85% DuPont Orlon Sayelle 15% rayon	machine wash & dry	solid 1½ oz. print 1½ oz.	280 / 210	—	—	—	—	—
Lisle Angora Lamb	USA	smooth & light	5	6	60% lambswool 40% Angora	hand wash cold water, ivory only	4, 8 & 16 oz. skein, solid colors in 16 oz. cones	2,300 ypp	4 oz. = 24.00 hand-dyed 4 oz. = 16.00 natural	3	3	2	1
Fairytails	USA	classic with pigtail	6	5.5	100% U.S. cotton	hand wash, cold water, ivory only	4, 8 & 16 oz. skeins, solid colors in 16 oz. cones	1,100 pp	4 oz. = 13.00 hand dyed 4 oz. = 6.00 natural	4	4	2-3	2
Navajo Sportweight	USA	smooth, soft	7	6	100% U.S. wool	hand wash, cold water, ivory only	4, 8 & 16 oz.	1,200 ypp	4 oz = 14.00 hand-dyed	4	4	2-3	2
Pretty Nubby	USA	classic European light slub	5	5	60% rayon 40% cotton	hand wash, cold water, ivory only	4, 8 & 16 oz. skeins, solid colors in 16 oz. cones	950 ypp	4 oz. = 13.00 hand-dyed 4 oz. = 6.00 natural	5	5	3	2
Silk Cord	USA	cotton string construction	6	5.5	100% very fine silk	hand wash, cold water, ivory only	3, 5 & 7 oz.	840 ypp	3.5 oz = 21.00 hand-dyed 3.5 oz. = 15.00 natural	5	5	3-4	2
Lo-Ran Hayfield Brushed DK	USA	variegated to run along with ribbon	10½	4	50% acrylic 50% nylon	machine wash & dry	100 gm	361	4.95	—	—	—	—
Silky Soft Ribbon	USA	⅛" ribbon	7	5	100% polyester	machine wash & dry	—	100	11.50	—	6	—	—
Macauslan Shetland	USA GB	—	5	7	100% Shetland wool	wool wash dry clean	1 oz. 1 lb. 2½ lb. 3 lb.	145 2,300 — —	2.50-3.25 — — —	12	10	7	3-4
Mark Yarns Moonlight Metallic	USA	shiny	5-6	6	55% viscose 15% polyamide 30% polyester	hand wash dry clean	20 gm	120	6.40	—	10-11	—	—
Venice	USA	smooth	5-6	5	70% viscose 30% cotton	hand wash dry clean	—	77	5.00	—	18	—	—

Brand and Yarn Name	Where Sold	Type	US Needle Size	Gauge/Tension per Inch	Fiber Content	Cleaning Care	Skein, Hank, Ball, or Cone Weight	Approx. Yardage	Approx. Price	Man	Woman	Child	Infant
Mary Lou Lustro	USA	baby novelty machine	—	—	50% DuPont Sayelle 50% Antron nylon	machine wash	1½ lb.	3,360	21.00	1	1	½	—
Trio 3/11	USA	novelty machine	—	—	100% DuPont acrylic	machine wash	1.1 lb.	2,100	11.00	1	1	½	—
Melrose Baby Camel	USA	—	6	6	50% baby camel 40% wool 10% acrylic	—	20 gm	117	5.99	—	—	—	—
Cottonette	USA	—	5	5.5	54% cotton 46% rayon	—	1.5 oz.	100	3.30	—	—	—	—
Lorie	USA	—	6	5-6	73% rayon 27% cotton	—	1-1¼ lb.	750	32.00	—	—	—	—
Memory Four	USA	—	6	5	98% cotton 2% stretch fibre	—	50 gm	160	3.50	—	—	—	—
Perlite	USA	—	5	5.5	45% rayon 55% Mylar	—	—	100	6.50	—	—	—	—
Rayonette	USA	—	5	5.5	100% rayon	—	1.5 oz.	100	3.25	—	—	—	—
Rombo	USA	novelty	6	6	rayon/beads	—	—	—	—	—	—	—	—
Rosette	USA	—	5	5.5	100% rayon	—	1.75 oz.	100	5.70	—	—	—	—
Suzette	USA	—	5	5.5	50% rayon 50% Mylar	—	1.25 oz.	70	6.50	—	—	—	—
Merino Altaga 5 Fils	—	—	6	5½	100% alpaca	—	50 gm	135	11.00	—	—	—	—
Cleopatra	—	terry multicolor	5	6	52% cotton 48% acrylic	—	50 gm	136	6.50	—	—	—	—
Cotton Club	—	classic, mercerized	5	6	100% cotton	—	50 gm	130	5.50	—	—	—	—
Cotton Gin	—	rustic-glimmer	8	5	75% cotton 24% rayon 1% nylon	—	50 gm	108	4.00	—	—	—	—
Laguna	—	rustic matte	5	5	23% silk 34% cotton 33% acrylic 10% nylon	—	50 gm	130	5.50	—	—	—	—
Lumi-Tweed	—	multicolor metallic	5	6	60% rayon 40% metalized polyester	—	20 gm	79	7.50	—	—	—	—

Approx. No. of Skeins for a Small-size Standard Knit Pullover Sweater with Long Sleeves and Crew Neck

B

Name	Country	Texture			Fiber	Care	Weight	Yards	Price				
Mohair Doux	—	soft fluffy	5	5½	80% super kid mohair 20% acrylic	—	50 gm	154	12.00	—	—	—	—
Ray-Cot	—	matte-shiny	4	6	60% rayon 40% cotton	—	50 gm	137	5.30	—	—	—	—
Rebelle	—	shiny with pigtails	5	5	66% rayon 17% cotton 17% acrylic	—	50 gm	126	6.40	—	—	—	—
Super Wash	—	smooth classic worsted	5	6	100% wool	—	50 gm	137	6.00	—	—	—	—
Tricheuse	—	soft, fluffy	5	5	53% kid mohair 25% wool 22% acrylic	—	50 gm	165	8.60	—	—	—	—
Millor Piropo	USA	smooth cabled	—	6	90% acrylic 10% nylon	machine wash & dry	9 oz.	861	—	3	2	—	—
Nature Spun Nature Spun 3/9	USA	worsted	5	6	100% wool	hand wash dry clean	3.5 oz 1 lb.	368 1,682	3.99-4.25 18.95	— —	— —	— —	— —
Nomis Conny	USA	hairy, brushed	5	7	100% brushed acrylic	machine wash & dry	40 gm	195	—	9	6	4	3
Excellence Sport	USA	smooth	5	6	100% DuPont acrylic	machine wash & dry	50 gm	245	—	9	6	4	3
Lustro Sport	USA	smooth shiny	5	6	100% DuPont acrylic	machine wash & dry	50 gm	245	—	9	6	4	3
Lustro Sport Ombre	USA	smooth ombré	5	6	100% DuPont acrylic	machine wash & dry	50 gm	245	—	9	6	4	3
Lustro Print	USA	smooth space-dyed	5	6	100% DuPont acrylic	machine wash & dry	50 gm	245	—	9	6	4	—
Nomotta Arabesque	USA	multicolor	5	5½	40% acrylic 33% cotton 27% viscose	hand wash do not bleach do not iron dry clean	50 gm	109	4.25	—	13	—	—
Extra	USA	basic	6	5½	100% new wool	machine wash, gentle do not bleach dry clean	50 gm	137	2.95	12	10	—	—
Femia	USA	textured	5	5	80% acrylic 20% viscose	machine wash, gentle do not bleach do not iron dry clean	50 gm	109	2.95	—	13	—	—
Frasquita	USA	bouclé	4	5½	75% cotton 25% viscose	hand wash do not bleach do not dry clean	50 gm	109	3.95	—	13	—	—

Brand and Yarn Name	Where Sold	Type	US Needle Size	Gauge/Tension per Inch	Fiber Content	Cleaning Care	Skein, Hank, Ball, or Cone Weight	Approx. Yardage	Approx. Price	Approx. No. of Skeins for a Small-size Standard Knit Pullover Sweater with Long Sleeves and Crew Neck			
										Man	Woman	Child	Infant
Viola	USA	textured	2	6	75% acrylic 18% cotton 7% polyamide	machine wash, gentle do not bleach do not iron dry clean	50 gm	159	3.95	10	9	—	—
Noro Koto	USA	—	7	5	100% silk	—	25 gm	106	9.50	—	8-10	—	—
Miho	USA	—	6	6	100% rayon	—	50 gm	500	9.00	—	4-6	—	—
Patons Arran	USA CA GB	smooth classic	6	5	70% acrylic 30% wool	machine wash & dry	50 gm	100	—	15	11	9	7
Astra	USA CA	smooth classic	5	6	100% acrylic	machine wash & dry	50 gm	182	—	11	9	4	2
Beehive DK	USA CA GB	smooth classic	6	5½	75% acrylic 25% wool	machine wash dry flat	50 gm	162	—	9	7	5	3
Beehive DK with Mountain Wool	USA CA GB	smooth classic	6	5½	50% acrylic 25% nylon 25% wool	machine wash dry flat	50 gm	158	—	9	7	5	3
Cotton Club	USA CA	slub	6	5½	56% acrylic 33% cotton 11% viscose	machine wash & dry	50 gm	175	—	10	8	5	2
Cotton Colada	dis.	nubby, shiny & matte	6	5½	54% rayon 44% cotton 2% nylon	hand wash dry flat	50 gm	88	—	16	13	10	7
Cotton Perlé	USA CA GB	perle mercerized	6	5½	100% cotton	hand wash dry flat	50 gm	115	—	14	11	8	5
Cotton Soft	dis.	smooth matte	6	5½	100% cotton	hand wash dry flat	50 gm	115	—	14	11	8	5
Cotton Splash	dis.	nubby, print dye	6	5	53% cotton 43% viscose 4% nylon	hand wash dry flat	50 gm	96	—	11	9	7	4
Cotton Top	USA CA AU GB	bouclé	6	5	100% cotton	hand wash dry flat	50 gm	126	—	10	8	6	3
Jenny	USA CA	basic	6	5	97% acrylic 3% nylon	machine wash & dry	50 gm	157	—	9	7	5	2
Linen Look	dis.	small slub	6	5¼	63% acrylic 17% cotton 13% linen 7% wool	hand wash dry flat	50 gm	137	—	12	9	5	2
Moorland DK	USA CA GB	smooth classic	6	5½	100% wool	hand wash dry flat	50 gm	150	—	15	12	9	3

Name	Country	Type	Needle	Gauge	Fiber	Care	Weight	Yards	Price				
Pearl Twist	USA CA	basic	6	5½	80% acrylic 20% nylon	machine wash & dry	50 gm	137	—	12	9	5	2
Solo DK	USA CA GB	brushed	6	5½	56% acrylic 24% wool 20% mohair	hand wash dry flat	50 gm	175	—	10	8	5	2
Tres Chic	USA CA	metallic nubby	6	5½	52% viscose 20% linen 10% acrylic 8% nylon 7% cotton 3% polyester	dry clean	50 gm	118	—	14	11	8	3
Peer Gynt/Norsk Engros USA Peer Gynt	—	sportweight, classic	2	6	100% wool	hand wash dry clean	100 gm	195	5.90	9	7	4	3
Peer Gynt/ Scandinavian House Imports Peer Gynt	NO	smooth	4	6	wool	hand wash dry clean	100 gm	197	7.10	—	8	—	—
Perendale Sportweight	USA	sportweight	4	6	100% Perendale wool	hand wash dry flat	50 gm	167	3.00	12	10	7	5
Pernelle Insouciance	USA	slub	5-6	6	72% acrylic 28% linen	hand wash dry clean	50 gm	135	4.20	—	9-10	—	—
Les Bouquet	USA	classic	5-6	6	51% wool 49% acrylic	machine	50 gm	140	2.85	—	7-8	—	—
Neige	USA	brushed	5-6	5½	50% acrylic 50% polyamide	hand wash dry clean	—	90	2.50	—	12	—	—
Nuage	USA	brushed mohair	5-6	6	80% acrylic 10% mohair 10% wool	hand wash dry clean	—	240	3.95	—	5	—	—
Touareg	USA	smooth	5-6	6	75% acrylic 25% wool	machine wash	50 gm	150	2.30	—	7-8	—	—
Phentex Galleria Avanti	USA CA	2-ply	9	4st-8R= 1po.	63% acrylic 20% wool 17% mohair	machine wash, cold; machine dry, gentle	50 gm	110	2.20	—	—	—	—
Baby Brite	USA CA	3-ply	3	8st-13R =1po.	80% acrylic 20% acetate	machine wash, cold; machine dry, gentle	45 gm	235	1.19	—	—	—	—
Baby yarn	USA CA	3-ply	8	5m/st-9R =1po.	100% acrylic	machine wash, cold; machine dry, gentle	50 gm	200	1.19	—	—	—	—
Cotton Acapulco	USA CA	2-ply	4	6st-12R= 1po.	60% viscose 40% cotton	machine wash, cold; machine dry, gentle	40 gm	110	3.50	—	—	—	—

Brand and Yarn Name	Where Sold	Type	US Needle Size	Gauge/Tension per Inch	Fiber Content	Cleaning Care	Skein, Hank, Ball, or Cone Weight	Approx. Yardage	Approx. Price	Man	Woman	Child	Infant
Cotton Jeannie	USA CA	6-ply	6	5st-8R=1po.	100% cotton	machine wash, cold; machine dry, gentle	40 gm	90	2.95	—	—	—	—
Cotton Sweet	USA CA	2-ply	7	5st-8R=1po.	61% acrylic 31% cotton 5% polyester 3% nylon	machine wash, cold; machine dry, gentle	40 gm	105	1.69	—	—	—	—
Harmony	USA CA	—	4	5st-10R=1po	100% brushed acrylic	machine wash, cold; machine dry, gentle	50 gm	140	1.19	—	—	—	—
Machine Knit Cotton Sport	USA CA	6-ply	6	5st-8R=1po	100% cotton	machine wash, cold; machine dry, gentle	1 lb.	1,020	27.95	—	—	—	—
Machine Knit Sport	USA CA	3-ply	4	7st-12R=1po.	100% acrylic	machine wash, cold; machine dry, gentle	1 lb.	1,815	9.95	—	—	—	—
Mohair	USA CA	2-ply	4	6st-10R=1po.	85% acrylic 15% mohair	machine wash, cold; machine dry, gentle	50 gm	175	1.79	—	—	—	—
Sterling	USA CA	2-ply	7	4st-6R=1po.	70% acrylic 30% nylon	machine wash, cold; machine dry, gentle	50 gm	90	1.49	—	—	—	—
Vegas	USA CA	3-ply	8	4st-9R=1po.	43% viscose 41% acrylic 10% mohair 4% polyester 2% nylon	machine wash, cold; machine dry, gentle	40 gm	75	4.50	—	—	—	—
Phildar Alpalima	dis.	alpaca blend	5	6	60% alpaca 40% acrylic	machine wash hand wash	50 gm	213	5.95	—	7	—	—
Canelis	USA	summer	5	6.5	67% acrylic 33% viscose	machine wash	50 gm	128	3.50	—	13	—	—
Indira	USA	fancy	5	6	31% cotton 27% acrylic 27% viscose 15% polyester	machine wash hand wash	50 gm	138	3.10	—	10	—	—
Nanette	USA	Angora blend	5	6.5	40% Angora 50% wool 10% polyamide	hand wash	10 gm	50	4.75	—	24	—	—

Approx. No. of Skeins for a Small-size Standard Knit Pullover Sweater with Long Sleeves and Crew Neck

Name		Description			Fiber	Care	Weight	Yards	Price		Needle		
Ovation	USA	fancy bouclé	5	5.5	77% acrylic 15% viscose 8% polyamide	machine wash hand wash	50 gm	132	3.75	—	10	—	—
Phil Douce	USA	mohair blend	6	5.25	75% acrylic 20% kid mohair 5% wool	hand wash	40 gm	149	3.50	—	9	—	—
Pronostic	USA	classic	5	6	80% acrylic 20% wool	machine wash	50 gm	175	2.35	—	8	—	—
Pingouin Boule de coton	USA FR	bouclé	6	14/4	100% cotton	machine wash dry clean	50 gm	71	3.45	—	10°	—	—
Bouclé Sport	dis.	—	11	9/4	68% acrylic 30% wool 2% polyester	—	—	55	—	—	—	—	—
Bouclette	USA FR	bouclé	4	22/4	60% cotton 40% acrylic	machine wash dry clean	50 gm	153	3.95	—	8°	—	—
Bourrette de Soie	USA FR	4-ply, soft sheen, raw silk	6	20/4	100% silk	—	50 gm	140	4.95	—	10°	—	—
Chenille	dis.	—	6	17/4	100% acrylic	hand wash dry clean	50 gm	100	—	—	9°	—	—
Confort	USA FR	heather 3-ply	4	23/4	50% wool 10% mohair 40% acrylic	machine wash dry clean	50 gm	140	2.45	—	9°	—	—
Confort Irise	dis.	3-ply with metallic strand	4	23/4	48% wool 39% acrylic 10% mohair 3% polyester	machine wash dry clean	50 gm	140	3.95	—	9°	—	—
Confortable	dis.	3-ply heather	4	21/4	55% wool 45% acrylic	machine wash dry clean	50 gm	140	—	—	9°	—	—
Coton et Lin	dis.	thick & thin 2-ply	3	29/4	80% cotton 20% linen	hand wash dry clean	50 gm	150	2.95	—	11°	—	—
Coton Naturel 8 Fils	dis.	8-ply, smooth	6	20/4	100% cotton	machine wash dry clean	50 gm	90	2.45	—	12°	—	—
Coton Ville	dis.	curly 2-ply	3	26/4	100% cotton	hand wash dry clean	50 gm	125	3.95	—	12°	—	—
Eaux Vives	dis.	—	3	22/4	70% acrylic 30% linen	—	50 gm	110	—	—	—	—	—
Eponge	dis.	bouclé 4-ply	4	19/4	95% cotton 5% viscose	hand wash dry clean	50 gm	77	—	—	14°	—	—
Etincelle	dis.	thick & thin 3-ply with metallic strand	6	21/4	92% cotton 5% viscose 3% polyester	hand wash dry clean	50 gm	95	3.95	—	12°	—	—

°Size 14

B

Brand and Yarn Name	Where Sold	Type	US Needle Size	Gauge/Tension per Inch	Fiber Content	Cleaning Care	Skein, Hank, Ball, or Cone Weight	Approx. Yardage	Approx. Price	Approx. No. of Skeins for a Small-size Standard Knit Pullover Sweater with Long Sleeves and Crew Neck			
										Man	Woman	Child	Infant
Fil d'Ecosse #3	—	4-ply beaded	6	20/4	100% cotton	machine wash dry clean	50 gm	95	3.45	—	12°	—	—
Flanerie	dis.	2-ply variegated blend	6	21/4	75% acrylic 25% mohair	hand wash, dry clean	50 gm	95	4.75	—	12°	—	—
4 Pingouins	USA FR	4-ply smooth	6	23/4	100% wool	machine wash dry clean	50 gm	140	2.95	—	8°	—	—
Givre	USA FR	fuzzy heather with white or grey base	8	16/4	32% polyamide 30% acrylic 25% mohair 13% wool	hand wash dry clean	50 gm	80	4.45	—	10°	—	—
Granitee	dis.	bouclé 2-ply	3	28/4	60% wool 40% polyamide	hand wash dry clean	50 gm	165	—	—	9°	—	—
Kirounal	USA FR	soft worsted	6	6	50% acrylic 40% wool 10% viscose	machine wash delicate	50 gm	132	—	—	—	—	—
Laine et Mohair	dis.	fuzzy heather	4	23/4	70% wool 24% mohair 5% polyamide	hand wash dry clean	50 gm	130	3.95	—	8°	—	—
Luciole	USA FR	shiny ribbon/ novelty	8	5	69% polyamide 20% viscose 11% polyester	hand wash	20 gm	132	—	—	—	—	—
Metis	USA FR	thick & thin 4-ply	6	15/4	60% cotton 40% linen	machine wash dry clean	50 gm	77	3.45	—	13°	—	—
Mistigri	dis.	2-ply blended colors	6	20/4	75% acrylic 25% wool	machine wash dry clean	50 gm	110	2.25	—	9°	—	—
Mohair et Soie	USA FR	fluffy soft	4	6	85% kid mohair 15% silk	hand wash	20 gm	66	—	—	8°	—	—
Pingofrance	USA FR	beaded 3-ply	4	23/4	75% acrylic 25% wool	machine wash dry clean	50 gm	150	1.69	—	8°	—	—
Pingoluxe	dis.	6-ply shiny crinkled	3	30/4	73% acetate 27% polyamide	hand wash dry clean	50 gm	130	—	—	12°	—	—
Pingorina	dis.	2-ply Angora blend heather	4	27/4	65% wool 25% Angora 10% polyamide	hand wash dry clean	20 gm	110	—	—	14°	—	—
Poudreuse	USA FR	fuzzy	6	21/4	80% acrylic 10% wool 10% mohair	hand wash dry clean	50 gm	155	2.25	—	7°	—	—
Soie & Laine	dis.	2-ply beaded, soft sheen	6	21/4	50% silk 50% wool	hand wash dry clean	20 gm	55	4.95	—	25°	—	—

Name	Origin	Description			Fiber	Care	Weight	Yards	Price				
Style Raphia	dis.	straw-like, matt	9	15/4	53% poly-propylene 47% polyester	machine wash dry clean	50 gm	125	3.95	—	10*	—	—
Tricotine	USA FR	tubular knit	7	20/4	100% cotton	machine wash dry clean	50 gm	77	3.95	—	12*	—	—
Type Shetland	dis.	heather 2-ply	6	23/4	100% wool	machine wash dry clean	50 gm	140	—	—	7	—	—
Whisper	dis.	fuzzy	4	23/4	100% acrylic	hand wash dry clean	50 gm	200	1.99	—	—	—	—
Plymouth Cairo Cotton	USA	—	5	6	100% cotton	hand wash	50 gm	165	2.80	—	8	—	—
Camel Hair	USA	—	5	6.5	100% camel hair	hand wash	20 gm	160	6.00	9	7	7	—
Cashmere	USA	—	5	6.5	100% cashmere	hand wash	20 gm	160	13.00	9	7	7	—
Emu Glimmer	USA	bouclé	5	5	100% acrylic	hand wash	50 gm	103	4.00	—	9	—	—
Emu Guernsey	USA	classic	3	7½	100% wool	hand wash	50 gm	123	3.00	18	14	9	—
Emu Perle	USA	sport	5	6	100% acrylic	hand wash	50 gm	134	2.50	—	11	—	—
Emu Spangle	USA	twist	5	5	66% viscose 31% acrylic 3% polyester	hand wash	50 gm	98	5.00	—	9	—	—
Indicieta 3-ply	USA	—	5	6	100% Peruvian alpaca	hand wash	50 gm	200	4.40	9	6	—	—
Indiecita 3-ply Dyed Heather	USA	sport	5	6	100% alpaca	handwash	50 gm	185	5.00	9	6	—	—
Lustre Ray	USA	—	5	6	70% wool 30% rayon	dry clean	2 oz.	260	3.50	—	6	—	—
Ric Rak	dis.	bouclé	5	6	100% cotton	hand wash	50 gm	170	2.60	9	7	5	—
Robin Diamante	USA	bouclé	5	5	87% acrylic 13% nylon	machine wash	50 gm	132	3.60	—	8	—	—
Saxony l	dis.	heather	—	—	100% wool	hand wash	50 gm	400	5.00	3-4	2-3	1-2	2-3
Woolray	USA	—	5	6	70% wool 30% rayon	hand wash	2 oz.	300	4.00	—	5 (10 double strand)	—	—
Rainbow Mills Crayons	USA	cotton cable cord, hand-dyed	8	4	100% mercerized cotton	hand wash dry clean	100 gm	140	11.00 variegated 8.00 solid	10	8	5	2-3
Paint Box	USA	hand-dyed	2	6	45% cotton 55% rayon	hand wash dry clean	100 gm	275	9.75 variegated 9.00 solid	5	4	2-3	1-2
Tango	USA	intertwined rayon/cotton ribbon tapes	8	4	rayon, nylon, cotton, metal, Pellon in some, polyester	dry clean	50 gm	70-80	5.70	—	12	—	—

*Size 14

B

Brand and Yarn Name	Where Sold	Type	US Needle Size	Gauge/Tension per Inch	Fiber Content	Cleaning Care	Skein, Hank, Ball, or Cone Weight	Approx. Yardage	Approx. Price	Approx. No. of Skeins for a Small-size Standard Knit Pullover Sweater with Long Sleeves and Crew Neck			
										Man	Woman	Child	Infant
Red Heart®													
Red Heart Cotton	USA	4-ply smooth	6	4½	100% cotton	machine wash dry flat	2½ oz.	115	1.85	14	11	5	4
Red Heart Cotton Sport Yarn	USA	3-ply smooth	5	5½	100% cotton	machine wash dry flat	2¼ oz.	180	1.99	9	7	3	2
Red Heart Luster Sheen	USA	cabled, smooth, lustrous	5	6	100% acrylic	machine wash & dry	2 oz.	180	1.59	10	8	6	3
Red Heart Mistelle	USA	3-ply brushed	7	5	100% acrylic	machine wash & dry	50 gm	150	1.69	11	9	5	3
Red Heart Sport Yarn	USA	2-ply smooth	5	5	100% Wintuk Orlon	machine wash & dry	2 oz.	240	1.29	8	6	4	2
Red Heart Super Sport Yarn	USA	3-ply smooth	7	5	100% Orlon acrylic	machine wash & dry	3 oz.	280	1.50	8	6	4	2
Reynolds Cashmere Sport	dis.	classic	5	6	65% cashmere 35% wool	dry clean	25 gm	85	—	—	13	—	—
Chesapeake	USA	—	6	5	70% wool 30% cotton	—	50 gm	110	—	—	11	—	—
Clover	USA	—	5	6	50% acrylic 50% linen	—	50 gm	135	—	—	10	—	—
Enjoue	dis.	bouclé	5	6	100% acrylic	wash	40 gm	165	—	—	8	—	—
Fireworks	USA	metallic glitter	4	6	100% Lurex	—	25 gm	150	—	—	10	—	—
Giselle	dis.	slub	4	6	100% cotton	wash	30 gm	90	—	—	12	—	—
Irish Linen	USA	—	3	5	100% linen	—	40 gm	100	—	—	12	—	—
Kalimousse	dis.	bouclé	3	6	100% wool	—	50 gm	158	—	—	15 / 2 piece suit	—	—
Mohair Classique	USA	fluffy	5	5½	52% mohair 48% acrylic	—	50 gm	215	—	—	5	—	—
Nature Yarn	dis.	vegetable-dyed	6	5½	100% natural	—	50 gm	115	—	—	10	—	—
Orient Express	dis.	luxury	4	6	47% silk 53% acrylic	—	30 gm	115	—	—	10	—	—
Pizzazz	USA	ray-rib, space-dyed	6	5½	100% nylon	—	50 gm	115	—	—	11	—	—

B

Name	Origin	Description			Fiber	Care	Ball	Yardage	Price				
Shetland de Sport	dis.	smooth classic worsted	6	5	100% wool	dry clean	40 gm	132	—	—	—	8	—	—
Slique	USA	wet look	4	6	56% cotton 44% rayon	—	40 gm	110	—	—	—	9	—	—
Sport Reynelle	dis.	smooth classic worsted	5	5½	100% Orlon	wash	2 oz	230	—	—	—	8	—	—
Town & Country	USA	smooth classic worsted	5	5½	85% wool 15% acrylic		50 gm	132	—	—	—	8	—	—
Une-Deux-Trois	USA	—	6 single 9 double	5½ single 4 double	80% acrylic 10% wool 10% nylon	—	40 gm	160	—	—	—	7 single	—	—
Richard Poppleton Carolin	USA CA GB AU	—	3-5	6	46% cotton 27% wool 19% acrylic 8% linen	hand wash	50 gm	153	3.75	6-8	5-7	5-7	4-5	—
Cotton for Baby	USA CA GB AU	—	3-5	6	100% cotton	machine wash	50 gm	156	2.95	—	—	—	—	2-3
Fiji	USA CA GB AU	—	3-5	6	100% cotton	hand wash	50 gm	156	2.95	5-6	5-7	3-6	3-4	—
Palette	USA CA GB AU	slub random dyed	3-5	6	70% acrylic 30% wool	machine wash	50 gm	157	3.85	8-10	7-9	7-9	5-7	—
Plaza	USA CA GB AU	cotton bouclé wrap	3-5	6	38% cotton 38% acrylic 13% wool 11% polyester	hand wash	50 gm	148	3.25	5-7	3-6	3-6	3-4	—
Plaza Plus	USA CA GB AU	multicolored cotton bouclé wrap	3-5	6	38% cotton 38% acrylic 13% wool 11% polyester	hand wash	50 gm	148	3.60	5-7	3-6	3-6	3-4	—
Rio Grande Wool Mill American Columbia	USA	2 single strands	6	6	100% wool	hand wash	4 oz.	175	10.00 dyed 8.75 white	8	6	6	4	—
Columbia/Kid Mohair	USA	2 single strands	8	6	100% wool	hand wash	4 oz.	216	12.00 dyed 8.00 white	6	4½	4½	3	N/A
Hand-Dyed Tweed	USA	2 single strands	8	6	100% wool	hand wash	4 oz.	200	10.00	6	4½	4½	3	2½
Montana Targhee/Mohair	USA	2 single strands (natural)	6	6	75% wool 25% mohair	hand wash	4 oz.	216	9.25	6	4½	4½	3	N/A

Brand and Yarn Name	Where Sold	Type	US Needle Size	Gauge/Tension per Inch	Fiber Content	Cleaning Care	Skein, Hank, Ball, or Cone Weight	Approx. Yardage	Approx. Price	Approx. No. of Skeins for a Small-size Standard Knit Pullover Sweater with Long Sleeves and Crew Neck			
										Man	Woman	Child	Infant
Montana Targhee/ Naturals	USA	2 single strands	8	5	100% wool	hand wash	4 oz.	194	8.00	7	6	3	2
Southwestern Naturals	USA	2 single strands	8	5	100% wool	hand wash	4 oz.	156	2.95	8	6	4	N/A
Rowan Yarns Rowan Designer DK	CA	smooth	6	6	100% wool	hand wash	50 gm	115 m	4.99	—	11	—	—
Rowan Flecks DK	CA	tweed	6	6	85% wool 15% cotton	hand wash	50 gm	120 m	6.99	—	10	—	—
Santa Fe Yarn Country Blend #501	USA	sport	5	5½	71% cotton 29% linen	dry clean	4 oz.	200	11.60	7	5	2	1
Crinkle Silk #201	USA	sport	6	5	73% silk 27% wool	dry clean	2 oz.	144	13.50	9	7	2½	1½
Linear Silk #222	USA	sport	8	5	100% silk	dry clean	100 gm	165	22.00	8	6	—	—
Nautical Cotton 1101	USA	sport	6	5	100% cotton	dry clean	4 oz.	210	8.80	6	5	2	1
Vintage #101	USA	sport	6	4½	100% rayon	dry clean	100 gm	227	9.70	6	4	2	1
Whisper #122 (used to double strand with yarns that stretch)	USA	sport	—	—	stretch nylon core wrapped with nylon	dry clean	25 gm	121	4.90	—	—	—	—
Schaffhauser Allround	USA	classic	4-5	6	100% wool	machine wash	50 gm	150	3.95	—	8	—	—
Bernina Sport	dis.	classic & tweed sock yarn	4-6	5	75% wool 25% polyamide	machine wash	50 gm	130	4.05	—	—	—	—
St. Tropez	USA	classic	3-5	6	50% lambswool 50% cotton	machine wash	—	142	4.60	—	10	—	—
Shetland for Men	USA	heathery & solid colors	3-5	6	100% wool	hand wash	50 gm	190	3.85	—	7	—	—
Summer Tweed	dis.	tweed	3-5	5½	60% cotton 34% acrylic 3% linen 3% viscose	machine wash	50 gm	150	3.75	—	8	—	—
Sunday	USA	classic	3-5	5½	77% cotton 16% viscose 7% linen	machine wash	—	134	4.10	—	10	—	—
Scheepjeswol Cotton Satin	US CA GB	slightly shiny, heavy	4	5½	100% cotton	machine wash, 30° C cool iron do not bleach	50 gm	110	4.50	14	12	10	—

B

Yarn	Texture	Country	Needle	Gauge	Fiber	Care	Ball wt	Yds	Price				
Cotton Supreme	heavy, slightly slubby	US / CA / GB	4	5½	86% cotton, 14% viscose	hand wash, lukewarm, cool iron, do not bleach	50 gm	115	3.50	14	12	—	—
Crystal	shiny, fuzzy	US / CA / GB	4	5¾	47% wool, 33% acrylic, 20% nylon	machine wash, 30°C, cool iron, do not bleach	50 gm	181	4.00	—	8	6	—
Kid Mohair 30%	soft, fluffy, heavy	US / CA / GB	5–6	5½	70% acrylic, 30% mohair	machine wash, 30°C, do not iron, do not bleach	50 gm	203	3.00	9	7	—	—
Linen	flat, cotton	US / CA / GB	4	6	60% cotton, 40% linen	machine wash, 30°C, do not iron, do not bleach	50 gm	187	4.00	13	8	6	—
Lurex (Fashion)	metallic, variegated	US / CA / GB	7	6	50% viscose, 25% cotton, 15% linen, 7% polyester, 3% nylon	hand wash, lukewarm, do not iron, do not bleach	50 gm	77	8.00	—	15	—	6
Raffia	fashionable, cotton	US / CA / GB	7	6¼	73% cotton, 24% viscose, 3% nylon	hand wash, lukewarm, do not iron, do not bleach	50 gm	104	4.50	—	9	—	—
Superwash Zermatt	basic, flat, heavy	US / CA / GB	4	5½	100% new wool	machine wash, & dry, do not iron, do not bleach	50 gm	99	3.00	22	16	10	6
Voluma	soft, fluffy, flat	US / CA / GB	5–6	5½	85% acrylic, 15% kid mohair	machine wash, 30°C, do not iron, do not bleach	50 gm	209	4.00	12	8	—	3
Voluma Colari	soft, variegated	US / CA / GB	5–6	5½	85% acrylic, 15% kid mohair	machine wash, 30°C, do not iron, do not bleach	50 gm	209	4.00	12	8	—	3
Schoeller Claire	smooth, classic	USA	5	5½	50% cotton, 50% acrylic	hand wash	50 gm	108	3.99	—	10	—	—
Sarah	smooth, classic	USA	5	6	40% alpaca, 30% wool, 30% acrylic	hand wash	20 gm	70	4.39	—	7	—	—
Tina	slubbed	USA	4	6	50% cotton, 25% viscose, 20% flax, 5% acrylic	machine wash, gentle, dry flat	50 gm	108	4.09	14	9	5	3
Romanze	glossy, smooth, classic	USA	5	6	20% wool, 50% viscose, 30% acrylic	hand wash	50 gm	97	4.59	—	12	—	—

Brand and Yarn Name	Where Sold	Type	US Needle Size	Gauge/Tension per Inch	Fiber Content	Cleaning Care	Skein, Hank, Ball, or Cone Weight	Approx. Yardage	Approx. Price	Approx. No. of Skeins for a Small-size Standard Knit Pullover Sweater with Long Sleeves and Crew Neck			
										Man	Woman	Child	Infant
Wollspass	USA	smooth classic worsted	6	6	100% wool	machine wash, gentle	50 gm	126	3.69	—	10	—	—
Scotts Woolen Mill Linnay	USA	2-ply rustic	5–7	6–8	50% rayon 50% linen	solid colors: hand wash, cold / mixed colors: dry clean	2 oz. skein ½ or 1 lb. cone	150 1,200	2.50 18.00/lb	8	6	4	2
Margo	USA	dressy textured novelty	4–6	4–6	76% acetate 24% nylon	solid colors: machine wash, cold water / mixed colors: dry clean	2 oz. skein ½ or 1 lb. cone	190 1,550	3.30 25.00	9	7	5	3
Number One	dis.	soft, glossy classic sport	4–7	4–6	100% kid mohair	solid colors: hand wash, cold / mixed colors: dry clean	2 oz. skein ½ or 1 lb. cone	155 1,250	6.70 52.00	8	6	4	2
Rapture	USA	nubby twisted novelty line has compatible space-dyed colors to go with plain colors	4–8	5–8	88% wool 12% nylon	solid colors: hand wash, cold / mixed colors: dry clean	2 oz. skein ½ or 1 lb. cone	135 1,100	4.70 36.00	8	6	4	2
Camelot II	USA	shiny braid	4–7	4–6	100% rayon	dry clean	2 oz. skein ½ or 1 lb. cone	100 800	4.00 30.00	14	12	8–10	5
Caress	USA	brushed	4–8	5–8	100% wool	solid colors: hand wash, cold / mixed colors: dry clean	2 oz. skein ½ or 1 lb. cone	230 1,850	4.75 36.50	10	8	6	3
Dynasty	dis.	single ply homespun texture	4–6	4–6	100% tussah silk	solid colors only: dry clean or cold wash	2 oz. skein ½ or 1 lb. cone	230 1,900	8.00 62.00	8	6	4	2
Galaxy	USA	bouclé shiny	5–7	5–6	100% rayon	dry clean	2 oz. skein ½ or 1 lb. cone	112 900	4.00 30.00	14	12	8–10	5
Shimmer	USA	chenille	8	4	100% rayon chenille	dry clean	2 oz. 1 or ½ lb. cone	125 1,000	3.50 26.00	9	6	4	2
Sonia	USA	ratiné	3	7½	80% rayon 20% cotton slub	hand wash	2 oz. 1 or ½ lb. cone	195 1,575	3.50 26.00	9	7	5	3

B

Name	Origin			Texture	Fiber Content	Care	Weight	Yards	Price				
Serendipity Skeins Dazzle	USA	5	6	2-ply cord hand-dyed	100% silk	dry clean	5 oz.	625	—	9	2	2	1
Glimmer	USA	8	5	hand-dyed	90% kid mohair 10% nylon	hand wash dry clean	6 oz.	750	—	2	2	2	1
North Star	USA	4	6	rivals velvet hand-dyed	100% silk	dry clean	2 oz.	187	—	7	5	5	3
Nostalgia	USA	6	5	nubby, textured hand-dyed	100% silk	dry clean	9 oz.	1,013	—	2	1	1	1
Pizzazz	USA	7	5	soft, classic 2-ply hand-dyed	50% silk 50% merino wool	dry clean	5 oz.	625	—	3	2	2	1
Spring	USA	6	5½	hand-dyed	65% silk 35% linen	dry clean	2 oz.	157	—	9	6	5	4
Summer	USA	7	5	fine, filigree flake hand-dyed	100% cotton	hand wash dry clean	8 oz.	825	—	2	2	1	1
Winter	USA	7	5	classic worsted hand-dyed	100% superwash wool	machine wash hand wash dry clean	2 oz.	173	—	8	6	5	4
Zing	USA	5	6	fine, lustrous bouclé hand-dyed	100% silk	dry clean	2 oz.	180	—	8	6	5	4
Shasha Yarn Portena (Aspen)	USA	6	5½	smooth	wool	dry clean	100 gm	109	4.00	—	8	—	—
Romance	USA	7	5	tweedy	wool	dry clean	100 gm	273	4.40	—	6	—	—
Senorita	USA	5	6	smooth	wool	dry clean	50 gm	166	2.40	—	7	—	—
Sirdar Casino	USA	5	6	specialty	48% cotton 24% polyamide 17% acrylic 11% metalized polyester	—	50 gm	132	6.90	—	—	—	—
Double Crepe	USA	4	6	wash & wear	55% bri-nylon 45% acrylic	—	40 gm	144	2.86	—	—	—	—
DK	USA	5	6	—	45% acrylic 15% wool 40% bri-nylon	—	50 gm	184	3.50	—	—	—	—
Gemini Brushed DK	USA	5	6	specialty	50% acrylic 50% bri-nylon	—	40 gm	142	2.68	—	—	—	—
Majestic DK	USA	5	6	—	100% wool	—	50 gm	130	4.50	—	—	—	—
Panorama DK	USA	5	6	—	100% wool	—	50 gm	140	4.00	—	—	—	—

Brand and Yarn Name	Where Sold	Type	US Needle Size	Gauge/Tension per Inch	Fiber Content	Cleaning Care	Skein, Hank, Ball, or Cone Weight	Approx. Yardage	Approx. Price	Approx. No. of Skeins for a Small-size Standard Knit Pullover Sweater with Long Sleeves and Crew Neck			
										Man	Woman	Child	Infant
Piazza DK	USA	specialty	5	6	50% wool 25% acrylic 25% bri-nylon	—	50 gm	150	5.20	—	—	—	—
Secrets DK	USA	specialty	5	6	65% acrylic 23% wool 10% nylon 2% metalized	—	50 gm	170	4.00	—	—	—	—
She	USA	specialty	6	5	55% acrylic 45% mohair	—	50 gm	167	6.50	—	—	—	—
Snuggly DK	USA	baby	5	6	55% bri-nylon 45% acrylic	—	40 gm	156	2.00	—	—	—	—
Snuggly QK	USA	baby	5	6½	55% bri-nylon 45% acrylic	—	40 gm	156	2.00	—	—	—	—
Snuggly Lustre DK	USA	baby	5	6	43% bri-nylon 35% nylon 22% viscose	—	40 gm	142	2.00	—	—	—	—
Sombrero	USA	—	3	6½	47% acrylic 39% cotton 14% nylon	—	50 gm	189	4.30	—	—	—	—
Sunseeker Boutonne DK	USA	—	5	6	48% cotton 32% acrylic 13% viscose 7% nylon	—	50 gm	121	4.50	—	—	—	—
Sunseeker Cloud 9 DK	USA	—	5	6	87% acrylic 13% nylon	—	50 gm	183	4.00	—	—	—	—
Sunseeker Cloud 10	USA	—	5	6	89% acrylic 11% nylon	—	50 gm	150	5.00	—	—	—	—
Sunseeker Cotton Contrast DK	USA	—	5	6	84% cotton 9% nylon 7% acrylic	—	50 gm	129	4.40	—	—	—	—
Sunseeker Linen Touch DK	USA	—	5	6	47% acrylic 34% cotton 19% linen	—	50 gm	123	4.00	—	—	—	—
Sunseeker Sensations	USA	—	5	6	70% viscose 25% acrylic 5% nylon	—	50 gm	170	4.40	—	—	—	—
Sunseeker Soufle	USA	—	5	6	59% nylon 41% acrylic	—	50 gm	178	4.90	—	—	—	—
Sunseeker Spree	USA	—	5	6	100% acrylic	—	50 gm	192	4.40	—	—	—	—

B

Name	Country	Type			Fiber	Care	Put-up	Yards	Price				
Temptation	USA	specialty	5	6	50% acrylic 50% nylon	—	50 gm	189	3.50	—	—	—	—
The Terry Look	USA	—	3	6½	90% acrylic 10% bri-nylon	—	50 gm	189	4.80	—	—	—	—
Tweed Double Crepe	USA	—	5	6	61% acrylic 28% bri-nylon 11% wool	—	50 gm	145	3.75	—	—	—	—
Skinner® Ultrasuede® Ultrasuede Yarn	USA	synthetic suede/ worsted	6	4.5	polyurethane	machine wash dry clean	45 yd. skein 230 yd. spool	45 230	10.90 46.00	24 5	21 4	14 3	11 2
Softball® Yarn Classic Softball Cotton Solid Color	USA	classic sport	6	7	100% combed cotton	machine wash & dry	2 lb. cone	3,700	20.80 lb.	1 lb.	1 lb.	7 oz.	5 oz.
Cotton Chine	USA	dressy	6	7	75% cotton 25% rayon	dry clean	50 gm ball 2 lb. cone	204 3,700	39.60 doz. 24.80 lb.	10 balls	10 balls	4 balls	3 balls
Cotton Ice	USA	fancy pigtail	5	6	75% cotton 25% nylon	machine wash & dry	50 gm ball 2 lb. cone	140 2,560	46.80 doz. 28.80 lb.	10 balls	10 balls	4 balls	3 balls
Cotton Tweed	USA	multicolored flecks	5	6	cotton blend	machine wash & dry	50 gm ball 2 lb. cone	204 3,700	43.20 doz. 28.80 lb.	10 balls	10 balls	4 balls	3 balls
Woolchine	USA	dressy	5	6	75% wool 25% rayon	dry clean	50 gm ball 2 lb. cone	204 3,700	43.20 doz. 28.00 lb.	10 balls	10 balls	4 balls	3 balls
Soie et Soie Brocade/Textured	USA JP	lustrous smooth with metallic accent	6	6	80% filament silk 13% polyester 7% rayon	dry clean	25 gm	100 m	—	—	10–11	—	—
Ramie/Silk	USA JP	summer weight cool	7–8	6–6½	52% filament silk 48% ramie	hand wash	30 gm	—	—	11	—	—	—
Textured Silk	USA JP	lustrous dressy smooth light weight	6	6	100% filament silk	dry clean	25 gm	100 m	—	—	10–11	—	—
Solberg Yarns Anitra	USA	tweed classic	5–7	5	100% cotton	machine wash	50 gm	93	2.99	12	8	—	—
Flamingo	USA	shiny bouclé	3–7	5½	52% cotton 48% viscose	machine wash	50 gm	130	2.99	—	11	—	—
Frotolett	USA	classic sport	8–10	3½	65% cotton 35% acrylic	machine wash	100 gm	165	5.99	7	5	3	—
Helios	USA	classic soft spot	8–10	3½	100% cotton	machine wash	50 gm	93	2.99	—	14	—	—
Spinnel	USA	shiny	5–7	5½	55% cotton 45% viscose	hand wash	50 gm	120	3.49	—	10	—	—

Brand and Yarn Name	Where Sold	Type	US Needle Size	Gauge/ Tension per Inch	Fiber Content	Cleaning Care	Skein, Hank, Ball, or Cone Weight	Approx. Yardage	Approx. Price	Approx. No. of Skeins for a Small-size Standard Knit Pullover Sweater with Long Sleeves and Crew Neck			
										Man	Woman	Child	Infant
SpringBrook Aurora	USA	slinky nubbed bouclé	4-6	4-6	96% rayon 4% nylon	dry clean	50 gm 1 lb.	95 900	3.60 30.00	—	10	—	—
Champagne	USA	light, airy bouclé	4-7	4-6	71% mohair 29% nylon	hand wash, cold water dry flat	50 gm 1 lb.	160 1,500	4.50 38.00	—	9	—	—
Lin d' Ete	USA	slightly shiny string	4-6	4-6	71% rayon 29% linen	dry clean	50 gm 1 lb.	130 1,200	1.60 11.20	—	11	—	—
Malibu	USA	looped slub	4-7	4-6	59% rayon 22% cotton 15% polyester 5% nylon	dry clean	50 gm 1 lb.	105 1,000	3.00 24.00	—	14	—	—
Melody	USA	fluffy with slub overlay	4-7	4-6	63% cotton 22% acrylic 15% nylon	machine wash, gentle, cold water dry flat	50 gm 1 lb.	105 1,000	2.65 21.00	—	14	—	—
Sheila	USA	—	4-6	4-6	96% cotton 4% nylon	machine wash, gentle, cold water dry flat	50 gm 1 lb.	130 1,200	3.40 28.00	—	11	—	—
Sport Yarn	USA	heather	4-6	4-6	85% acrylic 15% wool	machine wash, gentle, cold water tumble dry	50 gm 1 lb.	200 1,860	1.55 13.50	—	7	—	—
Sunbeam Cotton Trend DK	CA	DK	6	6	100% acrylic	machine wash	100 gm	248 m	5.50 (CA $)	—	5	—	—
Ecstasy DK	CA	DK	6	6	57% acrylic 30% wool 13% polyester	hand wash	50 gm	119 m	4.50 (CA $)	—	8	—	—
Mountain Maid Marls DK	CA	DK	6	6	100% acrylic	machine wash	50 gm	300 m	3.99 (CA $)	—	5	—	—
Sateen DK	CA	DK	6	6	70% cotton 30% nylon	machine wash	50 gm	126 m	3.39 (CA $)	—	8	—	—
Susan Bates Sonata	dis.	smooth shiny	5	6	100% acrylic	machine wash & dry	50 gm	145	—	17	14	12	6
Swiss Straw Swistraw	—	raffia-like synthetic	—	—	—	wash dry clean	—	24	.99	—	—	—	—
Tahki Imports Twiggy Tweed	FR	tweed	5	5½	100% wool	dry clean	3.5 oz.	380	6.40	—	4	—	—
Tamm Yarns Astracryl Perla Tamm	USA CA AU MX	3-ply cotton like	—	16/3 3-5	100% acrylic	machine wash	454 gm (1 lb.)	2,490	16.00	—	1 cone	—	—
Diamante Tamm	USA MX CA AU	2-ply smooth	—	8/2 5-6	75% acrylic 25% poly-nylon	machine wash	454 gm	2,133	16.10	—	1 cone	—	—

B

Name	Country	Type	Needle	Gauge	Fiber	Care	Weight	Yardage	Price		Amount	
Richeline Tamm	USA MX CA AU	2-ply mohair touch	—	17/2 3-4	70% acrylic 30% poly-nylon	machine wash	454 gm	4,210	16.65	—	1 cone	—
Sport Shetland	USA MX CA AU	2-ply wool look	—	20/2 4-6	92% acrylic 8% rayon	machine wash	454 gm	5,162	16.60	—	1 cone	—
Suavi Tamm	USA MX CA AU	2-ply fuzzy	—	16/2 2-5	80% acrylic 20% poly-nylon	machine wash dry flat	454 gm	3,323	17.90	—	1 cone	—
Unger Yarn Ariane	USA CA	metallic	4	6	80% acetate 20% metal plastic	dry clean only	3.5 oz (20 gm)	125	4.50	—	7	—
Britania	USA CA	Shetland	6	5½	100% wool	hand wash	50 gm	140	4.20	—	8	—
Cruise	USA CA	—	4	6½	60% acrylic 40% nylon	machine wash	50 gm	210	2.85	—	8	—
Electra	USA CA	metallic	4	6	80% acetate, 20% metal plastic	dry clean only	20 gm	125	5.95	—	7	—
French Tweed	USA CA	homespun tweedy textured	4	6	100% wool	hand wash dry clean	100 gm	384	7.20	—	3	—
Jewel	USA CA	shiny	4	6	50% cotton 50% rayon	dry clean	50 gm	135	4.00	—	8	—
Lumio	USA CA	metallic	3	6½	75% wool 22% polyester 3% nylon	dry clean	25 gm	160	4.80	—	8	—
Marbella	USA CA	perle	4	5½	100% acrylic	machine wash	50 gm	143	2.80	—	8	—
Moonbeam	USA CA	metallic novelty	4	5½	74% viscose 10% metallic 8% cotton 8% nylon	dry clean	40 gm	101	4.80	—	10	—
Roly Sport	USA CA	—	5	6	100% acrylic	machine wash	50 gm	290	1.90	—	5	—
Welcomme Akala	USA	smooth	5-6	6	100% cotton	hand wash dry clean	50 gm	95	5.25	—	12-13	—
Annees	USA	smooth	5-6	5	57% cotton 24% viscose 19% linen	hand wash dry clean	—	95	5.75	—	12	—
La Soie	USA	dressy	5-6	6	100% pure silk	hand wash dry clean	50 gm	140	16.50	—	7-8	—
Les Saisons	USA	classic	5-6	6	55% acrylic 30% wool 15% mohair	hand wash dry clean	50 gm	150	3.60	—	7-8	—
Les Sixtees	USA	shiny/slub	6	5¾	70% viscose 18% cotton 12% linen	hand wash dry clean	—	100	6.50	—	11	—

Brand and Yarn Name	Where Sold	Type	US Needle Size	Gauge/Tension per Inch	Fiber Content	Cleaning Care	Skein, Hank, Ball, or Cone Weight	Approx. Yardage	Approx. Price	Approx. No. of Skeins for a Small-size Standard Knit Pullover Sweater with Long Sleeves and Crew Neck			
										Man	Woman	Child	Infant
Pure Laine #4	USA	smooth	5-6	5½	100% wool	machine wash dry clean	—	138	4.50	—	7	—	—
Shetland et Alpaga 4	USA	Shetland twist	5-6	6	90% wool 10% alpaga	machine wash dry clean	50 gm	145	5.40	—	7-8	—	—
Wendy Darling DK	USA CA GB AU	baby	3-5	6	55% bri-nylon 45% Courtelle acrylic	machine wash	40 gm	148	2.45	—	—	—	2-4
Darling DK	USA CA GB AU	baby	3-5	6	55% bri-nylon 45% Courtelle acrylic	machine wash	20 gm	74	1.20	—	—	—	3-5
Darling Tinkerbell DK	USA CA GB AU	baby with viscose slub wrap	3-5	6	55% bri-nylon 45% Courtelle acrylic	machine wash	40 gm	148	2.25	—	—	—	2-4
Dolce	USA CA GB AU	brushed knits with donna	3-5	6	50% bri-nylon 50% Courtelle acrylic	hand wash	50 gm	174	2.90	6	4-6	4	2
Family Choice Opal	USA CA GB AU	—	3-5	6	48% viscose 26% Courtelle acrylic 21% bri-nylon 5% wool	machine wash	50 gm	145	2.50	4-6	4-6	4	—
Family Choice DK	USA CA GB AU	—	3-5	6	50% Courtelle acrylic 40% bri-nylon 10% wool	machine wash	50 gm	172	2.30	8	8	5	2-3
Matina	USA CA GB AU	knits with tempo	4-6	6	50% Courtelle acrylic 50% bri-nylon	hand wash	50 gm	164	3.30	8	6-8	5	2-3
Seta	USA CA GB AU	—	3-5	6	48% viscose 40% cotton 9% silk 3% nylon	hand wash	—	137	4.70	5-6	4-5	4	—
Shetland DK	USA CA GB AU	—	3-5	6	100% pure new wool	machine wash	50 gm	153	3.15	8	7	5	—
Soda Pops	USA CA GB AU	baby	3-5	6	55% bri-nylon 45% Courtelle acrylic	machine wash	40 gm	134	2.00	—	—	—	2-4

Brand / Yarn	Country	Description	Needle	Needle	Fiber Content	Care	Put-up	Yardage	Price				
Wilde Yarns Fine 2-ply Colors	USA	classic 2-ply	5	6	100% wool	hand wash dry clean	4 oz.	320	4.00	5	4	3	2
2-ply Dyed Softie	USA	classic 2-ply	5	6	100% wool	hand wash dry clean	8 oz.	720	8.60	3	2	1	1
2-ply Natural Softie	USA	classic 2-ply	5	6	100% wool	hand wash dry clean	8 oz.	720	7.60	17 oz.	12 oz.	9 oz.	6 oz.
Yarn Country/ Newton's Knits Rayon Bouclé	USA	bouclé	6 or machine	7	100% rayon	dry clean	1 lb.	1,600	16.00	22 oz.	19 oz.	18 oz.	16 oz.
Yarns Galore Acrylic Pompadour	USA	smooth classic acrylic sport weight with rayon sheen	6	5	82% acrylic 14% rayon 4% nylon	hand wash machine wash, cold water machine dry, delicate dry clean	16 oz. 2 oz.	1,650 206	20.00 2.50	18 oz. 9	14 oz. 7	10 oz. 5	5½ oz. 3
Capricorn ⅛ in. width ribbon	USA	smooth ⅛" width ribbon	6	7	100% nylon	hand wash dry flat dry clean	8 oz.	500 yds.	30.00	—	16 oz. 2 cones	10 oz. 1½ cones	—
Cotton Pompadour	USA	smooth classic sport weight with rayon sheen	6	6½	85% cotton 14% rayon 1% nylon	hand wash machine wash, cold water dry flat dry clean	16 oz. cone 2 oz.	1,500 187	20.00 2.50	20 oz. 10	15 oz. 8	10½ oz. 6	6 oz. 3
Frill	USA	ripple shine, double strand	6	5½	100% rayon	hand wash, cold water dry flat dry clean	8 oz.	725 yds.	16.00	19 oz. 2½ cones	15 oz. 2 cones	10 oz. 1½ cones	6 oz. 1 cone
Glitteray	USA	chainette	6	7	100% rayon	hand wash, cold water dry flat dry clean	8 oz.	600 yds.	16.00	20 oz. 2½ cones	16 oz. 2 cones	12 oz. 1½ cones	7 oz. 1 cone
Taurus	USA	smooth ⅛" width ribbon	6	7	100% rayon	hand wash dry flat dry clean	8 oz.	500 yds.	30.00	—	16 oz. 2 cones	10 oz. 1½ cones	—

CLASS C

Heavy Worsted Or 4-Ply Weight Yarns

Brand and Yarn Name	Where Sold	Type	US Needle Size	Gauge/Tension per Inch	Fiber Content	Cleaning Care	Skein, Hank, Ball, or Cone Weight	Approx. Yardage	Approx. Price	Approx. No. of Skeins for a Small-size Standard Knit Pullover Sweater with Long Sleeves and Crew Neck			
										Man	Woman	Child	Infant
Aarlan Alpaca/Silk	USA	worsted	5–7	5¼	55% wool 25% silk	hand wash	50 gm	120	5.50	14	12	10	8
Angora Deux	USA	worsted	7–8	5	100% Angora	hand wash	20 gm	65	10.00	—	12	10	8
Athas	USA	worsted	5–7	5¼	100% mercerized cotton	hand wash	50 gm	90	3.50	12–14	10–12	8–10	6–8
Carnaby	USA	worsted	8–10	4½–5	45% wool 35% acrylic 20% polyamide	hand wash	50 gm	105	4.00	12–14	11–13	9–11	7–9
Charmeuse	USA	worsted	7–10	5–6	30% mohair 70% acrylic	hand wash	50 gm	185	4.50	10–12	8–10	6–8	4–6
Classica	USA	worsted	6–8	5¼	100% pure wool	hand wash	50 gm	125	3.70	14–16	12–14	8–10	6–8
Codina	USA	worsted	7–8	5	100% mercerized cotton	hand wash	50 gm	87	5.00	14–16	12–14	8–10	6–8
Cotonova	USA	worsted	5–7	5–4½	100% mercerized cotton	hand wash	50 gm	80	4.00	12–14	10–12	8–10	6–8
Cristal	USA	worsted	7–8	5	100% wool	hand wash	50 gm	100	3.30	12–14	10–12	6–8	5–7
Darling	USA	worsted	7–9	5	42% viscose 38% acrylic 18% wool 2% polyester	hand wash	50 gm	105	5.00	12–14	8–10	7–9	5–7
Empress Silk	dis.	twisted	7–9	5–4	100% silk	dry clean	50 gm	60	13.60	—	10–12	—	—
Gypsy	dis.	nubby	7–8	5½–5	100% mercerized cotton	warm water wash	50 gm	150	3.60	—	8–10	—	—
Harmony	dis.	fluffy tweed	8–9	5–4½	45% wool 35% acrylic 20% mohair	warm water wash	50 gm	87	4.20	—	10–12	—	—
Kid/Silk	USA	worsted	8–10	4½	80% kid mohair 20% silk	hand wash	20 gm	80	4.00	14–16	12–14	9–11	7–9
Lucenter	USA	worsted	7–9	5	55% cotton 45% viscose	hand wash	50 gm	105	5.00	12–14	10–12	8–10	6–8

C

Name	Country	Description		Fiber	Care	Weight	Yards	Price				
Mohair	USA	worsted	7–9 / 4½–5	70% mohair 30% acrylic	hand wash	50 gm	170	6.50	9-12	7-9	6-8	5-7
Mon Amie	dis.	fluffy	9–10 / 4	100% kid mohair	hand wash dry clean	50 gm	120	7.00	—	8	—	—
Natch	dis.	smooth classic	8 / 5	100% wool	warm water wash	50 gm	97	2.90	—	10-12	—	—
Rustic	dis.	thick & thin	7–8 / 5–4	85% wool 15% acrylic	hand wash warm	50 gm	95	4.80	—	9-12	—	—
Safari-Color	dis.	thick & thin	7–8 / 5–4½	80% cotton 10% linen 10% wool	warm water wash	50 gm	110	4.50	—	10-12	—	—
Safari-Rustic	dis.	thick & thin	7–8 / 5–4½	80% cotton 20% linen	warm water wash	50 gm	110	4.00	—	10-12	—	—
Topaz	USA	worsted	7–9 / 5–4½	70% mohair 30% acrylic	hand wash	50 gm	160	6.50	11-13	9-11	7-9	5-7
Wool Alpaca	dis.	fluffy smooth	9–10 / 4–3½	85% wool 15% alpaca	warm water wash	50 gm	81	3.60	—	10-14	—	—
Andean Yarns Alpaquita	USA CA	4-ply natural	7 / 5	100% alpaca	hand wash dry flat	100 gm	220	9.00	6	5	4	3
Alpaquita	USA CA	4-ply misty hues	7 / 5	100% alpaca	hand wash dry flat	100 gm	220	9.00	6	5	4	3
Alpaquita	USA CA	Suprema	7–8 / 5	100% alpaca	hand wash dry flat	100 gm	200	10.00	6	5	4	3
Alpaquita	dis.	4-ply plant-dyed	7 / 5	100% alpaca	hand wash dry flat	50 gm	110	5.50	11	10	8	6
Chine	USA	2 ply Shetland twist soft, airy	7 / 4½	100% alpaca	hand wash dry flat	100 gm	190	10.00	6	5	4	3
Cusco	USA CA	4-ply dyed brights	7 / 5	100% alpaca	hand wash dry flat	100 gm	220	10.00	6	5	4	3
Anny Blatt Angora	USA CA AU GB	Angora	9–10 / 3½	100% Angora	hand wash dry clean	10 gm	27	9.95	—	35	16	8
Angora Givre	USA CA AU GB	Angora heather	6–9 / 4	50% Angora 50% lambswool	hand wash dry clean	20 gm	64	12.75	20	15	10	5
Dallas	USA CA AU GB	novelty, brushed spiral	6–8 / 4	55% wool 23% acrylic 22% polyester	hand wash dry clean	50 gm	90	9.95	15	12	8	5
Ecoss	USA	mercerized	7–8 / 4½–5	100% cotton	hand wash dry clean	50 gm	90	4.95	12	10	6	4

Brand and Yarn Name	Where Sold	Type	US Needle Size	Gauge/Tension per Inch	Fiber Content	Cleaning Care	Skein, Hank, Ball, or Cone Weight	Approx. Yardage	Approx. Price	Approx. No. of Skeins for a Small-size Standard Knit Pullover Sweater with Long Sleeves and Crew Neck			
										Man	Woman	Child	Infant
Flirt	USA CA AU GB	novelty thick & thin cotton/linen blend	8-10	3½	67% cotton 23% viscose 10% linen	hand wash dry clean	50 gm	60	5.50	18	14	6	3
Folie	USA	fluffy mohair blend	8-9	4½-5	53% mohair 34% wool 13% acrylic	hand wash dry clean	40 gm	118	3.50	11	9	5	3
Kid	USA	soft kid mohair blend	8-10	4-5	80% mohair 20% acrylic	hand wash dry clean	50 gm	112	8.95	11	9	5	3
Liberty	dis.	novelty rolled ribbon with yarn wrapped around	7	5	80% rayon 16% acrylic 4% nylon	hand wash	40 gm	70	9.95	—	14	—	—
Look	USA CA AU GB	smooth ribbon	9-10	3½	woven ribbon 94% viscose 6% nylon	hand wash dry clean	50 gm	60	9.25	—	14	—	—
Magnolia	USA CA AU GB	novelty fabric & singles	6-9	4	64% viscose 16% wool 20% polyamide	hand wash dry clean	50 gm	90	9.95	17	12	6	—
Mohair et Soie	USA CA AU GB	deluxe long haired	9-10½	3½	80% mohair 20% silk	hand wash dry clean	50 gm	70	12.95	18	14	7	—
No. 5	USA	smooth superwash	8	5	100% wool	superwash	50 gm	100	2.95	12	10	6	4
No. 6	USA CA AU GB	smooth heavy	9-10	4	100% wool	superwash	50 gm	68	4.50	17	12	5	3
Petunia	USA CA AU GB	novelty smooth & twisted	7-8	4	46% acrylic 34% viscose 20% polyester	hand wash dry clean	50 gm	80	12.95	—	13	6	—
Silk	USA CA AU GB	long-fibered luxury silk	7-8	4	100% silk	hand wash dry clean	40 gm	65	13.50	20	15	7	4
Star	USA CA AU GB	novelty looped metallic	6-7	3½	70% viscose 20% polyester-metalize 10% polyamide	hand wash dry clean	20 gm	55	7.50	—	16	—	—
Star Multico	USA CA AU GB	novelty looped metallic	6-7	3½	70% viscose 20% polyester-metalize 10% polyamide	hand wash dry clean	20 gm	55	8.50	—	16	—	—

C

Name	Country	Description			Fiber Content	Care	Weight	Yards	Price				
Starblitz	USA CA AU GB	mohair, long hair silky	4–7	4½	60% kid mohair 20% polyamide 20% Courtelle	hand wash dry clean	50 gm	135	7.95	14	10	5	—
Argyall Ltd Chameleon	CA	mohair	7	4½	50% mohair 2.5% nylon 47.5% acrylic	hand wash 40°C	50 gm	163 m	7.00 (CA $)	—	4	—	—
Pure Quality Cotton	CA	—	5	4½	100% cotton	hand wash	100 gm	164	4.99 (CA $)	—	7	—	—
Aurora Wellscroft Nub	USA	2-ply rich tweed with nubs	7–8	5–4½	100% wool	hana wash	100 gm	190	6.00	6	5	3–4	2
Bartlettyarns Fisherman	USA	2-ply	8 H	4	100% wool	hand wash dry clean	4 oz.	210	4.00	6	6	3	2
Glen Tweed	USA	2-ply	8 H	4	100% wool	hand wash dry clean	4 oz.	210	4.00	6	6	3	2
Homespun	USA	2-ply	8 H	4	100% wool	hand wash dry clean	4 oz.	210	4.50	6	6	3	2
Donegal Tweed	USA	2-ply	8 H	4	100% wool	hand wash dry clean	4 oz.	200	5.00	7	6	3	2
Baruffa Magellano	USA	multi-colored novelty	8	4	55% cotton 20% polyamide 15% viscose 10% acrylic	hand wash	50 gm	68	4.99	—	11	—	—
Maratona	USA	extra fine merino	9	4	100% wool	hand wash	50 gm	121	5.50	—	9	—	—
Navona	USA	soft & silky	8	4	38% silk 30% wool 20% kid mohair 12% acrylic	hand wash	50 gm	115	8.00	—	9	—	—
7Settembre	USA	premium superwash	6	5.5	100% wool	machine wash	50 gm	132	3.25	—	8	—	—
Spiaggia	USA	vibrant bouclé	7	5	50% acrylic 20% linen 15% viscose 10% silk 15% nylon	hand wash	50 gm	110	4.50	—	8	—	—
Vacanza	USA	cable twist	6	5	100% wool	hand wash	50 gm	135	4.50	—	8	—	—
Volley	USA	classic	8	4	50% cashmere 40% merino wool 10% nylon	hand wash	50 gm	152	9.50	—	9	—	—
Berger du Nord Brilliance	USA	—	8	4¾	95% viscose 5% polyester	—	50 gm	105	8.95	—	8	—	—
Cabourg	USA	—	7	4	66% cotton 34% viscose	—	50 gm	80	5.75	—	—	—	—
Cotton 5	USA	—	6	4¼	100% cotton	—	50 gm	75 •	3.75	—	—	—	—

Brand and Yarn Name	Where Sold	Type	US Needle Size	Gauge/Tension per Inch	Fiber Content	Cleaning Care	Skein, Hank, Ball, or Cone Weight	Approx. Yardage	Approx. Price	Approx. No. of Skeins for a Small-size Standard Knit Pullover Sweater with Long Sleeves and Crew Neck			
										Man	Woman	Child	Infant
Cottonelle	USA	—	4	4¾	100% cotton	—	50 gm	100	5.25	—	—	—	—
Douceur 5	USA	—	8	4¼	85% wool 15% kid mohair	—	50 gm	92	4.50	—	—	—	—
Entincelante A Lustrous Tisse	USA		8	4¼	65% rayon 35% cotton	—	50 gm	80	8.50	—	—	—	—
Ecosse 5	USA	—	7	4¼	100% cotton	—	50 gm	90	4.50	—	—	—	—
Flore	USA	—	8	4½	73% cotton 27% viscose	—	50 gm	90	8.30	—	—	—	—
Jeans	USA	—	6	4¼	100% cotton	—	50 gm	75	4.75	—	—	—	—
Kid Agneau	USA	—	6	4¾	52% kid mohair 28% lambswool 20% Courtelle	—	50 gm	135	7.95	—	—	—	—
Kid Mohair	USA	—	6	4¾	80% kid mohair 20% Chiro	—	50 gm	135	8.95	—	—	—	—
Linen/Cotton Colors	USA	—	7	4¼	55% linen 25% cotton 20% viscose	—	50 gm	85	5.25	—	—	—	—
Madras	USA	—	8	4¼	75% viscose 25% cotton	—	50 gm	75	8.50	—	—	—	—
Mode	USA	—	6	—	23% cotton 30% acrylic 47% polyester	—	20 gm	26	9.50	—	—	—	—
Noix de Coco	USA	—	8	4¾	71% cotton 29% viscose	—	50 gm	95	8.50	—	—	—	—
Prodige	USA	—	7	4¾	100% wool	—	50 gm	90	3.95	—	—	—	—
Silkid 4	USA	—	6	4½	12% kid mohair 22% wool 36% acrylic	—	50 gm	110	8.95	—	—	—	—
Tisse	USA	ribbon	8	4¼	79% cotton 21% viscose	—	50 gm	80	8.50	—	—	—	—
Bernat Berella 4	USA	smooth classic worsted	7–8	5–4½	100% blended acrylic	machine wash	100 gm	240 yds.	2.75	6	5	3	—
Bimini	USA	terry bouclé	6	5	100% cotton	hand wash	50 gm	92	3.95	16	10	7	—
Blarneyspun	USA	water repellant worsted	8	4½	100% wool	hand wash	50 gm	75	3.50	17	16	10	—

C

Name	Country	Description	Needle	Gauge	Fiber	Care	Weight	Yards	Price				
Cameo	USA	fashion basic	7	5	80% wool 20% alpaca	hand wash	50 gm	105	3.95	14	10	6	—
Carmen	USA	fashion basic	6	5	100% cotton	hand wash	50 gm	90	2.95	16	—	8	—
Fettuccia	USA	knitted ribbon	8	5	100% mercerized cotton	hand wash	50 gm	80	4.95	18	14	9	—
Fisherman	USA	classic worsted	8	5	100% wool with natural oils	hand wash	100 gm	220	3.95	7	5	3	—
Gelato	USA	slub tweed	6	5	70% rayon 30% cotton	hand wash	50 gm	70	4.95	20	14	10	—
Gloucester	USA	fashion basic	8	4½	100% cotton	hand wash	100 gm	145	4.25	9	8	5	—
Gossamer	USA	viscose tweed	6	5	64% acrylic 36% viscose	hand wash	50 gm	94	5.50	15	11	—	—
Panama	USA	tweed blend	6	5	40% cotton 31% acrylic 29% linen	hand wash	50 gm	90	3.50	16	15	8	—
Sesame 4	USA	classic worsted	8	5	100% virgin wool	hand wash	100 gm	220	4.25	6	5	3	—
Sorbetto	USA	novelty vrille	6	5	30% cotton 25% acrylic 20% linen 20% viscose 5% nylon	hand wash	50 gm	110	4.95	13	10	7	—
Stardust	USA	novelty tweed	7	5	75% wool 13% acrylic 12% bright nylon	hand wash	50 gm	95 Yds.	3.95	15	11	7	—
Berroco Avanti	dis.	heather flecked worsted	8 J hook	4½	100% wool	—	50 gm 1 lb. 2 lb.	80 725 1,450	3.65 —	12	8 matching fabric available	—	
Canterbury	USA	fleecy with loops	8 J hook	4	40% wool 15% mohair 33% acrylic 8% polyester	—	50 gm 1 lb. 2 lb.	110 1,000 2,000	4.65	8	6	—	—
Cheers	USA CA	fluffy	10½	3½	15% mohair 50% acrylic 35% acetate	hand wash	50 gm. 1 lb. 4-6 lb.	66	4.12	—	12	—	—
Dante	USA CA	slubbed bouclé	6 I hook	5	65% rayon 27% cotton 8% nylon	—	50 gm 1 lb. 2 lb.	90 815 1,630	4.65	12	10	—	—
Dji Dji	USA	fluffy soft	8 I hook	4	77% wool 23% viscose	—	50 gm 1 lb. 3-5 lb	110 1,000	4.90 — —	8	7	—	—
Flair	USA	loopy bouclé	6 H hook	4½	47% cotton 39% acetate 14% polyamide	—	50 gm 1 lb 7-10 lb	105 951	3.65 — —	10	8	—	—

Brand and Yarn Name	Where Sold	Type	US Needle Size	Gauge/Tension per Inch	Fiber Content	Cleaning Care	Skein, Hank, Ball, or Cone Weight	Approx. Yardage	Approx. Price	Approx. No. of Skeins for a Small-size Standard Knit Pullover Sweater with Long Sleeves and Crew Neck			
										Man	Woman	Child	Infant
Glace	USA CA	shiny ⅛ ribbon	6 H hook	5	95% rayon 5% polyester	—	100 gm	150	9.30	—	7	—	—
Pembroke	USA	multicolor twist	8 K hook	4	96% wool 4% polyester	—	50 gm	75	5.15	—	8	—	—
Bouquet Yarns Amberly	dis.	texture/nub	8	4½	100% virgin wool	hand wash dry clean	50 gm	80	2.59	16	13	9	6
Blossom	dis.	textured	8	4½	70% acrylic 30% wool	machine wash & dry	50 gm	90	2.35	14	11	7	—
Classic	USA CA	classic	8	4½	100% acrylic	machine wash & dry	100 gm	250	2.90	8	7	5	—
Emerald Irish	USA CA	natural	8	4½-5	100% virgin wool	hand wash dry clean	50 gm	75	2.25	16	14	10	6
Firecracker	USA CA	classic roving type	8	4½	56% acrylic 24% wool 20% viscose	—	50 gm	115	2.35	15	13	9	—
Islander	dis.	classic	8	4½-5	51% wool 49% nylon	machine wash & dry	100 gm	165	3.25	9	8	5	—
Jacana	USA CA	brushed	8	4½-5	70% acrylic 30% mohair	machine wash & dry	50 gm	150	3.45	—	8	5	—
Marina	—	shrink treated	8	4½-5	100% virgin wool	machine wash & dry	50 gm	115	2.45	12	10	7	4
Northern Lights	dis.	variegated	8	4½-5	70% acrylic 30% wool	machine wash & dry	100 gm	180	3.40	8	6	4	2
Ragg	USA CA	classic	8	4½-5	100% acrylic	machine wash & dry	100 gm	230	3.05	7	5	3	2
Special Canadian	USA CA	classic	8	4½-5	70% acrylic 30% wool	machine wash & dry	100 gm	210	3.49	7	5	3	2
Stitches	dis.	classic	8	4½-5	100% acrylic	machine wash & dry	300 gm	585	6.25	3	2	1	1
Trend	USA CA	classic	8	4½-5	70% acrylic 30% wool	machine wash & dry	100 gm	210	3.45	7	5	3	2
Vogue	USA CA	classic	8	4½-5	100% acrylic	machine wash & dry	50 gm	195	2.55	7	6	4	2
Brentwood Yarns Allegro	USA	bumpy	6	5	wool/rayon	hand wash	skein/cone	85/850	6.50/63.00	15	11	7	5
Angelica	USA	heavy/bump	6	5	acrylic/rayon	hand wash	hank/cone	80/800	9.00/67.00	16	13	8	6
Bella	USA	fluffy	6	5	wool/mohair	hand wash	skein/cone	150/1,500	6.50/63.00	10	7	5	3
Bellini	USA	heavy/bump	6	5	rayon/acrylic	hand wash	hank/cone	80/800	9.00/67.00	16	13	8	6

Name	Country	Texture			Fiber	Care	Put-up	Yardage	Price				
Blackstone 2	USA	bumpy/acryl	6	5	acrylic	hand wash	skein/cone	77/770	2.40/22.00	16	13	8	6
Chainette	USA	chain/rayon	6	5	rayon	hand wash	tube/cone	110/1,100	2.70/27.00	15	12	8	5
Charmer	USA	thick/thin	8	5	cotton/rayon	hand wash	skein/cone	70/700	3.20/30.00	15	11	8	5
Cheers	USA	multi/bump	9	4	cotton/acrylic	hand wash	skein/cone	55/550	4.50/43.00	15	12	8	5
De Como	USA	shiny/bump	5	5	rayon	hand wash	tube/cone	85/850	4.20/40.00	15	12	8	5
Dynasty	USA	textured	7	5	acrylic/rayon	hand wash	skein/cone	82/820	3.80/36.00	15	12	8	5
Essence	USA	bumpy/rayon	6	5	cotton/rayon	hand wash	skein/cone	80/800	4.80/46.00	15	12	8	5
Exotic	USA	multi/bump	6	5	cotton/rayon	hand wash	skein/cone	65/650	4.20/40.00	15	12	8	5
Flashdance	USA	chain/metal	8	5	metallic	hand wash	hank/cone	145/1,450	9.00/88.00	10	7	5	3
Le Posh	USA	twist/cotton	6	5	cotton	hand wash	skein/cone	80/800	3.75/36.00	15	12	8	5
Polar	USA	fluffy	7	5	mohair	hand wash	skein/cone	100/1,000	7.00/68.00	12	8	5	3
Woolen	USA	flat/shiny	7	5	wool/rayon	hand wash	skein/cone	120/1,200	4.20/40.00	12	8	5	3
Brown Sheep Co. Cotton Top	USA CA	worsted	8-9	4	50% cotton 50% wool	hand wash	—	160 yds.	4.00	9	7	5	3
Top of the Lamb	USA CA	worsted	8-10	4-5	100% wool	hand wash	4 oz skein 4 oz hank	190 190	3.50 3.50	8 8	6 6	4 4	2 2
Wool-Mohair Blend	USA CA	worsted	8-10	4-5	15% mohair 85% wool	hand wash	4 oz.	196 yds.	4.00	8	6	4	2
Brunswick Alaska	USA CA AU	smooth	8	5	80% acrylic 20% nylon	machine wash & dry, delicate	40 gm	130	—	—	9	—	—
Ballybrae	USA CA AU	natural tweed	6	4½	100% wool	dry clean only	100 gm	190	—	8	7	5	—
Breeze	USA CA AU	knobby	4	5	80% cotton 20% polyester	machine wash & dry, delicate	40 gm	100	—	NR	12	9	NR
Brigitte Angora	USA CA AU	fleecy	8	4	100% French Angora	dry clean only	10 gm	30	—	NR	47	35	NR
Classic	dis.	smooth	8	5	75% acrylic 25% wool	dry clean only	50 gm	115	—	12	9	7	NR
Cotton Ribbon	USA CA AU	smooth	10	4	100% cotton	hand wash dry clean	50 gm	80	—	19	15	—	—
Eleganza	dis.	fleecy	8	5	80% acrylic 20% mohair	machine wash & dry, delicate	50 gm	150	—	NR	10	5	NR
Finesse	dis.	fleecy	5	8	75% mohair 25% nylon	dry clean only	40 gm	180	—	NR	12	9	NR

C

Brand and Yarn Name	Where Sold	Type	US Needle Size	Gauge/Tension per Inch	Fiber Content	Cleaning Care	Skein, Hank, Ball, or Cone Weight	Approx. Yardage	Approx. Price	Approx. No. of Skeins for a Small-size Standard Knit Pullover Sweater with Long Sleeves and Crew Neck			
										Man	Woman	Child	Infant
Germantown	USA CA AU	smooth	8	5	100% wool	dry clean only	100 gm	220	—	6	5	3	NR
Heatherblend	USA CA AU	smooth	8	5	80% acrylic 20% wool	machine wash & dry, delicate	50 gm	115	—	12	9	7	NR
Heather Bouclé	USA CA AU	knobby	5	5	75% acrylic 18% wool 7% nylon	machine wash & dry, delicate	50 gm	170	—	NR	10	5	NR
Panache	USA CA AU	knobby	5	5	64% cotton 31% acrylic 5% nylon	hand wash machine wash, delicate	40 gm	100	—	12	8	—	—
Piccolo	USA CA AU	knobby	7	5	54% cotton 45% viscose 1% nylon	hand wash dry clean	50 gm	75	—	14	10	—	—
Safari	USA CA AU	natural tweed	8	5	82% wool 13% cotton 5% nylon		50 gm	120	—	12	9	7	0
Sloop	USA CA AU	smooth	7	5	100% mercerized cotton	hand wash machine wash	50 gm	90	—	16	13	—	—
Windmist	USA CA AU	fleecy	6	5	100% acrylic (brushed)	machine wash	50 gm	135	—	—	8	6	—
Windrush	USA CA AU	smooth	5	5	100% Orlon acrylic	machine wash gentle cycle	100 gm	230	—	7	6	3	3
Bucilla Bucilla Wool	dis.	worsted	8	5	100% virgin wool	hand wash	3½ oz.	235	4.00	6	5	3	2
Caprice	USA	pima cotton	6	5½	100% deluxe pima cotton	hand wash machine wash	1¾ oz.	102	3.00	14	10	5	3
Chenilla	USA	chenille	10	3½	100% acrylic	machine wash	1¾ oz.	109	4.00	12	9	NR	NR
Glisten Puff	USA	frosty worsted	8	9	60% acrylic 40% nylon	machine wash & dry	3 oz.	190	2.40	6	5	3	2
Halo	USA	frosty worsted	10	4	50% superwash wool 25% nylon 25% acrylic	machine wash & dry	1¾ oz.	120	4.00	10	8	4	NR
Melody	dis.	fuzzy	8	5	50% mohair 50% acrylic	machine wash & dry	1 oz.	100	2.60	10	8	5	3
Mirage	USA	mohair look	6	5	50% Perlon 50% acrylic	machine wash & dry	1¾ oz.	130	2.70	9	7	3	NR

C

Name	Origin	Description			Fiber Content	Care	Weight	Yards	Price				
Morocco	USA	cotton	6	4	100% cotton	hand wash	1¾ oz.	77	2.10	6	5	3	2
Premium Acrylic	USA	easy care	8	4	100% premium acrylic	machine wash & dry	3½ oz.	195	1.90	5	4	3	2
Safari	USA	elastic type yarn	8	4½	26% viscose 1% lycra spandex 73% cotton	hand wash	1¾ oz.	82	4.50	16	12	6	NR
Santa Fe	USA	rustic look	10	3½	35% camel hair 35% cotton 20% acrylic 10% wool	hand wash	1¾ oz.	98	4.00	16	12	6	NR
Snowfall	dis.	soft, dawny wool	6	4	64% acrylic 32% Australian wool 4% spandex	hand wash	1¾ oz.	105	2.75	8	6	4	3
Softex	USA	solid colors	6	5	100% DuPont Orlon	machine wash & dry	4 oz.	245	2.80	6	4	3	2
Softex Spectrum	USA	heathers & ombres	6	5	100% DuPont Orlon	machine wash & dry	3 oz.	185	2.90	7	5	3	2
Spice	USA	brushed	9	3½	76% acrylic 14% wool 10% polyester	hand wash	1¾ oz.	131	4.00	9	7	4	NR
Tiara	USA	glamorous	9	5	82% viscose 11% acrylic 7% polyester	hand wash	1¾ oz.	107	6.00	NR	8	NR	NR
Wonder Knit	USA	hardy yarn	8	4	100% DuPont acrylic	machine wash & dry	3 oz.	175	1.60	6	5	3	2
Busse Achat	USA	solid slub texture	6	5	60% cotton 40% linen	hand wash, cold	50 gm (1¾ oz.)	131	5.25	12	10	—	—
Alpaca-Flamme	USA	alpaca with cotton slub	6	4½	70% alpaca 30% cotton	hand wash	1¾ oz. (50 gm)	142	10.25	10	9	4	—
Diorit	USA	terry texture with "eyelash"	8	4½	70% cotton 30% rayon	hand wash	1¾ oz. (50 gm)	93	5.10	—	11	—	—
Gold	USA	worsted solid	8–9	4½	100% pure new wool	hand wash, cold	50 gm (1¾ oz.)	110	3.65	14	11	—	—
Granat	USA	multicolored yarn with "cocoon"	7	5	65% rayon 35% cotton	hand wash	1¾ oz. (50 gm)	93	5.10	—	11	—	—
Jaspis	USA	multicolored 3-strand lightly slubbed	7	5	60% rayon 40% cotton	hand wash	1¾ oz. (50 gm)	104	4.60	13	11	8	—
Jeany	USA	"denim" cotton blend	7	5	75% cotton	hand wash	1¾ oz. (50 gm)	98	4.35	14	12	8	—
Lapis	USA	soft cotton with subtle sheen	5	5	100% mercerized cotton	hand wash	1¾ oz. (50 gm)	104	3.50	12	10	8	—

Brand and Yarn Name	Where Sold	Type	US Needle Size	Gauge/ Tension per Inch	Fiber Content	Cleaning Care	Skein, Hank, Ball, or Cone Weight	Approx. Yardage	Approx. Price	Approx. No. of Skeins for a Small-size Standard Knit Pullover Sweater with Long Sleeves and Crew Neck			
										Man	Woman	Child	Infant
Mohair-Tweed	—	heather tweed	8-9	4	62% new wool 23% mohair 9% polyamide 6% acrylic	hand wash, cold	50 gm (1¾ oz.)	104	6.70	13	10	—	—
Noppa	USA	flecked tweed	7-8	4½	70% new wool 30% rayon	hand wash, cold	50 gm (1¾ oz.)	110	3.30	12	10	—	—
Ophir	USA	slub texture with silk-like sheen	6	5	52% cotton 48% rayon	hand wash, cold	50 gm (1¾ oz.)	110	4.40	—	10	—	—
Pearl	USA	crimped cotton	5	5	94% cotton 6% nylon	hand wash	1¾ oz. (50 gm)	137	5.00	11	9	6	3
Printo	USA	printed wool with bouclé thread	6	4½	40% new wool 24% acrylic 17% nylon 14% mohair 5% alpaca	hand wash	1¾ oz. (50 gm)	120	7.15	11	9	6	—
Pure Linen	USA	pure linen	6	5½	100% linen	hand wash	1¾ oz. (50 gm)	131	6.00	—	11	—	—
Pyrit	USA	3-strand, lightly slubbed	7	5	60% rayon 40% cotton	hand wash	1¾ oz. (50 gm)	104	3.80	13	11	8	—
Sapris	USA	worsted with cotton "eyelash" and rayon sheen	6	4½	60% new wool 23% cotton 10% rayon 7% alpaca	hand wash	1¾ oz. (50 gm)	93	5.55	14	12	8	—
Silk & Wool	USA	classic worsted	8	5	65% new wool 35% silk	hand wash, cold	50 gm (1¾ oz.)	125	7.60	11	9	—	—
Softino	USA	classic Shetland look	5-6	5	90% new wool 10% alpaca	hand wash, cold	50 gm (1¾ oz.)	142	4.90	10	8	—	—
Swing	USA	soft texture twisted with Lurex	6	5	82% new wool 9% alpaca 7% polyester 2% polyamide	hand wash, cold	50 gm (1¾ oz.)	142	7.60	—	8	—	—
Squash-Top	USA	classic worsted	8	4¾	75% new wool 25% nylon	machine wash	1¾ oz. (50 gm)	109	5.25	12	10	4	2
Tivoli	USA	polyacrylic with silvery "mohair" loft	7	4½	70% polyacrylic 30% nylon	hand wash	1¾ oz. (50 gm)	165	4.35	—	8	—	—
Topas	USA	multicolor slub texture	6	5	60% cotton 40% linen	hand wash, cold	50 gm (1¾ oz.)	131	5.50	12	10	—	—

C

Name	Origin	Type			Fiber	Care	Size	Yards	Price				
Twinny	USA	variegated yarn with curly bouclé	5	5	41% cotton 26% polyacrylic 19% rayon 14% nylon	hand wash	1¾ oz. (50 gm)	140	5.30	12	10	8	3
Venecia	USA	fine chenille with rayon contrast	9	4	55% rayon 45% acrylic	hand wash	1¾ oz. (50 gm)	98	7.00	12	10	—	—
Candide Candide Heavy Weight	USA	home spun type	8 10	4½ 4	100% wool	hand wash	4 oz. 113 gm	190 yd. 174 m	4.50	8	6	3-4	2
Caron Carefree Plus Solid	USA	classic worsted	8	4½	67% Orlon 33% Dacron	machine wash & dry	3 oz.	176	1.40	8	6	3	2
Christmas Ombre	USA	classic	8	4½	100% Dupont acrylic	machine wash & dry	3 oz.	176	1.29	7	6	3	2
Christmas Glitter	USA	sparkle	8	4½	95% Dupont acrylic 5% metallic thread	machine wash & dry	3 oz.	176	1.79	7	6	3	2
Dawn Sayelle Solid	USA	worsted solid	8	4.5	100% Orlon	machine wash & dry	3.5 oz.	215	1.59	7	6	3	2
Dawn Sayelle Ombre	USA	worsted ombre	8	4.5	100% Orlon	machine wash & dry	3 oz.	185	1.59	7	6	3	2
Dawn Sofgan	USA	worsted solid	8	4.5	100% DuPont acrylic	machine wash & dry	3 oz.	192	.99	8	7	4	3
Dawn Wintuk Solid	USA	worsted solid	8	4.5	100% DuPont Orlon	machine wash & dry	3.5 oz.	207	1.59	6	5	3	2
Dawn Wintuk Ombre	USA	worsted ombre	8	4.5	100% DuPont Orlon	machine wash & dry	3 oz.	186	1.59	7	6	3	2
Dazzleaire	USA	brushed specialty	8	4½	60% acrylic 40% nylon	machine wash & dry	3 oz.	190	1.79	7	6	3	2
Glencannon	USA	dressy worsted	8	4½	80% DuPont Orlon* 20% wool	machine wash & dry	3 oz.	175	2.05	7	6	3	NA
Highland Heathers	USA	classic multicolored yarn	8	4.5	67% Orlon 33% Dacron	machine wash & dry	3 oz.	168	1.59	7	6	3	2
Orlon Plus Dacron	USA	worsted	8	4.5	67% Orlon 33% Dacron	machine wash & dry	3 oz.	176	1.19	8	6	3	2
Ragg Wool	dis.	natural	8	4½	100% wool	hand wash	3 oz.	246	2.10	6	5	3	NA
Sayelle	USA	worsted ombre	8	4½	100% DuPont Orlon acrylic	machine wash & dry	3 oz.	185	1.70	7	6	3	2
Sayelle	USA	worsted solid	8	4½	100% DuPont Orlon acrylic	machine wash & dry	3.5 oz.	215	1.70	7	6	3	2

Brand and Yarn Name	Where Sold	Type	US Needle Size	Gauge/Tension per Inch	Fiber Content	Cleaning Care	Skein, Hank, Ball, or Cone Weight	Approx. Yardage	Approx. Price	Approx. No. of Skeins for a Small-size Standard Knit Pullover Sweater with Long Sleeves and Crew Neck			
										Man	Woman	Child	Infant
SnoSpun	USA	looped novelty	8	3	44% cotton 42% acrylic 14% polyester	hand wash, cool do not bleach dry flat do not iron	50 gm (1.75 oz.)	108	1.99	10	8	4	2
Soft 'n Easy	USA	worsted solid, has memory	8	4½	100% acrylic Remember	machine wash & dry	3.5 oz.	230	1.59	6	5	3	2
Soft 'N Easy	USA	worsted ombre	8	4½	100% acrylic Remember	machine wash & dry	3 oz.	197	1.59	7	6	3	2
Wintuk	USA	worsted solid classic	8	4½	100% DuPont Orlon	machine wash & dry	3.5 oz.	230	1.69	6	5	3	2
Wintuk	USA	worsted ombre	8	4½	100% DuPont Orlon	machine wash & dry	3 oz.	197	1.69	7	6	3	2
Wintuk Solid	USA	worsted	8	4½	100% Orlon	machine wash & dry	3.5 oz.	230	1.58	6	5	3	2
Wintuk Ombre	USA	worsted	8	4½	100% Orlon	machine wash & dry	3 oz.	197	1.58	7	6	3	2
Ultra	dis.	shiny	8	4½	100% acrylic	machine wash & dry	3 oz.	176	1.10	7	6	3	2
Chanteleine Adeline	USA	brushed mohair with shiny fibers	7-8	4½	50% kid mohair 30% bright nylon 20% acrylic	hand wash	50 gm	110	5.90	—	8-9	NR	NR
Agate	dis.	brushed with metallic	8	4-5	wool mohair acrylic Lurex	hand wash	50 gm	187	6.50	8-9	6-7	NR	NR
Alexandra	USA	marled color, linen texture	8-9	3½-4	82% wool 14% linen 4% polyester	hand wash	50 gm	99	4.95	10-14	8-9	5-6	NR
Celine	USA	super soft brushed heather	5	5½-6	76% wool 24% mohair	hand wash	50 gm	148	5.40	9	7	4	NR
Emotion	USA	brushed soft blend	6-7	5	30% mohair 30% wool 40% acrylic	hand wash	50 gm	165	4.90	8-10	5-6	3-4	2-3
Evelyne	USA	tweedy slub	6	6	46% cotton 31% acrylic 23% linen	hand wash	50 gm	148	3.60	9-10	7-8	4-5	3
Kid Mohair	US	brushed, super soft	5-7	4½-5	70% kid mohair 30% acrylic	hand wash	50 gm	165	7.70	8-10	6-7	—	NR

C

Name	Country	Description			Fiber	Care	Ball	Yds	Price				
Lea	USA	textured	7	5	36% cotton 41% viscose 23% linen	hand wash	50 gm	110	3.75	10	8	NR	NR
Marly	dis.	classic smooth	8	5	80% Courtelle 20% wool	hand wash	50 gm	99	—	12	10	7	4
Melanie	USA	smooth with lustre	6–7	5–5½	70% cotton 30% viscose	hand wash	50 gm	125	3.40	9–10	7–8	5	NR
Mod Ecosse	USA	classic Ecosse	7–8	4½–5	100% mercerized cotton	hand wash	50 gm	96	3.75	12–15	9–10	7–8	3–4
Myriam 2	USA	tweed	6	5½	84% wool 16% acrylic	hand wash	50 gm	150	4.20	8–9	6–7	4–5	NR
Queyras	USA	classic	7–8	4½–5	55% superwash wool 45% acrylic	machine wash	50 gm	99	3.20	11–14	8–9	6–7	3–4
Sega	dis.	nubby textured cotton	8–9	4–4½	100% cotton	hand wash machine wash & dry	50 gm	88	3.90	13	11	5–6	2–4
Sissi	dis.	very soft brushed	6–7	5–5½	80% Courtelle 10% mohair 10% wool	hand wash	50 gm	165	3.60	8	6–7	4	2
Sologne	USA	brushed printed multicolor	7–8	4½–5	80% acrylic 10% mohair 10% wool	hand wash	50 gm	165	5.00	8–10	5–6	3–4	2–3
Sonia	USA	smooth classic	6	5½	100% superwash wool	machine wash	50 gm	148	4.00	9	7	5	3
Sorbet	USA	pigtail vrille	6–8	4½	61% cotton 39% rayon	hand wash	50 gm	73	4.90	12–14	9–10	6–7	3–4
Tiana (formerly Sissi)	USA	very soft brushed	6–7	5–5½	80% Courtelle 10% mohair 10% wool	hand wash	50 gm	165	3.60	8–10	5–6	3–4	2–3
Tipshet	dis.	classic Shetland smooth	9	4–4½	100% wool Woolmark	hand wash	50 gm	83	2.95	14	12	7–8	NR
Tricadie	dis.	tube yarn solid & multicolor	8–10	5–5½	70% acrylic 30% cotton	hand wash	50 gm	95	5.50	8–9	6–7	4–5	2–3
Charity Hill Farm Charity Hill Farm	USA	classic woolen-spun fisherman's worsted 2-ply	8	4	100% pure wool	hand wash	4 oz. 1 lb. cone	210 840	4.89 19.80	6–7 —	4–5 —	3–4 —	2 —
Chat Botte Arcadie	USA CA AU	flat ribbon	8	5½	100% nylon	hand wash dry clean	50 gm	92	5.50	NR	10	NR	NR
Chaleureuse	USA CA AU	fleecy	9	3¾	40% wool 40% mohair 20% Vinyon	hand wash dry clean	50 gm	67	8.20	16	14	7	5

Brand and Yarn Name	Where Sold	Type	US Needle Size	Gauge/ Tension per Inch	Fiber Content	Cleaning Care	Skein, Hank, Ball, or Cone Weight	Approx. Yardage	Approx. Price	Approx. No. of Skeins for a Small-size Standard Knit Pullover Sweater with Long Sleeves and Crew Neck			
										Man	Woman	Child	Infant
Delicatesse	USA CA AU	bouclé with metallic	7	4½	49% cotton 21% rayon 28% acrylic 2% polyester	hand wash dry clean	50 gm	73	12.00	NR	12	NR	NR
Eldorado	USA CA AU	novelty	6	4	49% cotton 25% wool 16% rayon 10% nylon	hand wash dry clean	40 gm	86	5.20	NR	15	10	NR
Emily	USA CA AU	fleecy	6	4	90% wool 10% nylon	hand wash dry clean	50 gm	87	5.30	20	15	10	NR
Kiss Me	USA CA AU	smooth	5	5	55% wool 45% acrylic	machine wash	50 gm	78	3.30	15	12	8	6
Malicieuse	USA CA AU	novelty	8	4	55% cotton 40% rayon 5% nylon	hand wash dry clean	50 gm	95	6.60	NR	15	8	4
Mohair et Soie	USA CA AU	fleecy	6	4½	80% mohair 20% silk	hand wash hand stain removal	20 gm	44	4.70	26	24	NR	NR
Nomades	USA CA AU	cabled	5	4¼	100% cotton	hand wash dry clean	50 gm	93	4.50	12	10	6	4
Persane	USA CA AU	novelty	8	4	51% rayon 38% cotton 6% polyester 5% nylon	hand wash dry clean	50 gm	71	7.50	NR	8	NR	NR
Pussy Cat	USA CA AU	multicolor	6	4	80% acrylic 20% mohair	hand wash dry clean	50 gm	90	5.50	15	13	NR	NR
Schuss	USA CA AU	classic	8	4	90% wool 10% Vinyon	hand wash dry clean	50 gm	72	3.90	15	12	10	8
Scotland	USA CA AU	tweed	6	5	46% wool 45% acrylic 9% polyester	hand wash dry clean	50 gm	89	4.50	15	12	8	5
Sport Royal	USA CA AU	smooth	7	4½	90% wool 10% mohair	hand wash dry clean	100 gm	159	9.50	15	14	9	6
Sunshine	USA CA AU	novelty	6	4	70% rayon 30% cotton	hand wash dry clean	40 gm	40	4.80	NR	15	10	7

C

Yarn	Country	Description			Fiber	Care	Put-up	Yardage	Price				
Toison D'or	USA CA AU	fleecy	5	5	100% wool	hand wash / dry clean	100 gm	153	8.00	9	9	NR	NR
Variances	USA CA AU	multicolor novelty	8	3½	40% acrylic 34% acetate 20% wool	hand wash / hand stain removal	50 gm	62	5.00	17	15	8	NR
Chester Farms Chester Farms 2-ply	—	natural	8	5	100% wool	hand wash / dry clean	4 oz. / 1 lb.	210 / 840	5.45 / 21.80	6-8 / 2	4-6 / 2	2-3 / 1	2 / 1
Chester Farms 2-ply	—	natural colored	8	5	100% wool	hand wash / dry clean	4 oz. / 1 lb.	210 / 840	5.45 / 21.80	6-8 / 2	4-6 / 2	2-3 / 1	2 / 1
China Silk Co., Inc. Cloisonné	USA CA AU GB	cultivated mulberry bouclé, heavy textured	8	3.5	100% silk	dry clean	100 gm. / 1 lb.	180 / 800	22.00	7	6	4	2
Foo Lion	USA CA AU GB	cultivated mulberry 2-ply	9	4	100% silk	dry clean	100 gm / 1 lb.	140 / 620	21.20	7	6	4	2
Imperial Garden	USA CA AU GB	cultivated mulberry chenille	8	4	100% silk	dry clean	100 gm / 1 lb.	390 / 1,750	22.00	7	6	4	2
Pagoda #3	USA CA AU GB	spun cord, pearlized	9	4	100% silk	dry clean	100 gm / 1 lb.	165 / 750	19.20	7	6	4	2
Christopher Farms Firsherman Yarn	USA	2-ply worsted	6	5	100% wool	hand wash	402	210	3.80	6	4	3	—
Classic Elite Yarns, Inc. Cum Laude	dis.	machine washable wool	8	4½	100% wool	machine wash	50 gm	123	3.95	—	9	—	—
Elegant	dis.	fluffy bouclé	5	5	89% wool 11% nylon	dry clean	50 gm	200	4.50	—	8	—	—
Fame	USA CA	multicolor silk and rayon noil	6	5	75% rayon 25% silk	dry clean	50 gm	109	4.50	—	10	—	—
Futura	dis.	lustrous, pure mohair	9	4	100% mohair kid & adult mohair	dry clean	50 gm	92	5.95	—	10	—	—
Heather #1 4/8	dis.	smooth heather	6	5	100% wool	dry clean	40 gm	100	2.95	—	10	—	—
Impulse	USA	slub	9	4	90% silk 10% wool rayon/nylon binder	dry clean	50 gm	57	8.95	—	15	—	—

Brand and Yarn Name	Where Sold	Type	US Needle Size	Gauge/Tension per Inch	Fiber Content	Cleaning Care	Skein, Hank, Ball, or Cone Weight	Approx. Yardage	Approx. Price	Approx. No. of Skeins for a Small-size Standard Knit Pullover Sweater with Long Sleeves and Crew Neck			
										Man	Woman	Child	Infant
LaGran	USA	brushed	9	4	74% mohair 13% wool 13% nylon	dry clean	1½ oz.	92	5.25	—	10	—	—
Laswa Bouclé	dis.	randomly space looped bouclé	7	5	60% wool 40% silk	dry clean	40 gm	68	5.95	—	12	—	—
Manhattan	USA	brushed	6	5	63% mohair 18½% wool 18½% nylon	dry clean	1½ oz.	193	4.95	—	8	—	—
Sharon	USA	bouclé	9	4	74% mohair 13% wool 13% nylon	dry clean	1½ oz.	92	4.95	—	10	—	—
Tamara	dis.	subtle twist	10½	4	34% silk 33% mohair 33% wool	dry clean	50 gm	72	8.25	—	11	—	—
Columbia-Minerva Cancun	USA	smooth	8 G	4½ 3½	99% cotton 1% nylon	hand wash	50 gm	93	1.79	14	12	6	4
Cottrène	USA	novelty	8 G	4½ 3½	54% So-lara acrylic 45% cotton 1% nylon	machine wash & dry	50 gm	93	1.79	14	12	6	4
Dots et Laine	USA	novelty	8 G	4½ 3½	73% So-lara acrylic 19% acrylic 1% virgin wool 7% rayon dots 1% nylon	machine wash & dry	50 gm	93	1.79	11	9	5	4
Flavors	USA	novelty	8 G	4½ 3½	35% rayon 30% cotton 25% So-lara acrylic 10% nylon	machine wash & dry	50 gm	93	1.99	11	9	5	4
Nantuck Brushed	USA	fluffy	8 G	4½ 3½	99% So-lara acrylic 1% nylon	machine wash & dry	50 gm	93	1.29	11	9	4	3
Nordic Berbers	USA	novelty	8 G	4½ 3½	70% So-lara acrylic 29% virgin wool 1% nylon	machine wash & dry	50 gm	93	1.99	11	9	5	4
Roulette	USA	novelty	8 needle G hook	4½ 3½	60% cotton 23% rayon 16% So-lara acrylic 1% nylon	hand wash	50 gm	93	1.99	11	9	5	4

Name	Country	Description	Needle	Gauge	Fiber	Care	Weight	Yards	Price				
Sierra	USA	novelty	8 needle G hook	4½ 3½	65% So-lara 24% virgin wool 10% alpaca wool 1% nylon	hand wash	50	93	1.99	11	9	5	4
Ultra Wool	USA	worsted	8 needle G hook	4½ 3½	99% virgin wool 1% nylon	machine wash & dry	50	93	2.49	11	9	5	4
Condon's Yarns Knitting Worsted	USA	2-ply	5	5¼	100% wool	hand wash	—	200	2.10	6	5	4	—
Copley Cabana	USA GB	multishaded slubbed and textured	7	4	79% cotton 10% acrylic 11% polyester	hand wash, lukewarm water dry flat dry clean	50 gm	82	5.50	12	9	5	3
Cobweb	USA GB	chic, brushed fashion classic	9	4	42% acrylic 37% nylon 21% mohair	hand wash, lukewarm water dry flat dry clean	25 gm	63	3.29	17	13	8	4
Finesse	USA	brushed tweed classic	8	4	51% acrylic 25% nylon 14% polyester 10% wool	hand wash, 30°C dry flat dry clean	50 gm	110	4.50	11	9	6	3
Sandpiper	USA BR	raggletaggle with light terry texture	7	4½	71% cotton 27% acrylic 2% nylon	hand wash, lukewarm water dry flat dry clean	50 gm	107	4.95	10	8	5	3
Country Spun™ Country Spun Worsted	USA	woolen spun	7-10	3½-4½	100% wool	machine wash, delicate dry flat	4 oz.	190	5.50	7	6	4	3
Crystal Palace Yarns Appaloosa Silk	USA	textured, slight color variations	7-8	4½	60% wool 40% silk	hand wash	50 gm	126	6.20	11-13	8-9	5-6	—
Aran	dis.	classic	8	5	100% wool	hand wash	50 gm	85	2.80	18-20	14-17	—	—
Aurora	USA	multicolor tiny loop texture	8-9	4-4½	88% wool 5% rayon 4% polyester 3% acrylic	hand wash	50 gm	110	4.80	11-13	8-9	5-6	—
Belle Ecosse	USA	cabled classic ecosse	7-8	4½-5	100% mercerized cotton	hand wash	50 gm	92	3.75	12-15	9-10	6-7	—
BIWA	USA	pearlspun classic	6-7	5	100% mercerized pearl cotton	hand wash	50 gm	93	3.80	11-14	8-10	5-6	3-4
Chenille Coton	USA	classic non-shed chenille	9	4½-5	70% cotton 30% rayon	hand wash	50 gm	121	4.60	—	8-9	—	—
Colors	USA	slightly flamme, multicolor	7-8	5-5½	100% wool	hand wash	50 gm	110	5.40	11-12	9	4-5	2-3

C

Brand and Yarn Name	Where Sold	Type	US Needle Size	Gauge/Tension per Inch	Fiber Content	Cleaning Care	Skein, Hank, Ball, or Cone Weight	Approx. Yardage	Approx. Price	Approx. No. of Skeins for a Small-size Standard Knit Pullover Sweater with Long Sleeves and Crew Neck			
										Man	Woman	Child	Infant
Country Cotton	USA	flamme cotton many colors	5-6	5-5½	100% cotton	hand wash	50 gm	130	3.30	10-12	7-8	5-6	2-3
Country Ribbon (Solids/shaded print)	USA	classic ribbon	8-9	4½	100% mercerized cotton	hand wash	50 gm	81	4.70/4.90	—	9-10	6-7	—
Country Silk	USA CA	shantung classic	6-7	4½-5½	100% silk	hand wash dry clean	50 gm	180	6.20	9-10	6-7	—	—
Creme	USA CA	classic lustrous smooth	6	5	50% silk 50% merino wool	hand wash dry clean	50 gm	135	8.80	10-11	8-9	—	—
Dalesman	dis.	classic	7	5	100% wool	hand wash	50 gm	105	2.90	13	10	—	—
Firefly Metallic	USA	chainette metallic	7-9	4½-5	80% acetate 20% metallic	hand wash	50 gm	130	5.50	—	8-9	—	—
Georgia Mercerized	USA	classic 8-ply	6-8	5-5½	100% mercerized cotton	hand wash	50 gm	95	3.20	12-15	9-10	5-6	2-3
Heavy Metal Ribbon	USA	metallic ribbon	7	5-5½	47% copper 48% rayon 5% nylon	hand wash dry clean	50 gm	96	8.80	—	7-8	—	—
Jeans	USA CA	indigo-dyed cabled cotton	6-7	4½-5	100% cotton real indigo-dyed	hand wash	100 gm	215	7.20	7-8	5	2-3	1-2
Kaleidoscope	USA	multicolor spun wool	7-8	5	100% stock-dyed wool	hand wash	50 gm	110	5.40	10-13	9	5-7	2-3
Linen Rustique	USA	textured flamme	5-6	5-6	55% cotton 45% linen	hand wash	50 gm	146	3.80	8-10	6-7	4-5	NR
Mandarin Silk	USA CA	combed silk classic	6-7	5-5½	100% silk	dry clean	50 gm	126	11.20	10-12	8-9	—	—
Medici Silk	dis.	bouclé	8-9	4½	100% silk	hand wash dry clean	50 gm	103	7.90	9	7	—	—
Mikado Ribbon (Solid colors/printed colors)	USA	ribbon	7-8	4½-5	50-50 cotton/rayon	dry clean	50 gm	104	4.90/5.40	—	8-9	—	—
Parfaite	USA	ribbon with blips	6-7	5-5¼	70% rayon 30% acrylic	dry clean	50 gm	108	6.50	—	9-10	—	—
Sikiang	USA	filament silk sheen	5-6	5-6	100% reeled filament silk	hand wash dry clean	50 gm	165	15.00	—	9-10	—	—
Silk/Linen	USA	classic 4-ply	6-7	4½-5	50-50 silk/bleached linen	hand wash	50 gm	100	6.80	11-12	8-9	—	—
Silk/Ramie	dis.	smooth classic	9	4	70% silk 30% ramie	dry clean	50 gm	88	9.90	11-13	8-9	NR	NR

Name													
Silk Rustique	USA	textured	7-8	4-4½	60% silk 40% rayon	hand wash	50 gm	137	5.60	10-12	8-9	NR	NR
Silk Tweed	USA CA	tweedy colors/texture	7-8	4½-5	100% silk	hand wash dry clean	50 gm	125	6.80	9-10	8-9	—	—
Surf	USA	nubby texture	6-7	4-4½	67% rayon 33% cotton	hand wash	50 gm	86	3.20	NR	8-9	6	NR
Waikiki	USA	nubby texture printed colors	6	5	65% rayon 35% cotton	hand wash	50 gm	100	4.40	NR	9-10	—	—
Di. Vé Capriccio	USA	novelty with metallic	8	4.5	60% cotton 38% viscose 2% polyester	hand wash	50 gm	98	4.50	—	9	—	—
Farfalla	USA	bouclé	7	4.5	35% acrylic 30% viscose 20% linen 15% polyamide	hand wash	50 gm	87	3.75	—	5	—	—
Jeans	USA	smooth cotton	5	5	100% cotton	hand wash machine wash	50 gm	115	3.25	—	9	—	—
Kid Mohair	USA	lofty	6	5.5	80% kid mohair 20% polyamide	dry clean	20 gm	98	3.75	—	12	—	—
Miro	USA	ribbon	8	5	60% cotton 40% viscose	hand wash	50 gm	121	3.99	—	9	—	—
Olivina	USA	colored plys	7	4	35% cotton 38% viscose 20% linen	hand wash	50 gm	87	3.25	—	8	—	—
Polinesia	USA	wrapped with self color	7	5	75% cotton 25% viscose	hand wash	50 gm	93	3.25	—	8	—	—
Stellare	USA	twist with metallic	6	4.5	50% acrylic 22% nylon 15% cotton 11% viscose 2% polyester	hand wash	50 gm	140	3.99	—	10	—	—
Sorrento	USA	basic	8	5	100% acrylic	machine wash	100 gm	219	.80	—	5	—	—
Dorothee Bis Dingo	USA	—	8	4½	62% cotton 38% linen	—	50 gm	99	4.80	—	8-10	—	—
Fermette	USA	—	8	5	100% cotton	—	50 gm	99	4.80	—	8-12	—	—
Kartoum	USA	—	8	5	100% cotton	—	50 gm	115	3.50	—	9-11	—	—
Nostalgie	USA	—	8	5	100% viscose	—	50 gm	99	4.50	—	10-12	—	—
Drop Spindle 4-ply Silk	USA	silk noil	7	4½	100% silk	hand wash dry clean	9-11 oz.	1,100/lb.	37.00	2	2	—	—
Home-dyed	USA	brushed mohair	8	5-6	67% mohair 28% wool 5% nylon	—	8 oz.	490	—	—	2	—	—

C

Brand and Yarn Name	Where Sold	Type	US Needle Size	Gauge/Tension per Inch	Fiber Content	Cleaning Care	Skein, Hank, Ball, or Cone Weight	Approx. Yardage	Approx. Price	Man	Woman	Child	Infant
Dyed in the Wool 100% Alpaca	dis.	variegated worsted	6	5½	100% alpaca	dry clean	25 oz.	1,500	140.00	1	1	—	—
Cotton Cord	USA	mercerized cabled	7	4½	100% cotton	hand wash dry clean	24 oz.	1,200	80.00	1	1	—	—
Wool/Silk/ blend	USA	variegated thick & thin	7	5	60% merino wool 40% silk	dry clean	24 oz.	1,500	115.00	1	1	—	—
Worsted Merino	USA	hand painted	8	4½	100% merino wool	hand wash dry clean	24 oz.	1,680	75.00	1	1	—	—
Erdal Yarns Bouquet	USA	—	9	4	100% rayon	—	50 gm / 1½ lb.	70 / 650	2.05 / 14.00	— / —	15 / —	— / —	— / —
Bubbles	USA	—	8	5	81% acrylic 19% polyester	—	50 gm / 1½ lb.	100 / 950	2.00 / 13.00	— / —	12 / —	— / —	— / —
Capellini	USA	ribbon	10½	4	100% acrylic	—	50 gm / 1 lb.	115 / 1,050	3.00 / 24.00	— / —	12 / —	— / —	— / —
Cloud	USA	—	9	4½	100% acrylic	—	50 gm / 1½ lb.	85 / 775	1.60 / 10.00	— / —	14 / —	— / —	— / —
Duetto	USA	—	9	5	68% cotton 16% acrylic 16% rayon	—	50 gm	100	2.60	—	13	—	—
Himalaya	USA	—	9	4½	50% cotton 50% rayon	—	50 gm / 1½ lb.	77 / 700	2.00 / 13.00	— / —	12 / —	— / —	— / —
Izmir	USA	—	10	4	100% cotton	—	50 gm / 1½ lb.	80 / 720	2.00 / 13.00	— / —	12 / —	— / —	— / —
Jazz	USA	—	10	4	37% cotton 31% rayon 26% linen 6% silk	—	50 gm / 1½ lb.	85 / 775	2.80 / 17.00	— / —	12 / —	— / —	— / —
Linguini	USA	ribbon	10	4½	100% rayon	—	50 gm / 1 lb.	80 / 880	2.75 / 21.00	— / —	— / 16 mini-cones	— / —	— / —
Tweedy	USA	—	10	4	100% rayon	—	50 gm / 1½ lb.	85 / 775	2.25 / 16.00	— / —	11 / —	— / —	— / —
Esslinger Chanson	USA	worsted	6	5	80% acrylic 20% wool	hand wash, cold dry flat dry clean	50 gm	124	2.89	11	9	5	—
Ingrid	USA	cotton blend slubbed 2-ply	7	5	50% cotton 30% mohair 20% acrylic	machine wash, gentle cycle	50 gm	81	5.49	12	9	7	—

Approx. No. of Skeins for a Small-size Standard Knit Pullover Sweater with Long Sleeves and Crew Neck

C

Name	Country	Type	Needle	Gauge	Fiber	Care	Put-up	Yardage	Price				
Estelle Yarns Filette	CA	dressy shiny	6	5	65% rayon 35% cotton	hand wash	50 gm	80 m	4.39	—	10	—	—
Reverie	CA	shiny bouclé	10	5	100% viscose	hand wash	50 gm (1,000 gm cone available)	60 m	4.99	—	—	—	—
Fiesta Yarn Alizia	USA	2 strand hand-dyed novelty	7–8	4½	rayon silk	dry clean	2 oz. / 8 oz.	680 yd./lb.	64.00 lb.	—	1¼	—	—
Antigua	—	hand-dyed novelty	8	5	cotton	dry clean / hand wash	1 lb. skein / 2 oz. ball	1,085 / 129	60.00 / 8.50	—	— / —	—	—
La Boheme	USA	2 strand hand-dyed novelty	9	4½	mohair & rayon bouclé	dry clean	8 oz. / 2 oz.	675 lb.	86.00 lb. / 11.75 2 oz.	1¾	1¼	1	—
Prelude	USA	ribbon hand-dyed	10	4½	100% cotton	dry clean	2 oz. / 8 oz.	575 lb.	48.00 lb.	—	1½	—	—
Rio Grande	USA	2 strand hand-dyed novelty	9	4	100% rayon	dry clean	8 oz. hank / 2 oz. skein	500 lb.	54.00 lb. / 7.76	2	1½ / —	1 / —	—
Terra	USA	1-ply hand-dyed	9	4	100% wool	dry clean	2 oz. / 8 oz.	772 lb.	50.00 lb.	—	1½	—	—
Flere Troder USA Flere Troder (4 strands)	USA	basic	8	5–4½	100% acrylic	hand wash machine wash	1 lb.	5,200	—	—	—	—	—
Froehlich Bergschaf	USA	thick & thin	8–9	5	100% mountain sheep's wool	hand wash, warm water machine wash, delicate	100 gm	192	7.25	—	—	—	—
Duo-Sano	USA	classic viyella	8–10	5–6	50% wool 50% Egyptian cotton	hand wash dry clean	50 gm	115	5.40	—	—	—	—
Swiss Chalet	USA	thick & thin	8–9	4½–5	100% wool	hand wash, warm water dry clean	100 gm	176	10.20	—	—	—	—
Gemini Angora	USA	fluffy	8	4½	100% Angora rabbit hair	hand wash	—	33	6.50	—	14–16	—	—
Arielle	USA	twisted bouclé type	8 double	4	72% rayon 28% acrylic	dry clean only	—	133	6.50	14	12–14 double	—	—
Butterfly	USA	tulle fabric in yarn	9	4½	72% wool 15% nylon 13% polyester	dry clean	50 gm	105	9.50	—	—	—	—
Featherspun	USA	fluffy mohair	9	4½	15% wool 85% acrylic	hand wash	50 gm	162	4.00	—	—	—	—
Mood Indigo Denim	USA	dyed cotton	8	4½	100% cotton	hand wash	50 gm	86	5.50	—	—	—	—

Brand and Yarn Name	Where Sold	Type	US Needle Size	Gauge/Tension per Inch	Fiber Content	Cleaning Care	Skein, Hank, Ball, or Cone Weight	Approx. Yardage	Approx. Price	Approx. No. of Skeins for a Small-size Standard Knit Pullover Sweater with Long Sleeves and Crew Neck			
										Man	Woman	Child	Infant
Starlight Satin	—	trim yarn, shiny	8	4	100% rayon	dry clean	—	700	9.00	—	use for trim	—	—
Sun-Day	USA	all year round yarn	8	4½	50% cotton 50% acrylic	machine wash	100 gm	206	4.00	—	—	—	—
Grandor Aran Bainin	USA	smooth	7	5	100% pure new wool	hand wash	50 gm	77	—	17	14	7	NR
Bouclé	USA	smooth textured	5	7	100% cotton	hand wash	1 oz.	80	1.30	—	—	—	—
Chenille 5	USA	chenille	7	4	95% cotton 5% nylon	hand wash	1 oz.	32	.80	—	—	—	—
Festival	dis.	knubby	6	6	84% cotton 11% nylon 5% acrylic	machine wash	25 gm	54	1.90	NR	15	NR	NR
Flake	USA	knubby	5	7	100% cotton	hand wash	1 oz.	68	1.50	—	—	—	—
Gimp	USA	textured	7	5	100% cotton	hand wash	1 oz.	31	1.50	—	—	—	—
Knop	USA	knubby	6	6	85% cotton 15% acrylic	hand wash	1 oz.	31	1.68	—	—	—	—
Linen Knop	USA	knubby	6	6	100% linen	hand wash	1 oz.	42	1.59	—	—	—	—
Small Gimp	USA	smooth textured	5	7	100% cotton	hand wash	1 oz.	50	1.68	—	—	—	—
Soft Snarl	USA	novelty twist	6	5	100% cotton	hand wash	1 oz.	20	1.70	—	—	—	—
Spikey Snarl	USA	novelty twist	6	5	100% cotton	hand wash	1 oz.	20	1.95	—	—	—	—
2/2 Soft	USA	smooth	7	5	100% cotton	hand wash	1 oz.	42	.68	—	—	—	—
Grignasco Griflorette	USA	mohair type fuzzy solid colors	8	5	34% mohair 33% wool 33% acrylic	hand wash, cool	40 gm	153	3.95	8	7	5	2
Grimoment	USA	mohair type fuzzy, tweed colors	8	5	50% mohair 30% wool 20% acrylic	hand wash, cool	50 gm	165	4.95	8	6	5	2
Grirudy	USA	mohair type fuzzy, broad subtle color changes	6	5	50% acrylic 40% mohair 10% wool	hand wash, warm	50 gm	219	5.29	7	5	3	2
Grisnow	USA	Shetland type classic twist	7	5	80% wool 15% mohair 5% acrylic	hand wash, warm	50 gm	150	3.39	8	7	5	2
Gristarlet	USA	mohair type fuzzy, tweed with Lurex	8	4.5	48% mohair 47% acrylic 5% PE	hand wash, cool	50 gm	142	6.75	9	7	5	2

C

Name	Origin	Description	Needle	Gauge	Fiber Content	Care	Weight	Yards	Price				
Gritommy	USA	basic yarn broad color range	8	4.25	50% wool 50% acrylic	hand wash, warm	50 gm.	126	2.15	10	8	6	2
Gritweed	USA	classic tweed with flecks of color	8	4.75	92% wool 8% acrylic	hand wash, warm	100 gm	235	6.75	6	5	3	1
Halcyon Yarn Scottish Tapestry Wool	USA	lustrous 2-ply worsted	5-9	4-5½	100% wool	hand wash dry clean	4 oz.	170 yd	—	9	7	4	3
Victorian Bouclé	USA	loop	5-8	4-6	70% mohair 25% wool 5% nylon	handwash dry clean	approx. 3 oz.	200	—	20 oz.	14 oz.	10 oz.	—
Victorian Mohair	USA	brushed	8-9	4-4½	70% mohair 25% wool 5% nylon	hand wash dry clean	2 oz. approx. 14 oz.	135 965	— —	20 oz.	14 oz.	10 oz.	—
Hayfield of England Lugano	USA CA GB	fashion mohair-like	8	4	51% mohair 37.5% nylon 11.5% acrylic	hand wash	50 gm	111	6.75	9	8	—	—
Lugano Fancy	USA CA GB	fashion mohair-like multitone	8	4	52% mohair 40% acrylic 4% nylon 4% polyester	hand wash	50 gm	111	6.95	9	8	—	—
Lugano Fancy Glitter	USA CA GB	fashion mohair-like multitone	8	4	52% mohair 25.5% acrylic 14.5% nylon 8% metalized fiber	hand wash	50 gm	111	7.50	9	8	—	—
Twilight	USA CA GB	cashmere look	8	4	30% viscose 42½% acrylic 4½% polyester 23% nylon	hand wash	50 gm	113	4.75	8	7	—	—
Heirloom Nordic	USA CA	worsted solids & heathers	6	5	100% virgin wool	dry clean, hand wash	1 lb. cone	1,250	12.50	—	—	—	—
Reflection	USA CA	worsted smooth	8	4	100% Wintuk Orlon	machine wash & dry	1 lb. cone	1,000	6.95	—	—	—	—
Ironstone Butterfly	USA	smooth shiny	8	5	74% cotton 26% rayon	hand wash	100 gm	260	4.50	—	5	—	—
Silk Wing	USA	smooth	8	4-5	70% silk 19% wool 11% ramie	dry clean	50 gm	122	8.00	—	8	—	—
Jack Frost 7 oz. afghan & sweater yarn	USA	smooth	7	5	100% olefin	machine wash & dry	7 oz.	—	—	—	—	—	—
Cotton "4"	USA	smooth	6	9	100% cotton	machine wash	2.5 oz.	—	—	—	—	—	—
Designer 12	USA	worsted	7	5	100% DuPont Comfort 12	wash	50 gm	111	1.89	9	7	5	2

Brand and Yarn Name	Where Sold	Type	US Needle Size	Gauge/Tension per Inch	Fiber Content	Cleaning Care	Skein, Hank, Ball, or Cone Weight	Approx. Yardage	Approx. Price	Approx. No. of Skeins for a Small-size Standard Knit Pullover Sweater with Long Sleeves and Crew Neck			
										Man	Woman	Child	Infant
100% DuPont Acrylic	USA	smooth	7	5	100% DuPont acrylic	machine wash & dry	3 oz.	—	—	—	—	—	—
Heathcliff "4"	USA	—	7, 10	5, 4	90% polyester 10% olefin fibre	machine wash & dry	2 oz.	—	—	—	—	—	—
Melange "4"	USA	mohair look with flecks	7, 10	5, 4	75% DuPont Orlon 25% rayon for fleck	machine wash & dry	1½ oz.	—	—	—	—	—	—
Morlana	USA	mohair look, brushed or fuzzy	7	5	100% DuPont Orlon	machine wash & dry	2 oz.	—	—	—	—	—	—
Morlana-Multi	USA	mohair look, brushed or fuzzy	7	5	100% DuPont Orlon	machine wash & dry	1½ oz.	—	—	—	—	—	—
Tropical "4"	USA	knubby	7	5	90% DuPont Wintuk 10% rayon for fleck	machine wash & dry	2 oz.	—	—	—	—	—	—
Wintuk Ombre	USA	worsted ombré, smooth	7	5	100% DuPont Wintuk Orlon acrylic	machine wash & dry	3 oz.	—	—	—	—	—	—
Wintuk Worsted	USA	worsted solid, smooth	7	5	100% DuPont Wintuk Orlon acrylic	machine wash & dry	3½ oz.	—	—	—	—	—	—
Jaeger Jaeger Michelle	dis.	brushed	7	5	70% acrylic 15% wool 15% mohair	hand wash dry flat	50 gm	161	—	9	6	4	2
Jaeger Winter Ribbon	dis.	ribbon	10½	4¼	70% wool 30% acrylic	hand wash, dry flat	50 gm	88	—	13	10	7	4
Joseph Galler, Inc. Belangor©	USA	luxurious fluffy Angora	9-10	4½	100% Angora	hand wash	10 gm	33	6.50	—	24	12	—
Bamboo Silk Ribbon	USA	lustrous silk knitting ribbon	9	4-3½	100% filament silk	hand wash dry clean	50 gm	100	15.00	12	8	—	—
Casablanca	USA	bright thick & thin	9-10	4½	62% cotton 38% rayon	hand wash dry clean	50 gm	102	3.40	16	14	—	—
Cashmere Belangor	USA	fluffed cashmere/Angora	8-9	5	80% cashmere 20% Angora	hand wash	20 gm	70	13.60	20	16	—	—

Name	Origin	Description			Fiber	Care	Ball	Yards						
Cotton Club	USA	pigtail cotton	9	4½	100% cotton	machine wash / hand wash	50 gm	129	5.00	12	10	—	—	—
Cotton Express	USA	quick knit cable twist	7–8	4½–5	100% cotton	machine wash / hand wash	50 gm	93	3.30	16	12	10	5	—
Flores	USA FR	soft fluffy brushed	10	4	76% kid mohair 24% wool	hand wash	50 gm	109	8.00	14	10	8	—	—
Harvard	USA SW	soft tweedy classic twist	8–9	5–4½	40% wool 30% cotton 30% baby alpaca	hand wash / dry clean	50 gm	110	6.60	16	14	8	—	—
Joelle	USA SW	novelty fluffy, soft	8–9	4½–3	53% mohair 47% polyamide ribbon	hand wash	40 gm	132	7.50	14	12	8	5	—
Musarde	USA FR	heather	8	4	55% wool 45% alpaca	hand wash	50 gm	93	7.60	12	10	8	—	—
Olympic-Supra	USA SW	classic worsted	8–9	4½	100% wool	hand wash / machine wash	50 gm	120	3.50	12	10	8	—	—
Royal	USA FR	glamorous, multishades	8–9	4½	40% wool 30% silk 30% kid mohair	hand wash	50 gm	132	10.50	14	10	8	—	—
Tiffany-Tweed	USA	soft tweed	9	4½	60% acrylic 40% wool	hand wash / machine wash	50 gm	110	3.25	14	10	8	—	—
Virginia	USA SW	nubby fuzzy	10–10½	4	50% wool 37% mohair 9% acrylic 4% rayon	hand wash	50 gm	79	6.00	12	8	6	—	—
Katia Alpaca	USA	—	7	5	68% acrylic 32% alpaca	—	50 gm	150	4.60	—	7	—	—	—
Aran	USA	—	7	5	100% wool	—	50 gm	142	3.20	—	7	—	—	—
Keops	USA	—	8	4½	100% cotton	—	50 gm	87	4.00	—	10	—	—	—
Royal Mohair	USA	—	8	5	58% kid mohair 42% acrylic	—	40 gm	164	6.50	—	7	—	—	—
Knitting Fever Dynasty	USA	—	7	5	47% silk 43% acrylic 10% nylon	—	40 gm	143	4.50	—	8	—	—	—
Ipanema	USA	—	8	5	50% cotton 50% rayon	—	50 gm	92	3.50	—	10–12	—	—	—
Super Worsted	USA	—	8	5	100% wool	—	50 gm	120	3.00	—	7	—	—	—
Lana Moro Astra	dis.	—	6	5½	100% acrylic	machine wash	50 gm	180	1.80	—	—	—	—	—
Cotton D'Ecosse	USA	mercerized	7	5	100% cotton	dry clean	50 gm	95	4.00	—	13	—	—	—
Diamante	USA	tape	8	5	cotton tape	dry clean	50 gm	90	5.10	—	14	—	—	—
Diamante print	USA	printed tape	8	5	cotton tape	dry clean	50 gm	90	5.50	—	14	—	—	—

C

Brand and Yarn Name	Where Sold	Type	US Needle Size	Gauge/Tension per Inch	Fiber Content	Cleaning Care	Skein, Hank, Ball, or Cone Weight	Approx. Yardage	Approx. Price	Approx. No. of Skeins for a Small-size Standard Knit Pullover Sweater with Long Sleeves and Crew Neck			
										Man	Woman	Child	Infant
D'Milano	USA	—	8	4	50% mohair 50% acrylic	dry clean	50 gm	128	4.60	—	10	—	—
D'Prato	USA	textured	8	4	64% cotton 34% viscose 2% nylon	dry clean	50 gm	70	5.00	—	15	—	—
D'Prato print	USA	textured	8	4	64% cotton 34% viscose 2% nylon	dry clean	50 gm	70	4.60	—	15	—	—
D'Roma	USA	—	8	4	50% mohair 50% acrylic	dry clean	50 gm	128	4.00	—	10	—	—
Firenza Brushed	USA	printed	8	5	100% acrylic	machine wash	50 gm	180	2.20	—	—	—	—
Firenza print	USA	printed	8	5	100% acrylic	machine wash	50 gm	180	2.10	—	—	—	—
Lana Moro 4-ply	dis.	classic	8	4½	100% acrylic	machine wash	3 oz.	—	2.40	—	—	—	—
Pelage	dis.	classic	7	5	50% acrylic 50% wool	machine wash	50 gm	126	2.15	—	—	—	—
Polo	USA	brushed	6	5	100% acrylic	machine wash	50 gm	187	2.00	—	—	—	—
Super cotton	dis.	mercerized	3	7	100% cotton	dry clean	50 gm	150	2.40	—	—	—	—
Lanas Margarita Acuario	USA ES FR IT DE GB	novelty	8	4	16% mohair 30% wool 38% acrylic 15% nylon	hand wash	—	87	6.00	12	10	8	—
Ankara Tweed	USA ES FR IT DE GB	novelty	8	4	77% nylon 27% rayon 17% polyester 8% viscose	hand wash	—	98	5.50	11	10	8	—
Australia Cable	USA ES FR IT DE GB	classic	8	4½	50% wool 50% acrylic	hand wash	—	123	3.80	10	8	6	3
Cindy	USA ES FR IT DE GB	novelty	8	4	45% rayon 45% viscose 10% acrylic	—	—	120	5.50	—	10	—	—
Estela	USA dis.	mohair novelty	6	5	36% acrylic 57% mohair 7% nylon	hand wash	50 gm	169	7.50	—	8	—	—
Feria	USA ES FR IT DE GB	novelty	7	5	52% rayon 43% acrylic 5% nylon	machine wash & dry	—	104	3.50	—	10	—	—

C

Name	Origin	Type	Needle	Gauge	Fiber content	Care	Weight	Yds	Price				
Garden	USA ES FR IT DE GB	fancy / mohair	8	4	28% acrylic 42% mohair 7% nylon 13% polyester 4% wool 6% rayon	hand wash	50 gm	136	6.00	—	8	—	—
Gentile	USA ES FR IT DE GB	tweed	8	5	42% cotton 41% acrylic 14% mohair 3% nylon	hand wash	50	114	5.50	10	8	6	3
Gormaya	USA	novelty slub multicolored	7	4	52% cotton 37% mohair 11% nylon	hand wash	50 gm	100	6.30	—	10	—	—
Magic	dis.	mohair with shiny slub	10	4	24% acrylic 6% wool 44% nylon 6% polyester 20% mohair	hand wash	50 gm	87	7.00	—	12	—	—
Malibu	USA ES FR IT DE GB	novelty	6	5	35% cotton 58% rayon	hand wash	50	103	4.00	—	9	—	—
Mercurio	USA ES FR IT DE GB	novelty holiday	8	5	46% nylon 29% rayon 17% polyester 8% viscose	hand wash	50	98	5.00	11	10	—	—
Mongora 80	USA	mohair	8	4	86% mohair 6% wool 8% nylon	hand wash	50 gm	120	7.00	—	8	—	—
Perle Cuatro	USA	silky acrylic	7	5	100% acrylic	machine wash	100 gm	246	6.80	—	5	—	—
Rex Mohair	USA	mohair	7	4	90% mohair 10% nylon	hand wash	25 gm	129	6.00	—	8	—	—
Seracs	USA	novelty slub	6	4½	47% rayon 11% mohair 42% cotton	hand wash	50 gm	87	4.60	—	10	—	—
Top	USA ES FR IT DE GB	classic	8	5	70% acrylic 20% mohair 10% wool	machine wash	50	148	3.50	7	6	4	2
Vulcano	USA ES FR IT DE GB	novelty	7	5	43% rayon 16% mohair 16% acrylic 12% polyester 8% nylon 5% rayon	hand wash	50	117	6.00	12	10	—	—
Lane Borgosesia Cotone del Borgo	USA	cotton	5	5	100% cotton	hand wash	50 gm	95	3.75	—	8	—	—
Diamante (diamante print)	USA	ribbon	8	5	100% rayon	dry clean	50 gm	92	4.99	—	12	—	—

Brand and Yarn Name	Where Sold	Type	US Needle Size	Gauge/Tension per Inch	Fiber Content	Cleaning Care	Skein, Hank, Ball, or Cone Weight	Approx. Yardage	Approx. Price	Approx. No. of Skeins for a Small-size Standard Knit Pullover Sweater with Long Sleeves and Crew Neck			
										Man	Woman	Child	Infant
Galaad	USA	mohair blend	7	5	50% mohair 50% acrylic	dry clean	40 gm	125	3.25	—	8	—	—
Golfo	USA	cotton with a twist	7	5	100% cotton	hand wash	50 gm	103	3.99	—	10	—	—
Knitaly®	USA	basic	7	5	100% wool superwash	machine wash	100 gm	215	5.30	—	5	—	—
Knitaly Melange	—	tweed	7	5	100% wool superwash	machine wash	100 gm	215	5.99	—	5	—	—
Knitaly Mouline	USA	3 color tweed	7	5	100% wool superwash	machine wash	100 gm	215	5.99	—	5	—	—
Parsifal	USA	Shetland	8	4.5	83% wool 10% mohair 7% acrylic	hand wash	50 gm	170	3.75	—	5	—	—
Stop Tweed	USA	soft flecked tweed	8	5	68% wool 25% lambswool 7% viscose	hand wash	50 gm	126	4.99	—	8	—	—
Lee Wards Orlon Ombre	USA	basic	8	4½	100% Orlon	hand wash machine wash	3.5 oz.	230	—	used for afghans			
Orlon Sayelle	USA	basic	8	4½	100% Orlon	hand wash machine wash	4 oz.	270	—	used for afghans			
Soft 'n Carefree	USA	basic	8	4½	67% Orlon 33% Dacron	hand wash machine wash	8 oz.	540	—	used for afghans			
Lily Art. 930H Sugar 'n Cream Original	USA CA	4-ply classic worsted weight	7	4	100% cotton	hand wash machine wash	solids 2.5 oz. ombres 2 oz.	solids 125 ombres 100	2.12	11	8	6	5
Sugar 'n Cream Wool	USA	4-ply worsted	9	9	100% wool	hand wash machine wash	2 oz.	135	2.00	13	10	8	6
Lion Brand Bianca	USA	brushed multicolored tweed	6 G hook	5 4 sc	100% acrylic	machine wash & dry	1.4 oz.–40 gm	112	—	—	—	—	—
Brigette	USA	tweed wool blend	—	—	42% wool 58% acrylic	hand wash	1.4 oz.–40 gm	110	—	—	—	—	—
Cape Cod	USA	4-ply worsted weight	—	4½–5	100% virgin wool	hand wash	50 gm	122	—	—	—	—	—
Cape Cod Knitting Worsted	USA	4-ply knitting worsted, containing natural oils	8	4½–5	100% virgin wool	hand wash	—	—	—	—	—	—	—
Discover	USA	4-ply knitting worsted thermal yarn	—	—	100% olefin	machine wash & dry	85.05 gm, 3 oz.	—	—	—	—	—	—

C

Name	Origin	Description	Hook	Gauge	Fiber Content	Care	Put-up	Yards	Price				
French Angora	USA	long hair	—	—	100% Angora	hand wash & dry	10 gm	32	—	—	—	—	—
Happy Holiday Craft Yarn	USA	holiday craft yarn worsted weight	K hook	2	100% virgin acrylic	machine wash & dry	3 oz.	—	—	—	—	—	—
Joy	USA	4-ply	—	—	100% virgin acrylic	machine wash & dry	3 oz.	—	—	—	—	—	—
Lamé Gold & Silver	USA	heavy craft, metalized (3-ply) thread	—	—	65% rayon 35% metalized polyester	—	—	75	—	—	—	—	—
Le Twist	USA	fashion tweed bouclé	—	—	64% acrylic 24% wool 12% rayon	machine wash & dry	50 gm	56	—	—	—	—	—
Lion Brand Sayelle	USA	classic worsted weight	8	4½-5	100% DuPont Orlon	machine wash & dry	solids 3½ oz. ombre 3 oz.	—	—	—	—	—	—
Lion Brand Pamela	USA	knitting worsted weight	8	4½	100% virgin acrylic	machine wash & dry	solids 3½ oz. ombre 3 oz.	—	—	—	—	—	—
Nicole	USA	fashion cotton slub yarn	G Hook	4 DC	54% cotton 23% linen 23% acrylic	hand wash	1.4 oz. 40 gm	105	—	—	—	—	—
Printelle	USA	multicolored knitting worsted	H hook or #8 needle	3½ sc 4½ ts	100% DuPont Orlon Sayelle	machine wash & dry	85.05 gm 3 oz.	210	—	—	—	—	—
Softy	USA	brushed mohair look, kit	6 & 8	4	100% pure acrylic	machine wash & dry	200 gm per ball	660	—	2	1-1½	1	1
Woolana	USA	classic heather wool	8	4½	100% wool	hand wash	40 gm	—	—	—	—	—	—
Lisle Lizzy	USA	soft, textured	7	5	74% rayon 24% cotton 2% silk	hand wash cold	4, 8 & 16 oz.	750 ypp	4 oz.—12.00 hand-dyed 4 oz.—5.00 natural	5-6	5	3-4	2-3
Navajo Worsted	USA	soft worsted	8	5	100% wool	hand wash cold	4, 8 & 16 oz.	784 ypp	4 oz.—14.00 hand-dyed	5-6	5	3-4	2-3
Real Nubby	USA	nubs & slubs	8	5	50% rayon 50% cotton	hand wash cold	4, 8 & 16 oz.	750 ypp	4 oz.—13.00 hand-dyed 4 oz.—6.00 natural	5-6	5	3-4	2-3
Lo-Ran "Silky Soft" Ribbon	USA	⅛" knitting ribbon	10	4	100% polyester	machine wash & dry	—	100	11.50	—	5	—	—
Malina Sayelle	USA	4-ply knitting worsted	8	4½	100% DuPont Orlon	machine wash	4 oz.	252	—	7	6	4	2

Brand and Yarn Name	Where Sold	Type	US Needle Size	Gauge/Tension per Inch	Fiber Content	Cleaning Care	Skein, Hank, Ball, or Cone Weight	Approx. Yardage	Approx. Price	Approx. No. of Skeins for a Small-size Standard Knit Pullover Sweater with Long Sleeves and Crew Neck			
										Man	Woman	Child	Infant
Wintuk	USA	4-ply knitting worsted	8	4½	100% DuPont Orlon	machine wash	4 oz.	248	—	7	6	4	2
Mark Yarns Angora	USA	dressy	7-8	4½-5	100% French Angora	hand wash dry clean	10 gm	30	6.25	—	23	—	—
Carnival Light	USA	nubby multicolored	7-8	4½	60% cotton 30% viscose 10% polyamide	hand wash dry clean	—	66	4.50	—	16	—	—
Mayflower Mayflower Cotton Helarsgarn	USA CA GB	classic cotton worsted	5-6	5	100% cotton	machine wash, 60°C hot iron no bleach	50 gm	88	2.00	15	13	10	4
Melrose Angora Deluxe	USA	—	6	4	100% rabbit hair	—	10 gm	35	6.50	—	—	—	—
Cablenella	USA dis.	twisted	9	4½	80% wool 20% rayon	—	2 oz.	100	5.00	—	—	—	—
Cablenella Print	dis.	twisted	9	4½	80% wool 20% rayon	—	2 oz.	100	5.65	—	—	—	—
Handsome	USA	basic smooth	8	4½-5	50% wool 50% acrylic	—	50 gm	115	3.00	—	—	—	—
Lorie	USA	—	4-6	5	73% rayon 27% cotton	—	50 gm	85	3.75	—	—	—	—
Miniswade	dis.	—	7	4½	100% rayon pile	—	—	50	15.00	—	—	—	—
Silky Spun Print	USA	—	8	4	100% bright acrylic	—	2 oz.	84	4.40	—	—	—	—
Supraswade	USA	⅛" ribbon	8	4½	100% rayon pile	—	—	50	15.00	—	—	—	—
Merino Angora Lame	—	fluffy with iridescent	7	4½	39% wool 29% Angora 29% silk 3% metal polyester	—	10 gm	35	8.80	—	—	—	—
Country	—	multicolored, fuzzy	6	5	80% mohair 20% acrylic	—	40 gm	125	9.00	—	—	—	—
Crinoline	—	shiny	6	4½	100% viscose	—	50 gm	100	6.00	—	—	—	—
Faguce	—	oat textured	5-6	4½-5	66% cotton 34% viscose	—	50 gm	130	5.00	—	—	—	—
Fascination	—	shiny, novelty	6-7	4-4½	100% nylon	—	50 gm	120	6.00	—	—	—	—

Laguna	—	rustic matte	5	5	23% silk 34% cotton 33% acrylic 10% nylon	—	50 gm	130	5.50	—	—	—	—
Natura 100% Acrylic	USA	smooth classic worsted	8	4½–5	100% acrylic	machine wash & dry	3 oz.	—	—	used for afghans			
100% DuPont Acrylic	USA	smooth classic worsted	8	4½–5	100% DuPont acrylic	machine wash & dry	3 oz.	—	—	used for afghans			
Sayelle	USA	smooth classic worsted	8	4½–5	100% DuPont Sayelle	machine wash & dry	3½ oz.	—	—	—	—	—	—
Sayelle Ombre	USA	smooth classic worsted	8	4½–5	100% DuPont Sayelle	machine wash & dry	3 oz.	—	—	—	—	—	—
Ultra-Aire	USA	brushed worsted	8	4½–5	50% acrylic 50% nylon	machine wash & dry	3 oz.	—	—	—	—	—	—
Wintuk®	USA	smooth classic worsted	8	4½–5	100% DuPont Wintuk	machine wash & dry	3½ oz.	—	—	—	—	—	—
Wintuk Ombre	—	smooth classic worsted	8	4½–5	100% DuPont Wintuk	machine wash & dry	3 oz.	—	—	—	—	—	—
Nature Spun Yarn Nature Spun 1/1.4	USA	worsted	9	4	100% wool	hand wash dry clean	3.5 oz. pull skein 1 # cone	169 784	3.99– 4.25 18.95	—	—	—	—
Nature Spun 3/6	USA	worsted	7	5	100% wool	hand wash dry clean	3.5 oz. pull skein 1 # cone	245 1,120	3.99– 4.28 18.95	—	—	—	—
Nomis Allison	USA	brushed, hairy	8	4	74% mohair 13% wool 13% nylon	hand wash, cold dry flat	40 gm	95	—	12	9	6	4
Angora	USA	hairy trim yarn	10	4	100% Angora	dry clean	10 gm	33	—	—	—	—	—
Excellence 80/20	USA	smooth, heather	8	4½	80% acrylic 20% wool	machine wash & dry	100 gm	235	—	6	5	3	2
Excellence Heather	USA	smooth	8	4½	100% DuPont acrylic	machine wash & dry	100 gm	235	—	6	5	3	2
Excellence Ombre	USA	smooth	8	4½	100% DuPont acrylic	machine wash & dry	100 gm	235	—	6	5	3	2
Excellence Print	USA	smooth	8	4½	100% DuPont acrylic	machine wash & dry	100 gm	235	—	6	5	3	2
Excellence worsted	USA	smooth	8	4½	100% DuPont acrylic	machine wash & dry	100 gm	235	—	6	5	3	2

C

Brand and Yarn Name	Where Sold	Type	US Needle Size	Gauge/Tension per Inch	Fiber Content	Cleaning Care	Skein, Hank, Ball, or Cone Weight	Approx. Yardage	Approx. Price	Approx. No. of Skeins for a Small-size Standard Knit Pullover Sweater with Long Sleeves and Crew Neck			
										Man	Woman	Child	Infant
Fisherman Mohair	USA	brushed, hairy	8	4	mohair blend	hand wash, cold dry flat	12 oz.	840	—	1+	1	partial	partial
Fisherman wool	USA	smooth	8	4½	100% fisherman wool	hand wash, cold dry flat	100 gm	235	—	6	5	3	2
Lustro	USA	smooth	8	4½	50% acrylic 50% nylon	machine wash & dry	100 gm	235	—	6	5	3	2
Lustro Ombre	USA	smooth	8	4½	—	machine wash & dry	100 gm	235	—	6	5	3	2
Wolle	USA	smooth	8	4½	100% wool	hand wash, cold dry flat	100 gm	235	—	6	5	3	2
Nomotta Alpha	USA	basic	5	5½	100% cotton	machine wash, gentle do not bleach dry clean	50 gm	98	3.25	—	14	—	—
Bossa Nova	USA	brushed tubular	8	4½	80% new wool 10% alpaca 10% pure silk	hand wash do not bleach dry clean	50 gm	137	4.50	16	14	—	—
Bossa Nova Jarre	USA	tubular	8	4½	76% new wool 10% alpaca 10% pure silk 4% viscose	hand wash do not bleach dry clean	50 gm	137	4.75	—	14	—	—
Habanera	USA	bouclé	8	4½	70% new wool 30% cotton	hand wash do not bleach dry clean	50 gm	115	3.50	—	12	—	—
Lido	USA	bouclé	6	4½	64% cotton 18% linen 17% viscose	machine wash do not bleach dry clean	50 gm	87	3.75	—	12	—	—
Marilyn	USA	fluffy	6	4½	44% viscose 33% acrylic 23% mohair	hand wash do not bleach do not iron dry clean	50 gm	93	4.95	—	10	—	—
Melodia	USA	fluffy textured	8	4½	40% acrylic 30% mohair 10% wool 10% polyamide	hand wash do not bleach do not iron dry clean	50 gm	120	4.95	—	12	—	—
Saskia	USA	lustrous twisted 2-ply	5	5½	60% silk 40% wool	hand wash dry clean	50 gm	153	6.25	—	8	—	—

Name													
Super Show	USA	fluffy	8	5	70% acrylic 30% mohair	machine wash, gentle, do not bleach, do not iron, dry clean	50 gm	164	3.75	—	8	—	—
Noro Hakuhou	USA	—	8	5	53% wool 28% acrylic 19% polyester	—	50 gm	182	9.50	—	6-7	—	—
Katsura	USA	—	8	5 (triple)	59% acrylic 41% polyester		50 gm	770	11.50	—	4	—	—
Koto	USA	—	7	5	100% silk	—	25 gm	106	9.50	—	8-10	—	—
Miyabi	USA	—	7	5	100% silk	—	50 gm	160	19.00	—	6	—	—
Renge	USA	—	7	5	100% cotton	—	50 gm	106	9.00	—	7	—	—
Sumire	USA	—	8	4½	86% cotton 14% silk	—	50 gm	140	9.50	—	6-8	—	—
Tachibana	USA	—	11	3	65% wool 30% Angora 5% silk	—	50 gm	75	16.50	—	10-12	—	—
Yamabuki	USA	—	7	5	50% silk 25% acrylic 17% polyester 8% nylon	—	50 gm	170	16.00	—	6	—	—
Offray Knitting Ribbon Offray Knitting Ribbon	USA	¼" wide silk-like ribbon	5 / 4 18=4"	4-5½ E hook G hook	100% polyester	machine wash & dry, dry clean	—	100	11.00	—	8-9	—	—
Patons Allure	USA CA	brushed, shaded coloration	8	4¼	50% mohair 50% acrylic	hand wash dry flat	50 gm	185	—	7	5	3	2
Canadiana	USA CA	basic	7	5	100% acrylic	machine wash & dry	100 gm	247	—	9	6	3	1
Capstan	dis.	showerproof fisherman	7	4¾	100% wool	hand wash dry flat	50 gm	114	—	16	12	8	4
Cotton Ribbon	dis.	ribbon	9	5	100% cotton	hand wash dry flat	50 gm	88	—	13	10	7	4
Cotton Ribbon (Stonewash)	dis.	ribbon	9	5	100% cotton	hand wash dry flat	50 gm	88	—	13	10	7	4
Promise	USA CA GB	brushed	8	4¾	67% acrylic 33% nylon	machine wash dry flat	40 gm	132	—	9	6	4	2
Perendale Softwist	USA	soft	7	5	100% Perendale wool	hand wash dry flat	50 gm	120 yds	2.80	10	8	6	4
Worsted	USA	smooth worsted 4-ply	8	5	100% Perendale wool	wash with pure soap dry flat	100 gm	170	4.50	8	6	4	3
Pernelle Bouclé	USA	bouclé	7-8	4¼	98% cotton 2% polyamide	hand wash dry clean	—	110	3.60	—	8	—	—

C

Brand and Yarn Name	Where Sold	Type	US Needle Size	Gauge/Tension per Inch	Fiber Content	Cleaning Care	Skein, Hank, Ball, or Cone Weight	Approx. Yardage	Approx. Price	Approx. No. of Skeins for a Small-size Standard Knit Pullover Sweater with Long Sleeves and Crew Neck			
										Man	Woman	Child	Infant
Enjoleuse	USA	smooth	7–8	4½	67% cotton 37% viscose	hand wash dry clean	—	90	3.80	—	10	—	—
Escalade	USA	smooth	7–8	4½–5	75% acrylic 25% wool	machine wash	50 gm	90	2.15	—	8–9	—	—
Fanette	USA	multicolor slub	7–8	4	37% acrylic 31% wool 27% polyester 5% polyamide	hand wash dry clean	—	95	3.95	—	9	—	—
Fugue	USA	slub	7–8	4½	86% cotton 12% viscose 2% polyamide	hand wash dry clean	—	110	4.00	—	10	—	—
Jaspe	USA	multicolor	7–8	4½–5	67% acrylic 33% wool	hand wash dry clean	50 gm	90	3.25	—	8–9	—	—
Les Bouquets	USA	smooth	7	5	51% wool 49% acrylic	machine wash dry clean	—	140	3.60	—	7	—	—
Moire	USA	ribbon	7	4¾	52% cotton 48% viscose	hand wash dry clean	—	95	4.75	—	13	—	—
New Gentry	USA	brushed	7	5	60% acrylic 25% mohair 10% wool	machine wash dry clean	—	145	4.50	—	6	—	—
Passacaille	USA	brushed/metalic	7	4¾	62% polyamide 27% acrylic 7% viscose 4% lame	hand wash dry clean	—	145	5.95	—	7	—	—
Poemes	USA	brushed multicolor	7–8	4¼	50% acrylic 25% polyamide 15% mohair 10% wool	hand wash dry clean	—	137	4.50	—	7	—	—
Pur Cotton	USA	smooth	7–8	4	100% cotton	machine wash dry clean	—	90	3.70	—	12	—	—
Phentex Galleria Elite	USA CA	4-ply	7	5st.–9R= 1po.	100% olefin	machine wash, cold machine dry, gentle	200 gm	415	2.49	—	—	—	—
Galaxie	USA CA	2-ply	8	5st.–9R= 1po.	30% acrylic 30% wool 29% viscose 11% polyester	machine wash, cold machine dry, gentle	40 gm	90	3.50	—	—	—	—
Lotus	USA CA	2-ply	4	5st.–6R= 1po.	60% acrylic 20% wool 20% nylon	machine wash, cold machine dry, gentle	50 gm	130	1.99	—	—	—	—
Machine Knit Mohair	USA CA	2-ply	4	6st.–10R= 1po.	85% acrylic 15% mohair	machine wash, cold machine dry, gentle	1 lb.	1,590	14.95	—	—	—	—

C

Name	Source	Type	Needle	Gauge	Fiber Content	Care	Weight	Yards	Price			
Machine Knit Worsted	USA CA	4-ply	8	4st.–8R= 1po.	100% acrylic	machine wash, cold / machine dry, gentle	1 lb.	770	8.95	—	—	—
Monaco	USA CA	2-ply	8	5st.–9R= 1po.	57% acrylic 19% nylon 19% mohair 5% cotton	machine wash, cold / machine dry, gentle	40 gm	100	3.75	—	—	—
Orchid	USA CA	4-ply	8	4st.–8R= 1po.	100% acrylic	machine wash, cold / machine dry, gentle	100 gm	170	1.89	—	—	—
Rainbow	USA CA	2-ply	7	5st.–6R= 1po.	33% viscose 30% wool 20% mohair 10% polyamide 7% acrylic	machine wash, cold / machine dry, gentle	40 gm	100	3.95	—	—	—
3-ply	USA CA	3-ply	8	5st.–9R= 1po.	100% Olefin Celaspun	machine wash, cold / machine dry, gentle	85 gm	160	1.29	—	—	—
Phildar Akala	USA	perle cotton	8	5	100% cotton	hand wash	50 gm	95	3.50	—	13	—
Badge	dis.	fancy	6	4.5	66% linen 19% cotton 15% acrylic	hand wash	40 gm	67	3.75	—	12	—
Brisants	USA	Shetland	6	5.5	65% acrylic 30% wool 15% viscose	hand wash machine wash	50 gm	142	3.25	—	9	—
Broadway	USA	novelty	8	4¼	34% acrylic 20% polyester 18% kid mohair 18% nylon 10% cotton	machine wash	50 gm	111	4.95	—	9	—
Corsaire	dis.	fancy	7–8	5	40% cotton 40% wool 15% viscose 5% nylon	hand wash	40 gm	70	3.50	—	12	—
Coton Cable	USA	mercerized cabled cotton	7	4½–5	100% cotton	hand wash	50 gm	114	3.95	—	13	—
Cyclades	dis.	classic	7–8	5	70% acrylic 18% wool 12% mohair	hand wash machine wash	50 gm	93	2.75	—	12	—
Dedicace	dis.	mohair blend	6	5	75% acrylic 20% mohair 5% wool	hand wash	50 gm	174	3.95	—	9	—
Detente	—	cotton	6	5	100% cotton	hand wash	50 gm	140	3.25	—	13	—
Flamme Cotton	dis.	fancy	5–6	5.5	81% cotton 19% viscose	hand wash	50 gm	92	3.95	—	15	—
Kid Mohair	USA	kid mohair	8	5	70% kid mohair 30% acrylic	hand wash	50 gm	100	6.95	—	9	—

Brand and Yarn Name	Where Sold	Type	US Needle Size	Gauge/ Tension per Inch	Fiber Content	Cleaning Care	Skein, Hank, Ball, or Cone Weight	Approx. Yardage	Approx. Price	Approx. No. of Skeins for a Small-size Standard Knit Pullover Sweater with Long Sleeves and Crew Neck			
										Man	Woman	Child	Infant
Leader	USA	classic	7–8	5	100% acrylic	hand wash machine wash	100 gm	230	2.95	—	5	—	—
Lenox Superwash	USA	—	7–8	5	100% virgin wool	machine wash	100 gm	219	4.95	—	6	—	—
Linbel	dis.	linen blend	6	5½	55% acrylic 37% linen 8% wool	hand wash machine wash	50 gm	132	3.25	—	9	—	—
Mistigri	USA	Shetland type	8	4½–5	60% wool 25% acrylic 15% viscose	hand wash	50 gm	114	3.50	—	11	—	—
Option 4	dis.	classic	7–8	5	100% acrylic	machine wash	50 gm	113	1.15	—	11	—	—
Palmares	dis.	tweed	4–6	5½	80% acrylic 20% wool	hand wash machine wash	50 gm	154	2.50	—	9	—	—
Pegase	USA	classic	7–8	5	80% acrylic 20% wool	machine wash	50 gm	98	2.15	—	11	—	—
Sagittaire	USA	classic	6	5½	70% acrylic 30% wool	hand wash machine wash	50 gm	145	2.75	—	9	—	—
Show	dis.	fancy mohair	8	4½	33% acrylic 26% wool 17% mohair 16% polyamide 8% polyester	hand wash machine wash	50 gm	104	4.25	—	11	—	—
Suffrage	dis.	100% virgin wool	4–6	5	100% virgin wool	hand wash machine wash	50 gm	108	2.75	—	11	—	—
Whisper	USA	brushed acrylic	8	4½–5	100% brushed acrylic	machine wash	50 gm	154	2.49	—	9	—	—
Wilky	USA	fancy meche	7–8	5	48% wool 41% acrylic 11% mohair	machine wash	50 gm	93	3.25	—	12	—	—
Pingouin Astrakan	dis.	bouclé heather	4	17/4	52% acrylic 35% wool 13% polyester	hand wash dry clean	50 gm	55	—	—	13°	—	—
Confortable Sport	USA FR	3-ply, beaded heather	7	16/4	55% wool 45% acrylic	machine wash dry clean	50 gm	77	2.95	—	11°	—	—
Corrida 4	USA FR	smooth 4-ply	6	21/4	60% cotton 40% acrylic	machine wash dry clean	50 gm	120	2.95	—	12°	—	—
Coton Torsade	USA FR	designer novelty	4–6	5	97% cotton 3% polyamide	machine wash	50 gm	82	—	—	—	—	—

C

Name		Description			Fiber	Care	Weight			Price		Size		
Ecapade	USA FR	basic worsted	7	5	50% wool 25% acrylic 15% flax 10% viscose	hand wash	50 gm	110	—	—	—	—	—	—
Feerique	USA FR	novelty gold & silver	8	4¼	29% wool 20% acrylic 20% polyamide 19% viscose 12% polyester	hand wash	50 gm	121	—	—	—	—	—	—
File de Laine	USA FR	thick & thin variegated	8	15/4	100% wool	hand wash dry clean	100 gm	155	—	6.95	—	7°	—	—
Fleur de Laine	USA FR	—	7	20/4	100% wool	dry clean	100 gm	150	—	3.35	—	—	—	—
Jarre	USA FR	speckled with white	8	16/4	33% cotton 33% acrylic 27% wool 7% viscose	machine wash dry clean	50 gm	88	—	2.95	—	12°	—	—
Le Yarn	USA FR	4-ply	9	18/4	80% acrylic 20% wool	machine wash dry clean	100 gm	200	—	3.35	—	5°	—	—
Mohair	dis.	fuzzy heather	7	17/4	85% mohair 15% polyamide	hand wash dry clean	40 gm	95	—	—	—	10°	—	—
Multicolore	dis.	bright color with black base, 3-ply	9	15/4	49% acrylic 26% mohair 25% wool	hand wash dry clean	50 gm	60	—	4.95	—	12°	—	—
New Zealand Wool	dis.	loosely twisted heather	9	15/4	100% wool	hand wash dry clean	100 gm	110	—	—	—	7°	—	—
Orage	USA FR	fuzzy	6	17/4	60% acrylic 20% wool 20% mohair	hand wash dry clean	50 gm	90	—	3.95	—	8°	—	—
Pingochamp	dis.	4-ply	9	18/4	100% acrylic	machine wash dry clean	100 gm	200	—	2.49	—	5°	—	—
Pingoram	dis.	4-ply	9	16/4	100% wool	hand wash dry clean	100 gm	220	—	3.49	—	5°	—	—
Pingostar	USA FR	3-ply	7	19/4	75% acrylic 25% wool	machine wash dry clean	50 gm	90	—	1.69	—	10°	—	—
Ruban	USA FR	tubular shiny	10½	15/4	100% polyamide	machine wash dry clean	50 gm	50	—	4.95	—	17°	—	—
Sport Laine	dis.	3-ply	8	18/4	100% wool	machine wash dry clean	50 gm	70	—	2.95	—	12°	—	—
Suedine	USA FR	suede finish	9	15/4	59% acrylic 27% cotton 14% viscose	hand wash dry clean	—	—	—	12.95	—	—	—	—

°Size 14

Brand and Yarn Name	Where Sold	Type	US Needle Size	Gauge/Tension per Inch	Fiber Content	Cleaning Care	Skein, Hank, Ball, or Cone Weight	Approx. Yardage	Approx. Price	Approx. No. of Skeins for a Small-size Standard Knit Pullover Sweater with Long Sleeves and Crew Neck			
										Man	Woman	Child	Infant
Tweede	dis.	variegated blend	10	15/4	53% wool 41% acrylic 4% viscose 2% polyester	hand wash dry clean	50 gm	66	—	—	12*	—	—
Typico	dis.	thick & thin, mix of colors	6	22/4	73% cotton 23% acrylic	machine wash dry clean	50 gm	120	—	—	6*	—	—
Vrilles	dis.	loopy, variegated color with fuzzy mohair	7	17/4	58% acrylic 20% mohair 20% wool 2% polyamide	hand wash dry clean	50 gm	101	4.95	—	11*	—	—
Voile	USA FR	sheer ribbon	9	5	100% polyamide	hand wash	50 gm	192	—	—	—	—	—
Plymouth Aloha	dis.	—	8	4½	20% silk 30% cotton 50% polyester	hand wash	150 gm	150	3.40	—	—	—	—
Bristol Cotton	USA	—	8	5	100% cotton	hand wash	50 gm	80	2.60	12	10	6	—
Emu Autumn Leaves	USA	veriegated	6	4	70% wool 23% acrylic 5% rayon 2% nylon	hand wash	50 gm	91	4.80	10	9	4	2
Emu Coolspun	USA	knubby worsted	8	5	100% cotton	hand wash	50 gm	113	4.40	11	9	7	—
Emu Coolspun Confetti	USA	knubby multicolor	8	5	49% cotton 44% acrylic 7% nylon	hand wash	50 gm	113	4.40	11	9	7	—
Emu Superwash DK	USA	smooth worsted	6	5½	100% wool	machine wash	50 gm	124	2.95	13	11	5	—
Galway Irish	USA	—	8	5	100% wool	hand wash	100 gm	245	3.80	8	6	4	—
Indicieta Pacette	USA	—	8	5	100% Peruvian alpaca	hand wash	50 gm	110	4.40	12	10	—	—
Indicieta 4-ply	USA	—	8	5	100% Peruvian alpaca	hand wash	100 gm	180	8.40	10	8	—	—
Lady Angora	USA	—	8	5	70% Angora 15% lambswool 15% nylon	hand wash	20 gm	98	7.60	—	10	—	—
Naturewoole	dis.	—	8	5	100% wool	hand wash	100 gm	220	4.60	8	6	4	—
100% Pure Angora	USA	—	8	5	100% imported rabbit hair	hand wash	10 gm	40	7.00	—	20	—	—

C

Name	Origin	Description	Needle (lg)	Needle (sm)	Fiber	Care	Ball	Yards	Price				
Ragwolle	dis.	—	8	5	85% wool 15% nylon	hand wash	100 gm	300	3.40	—	4	5	6	—
Robin Bambino DK	USA	worsted	6	5½	60% acrylic 40% nylon	machine wash & dry	40 gm	133	2.19	2	—	—	—
Robin Bambino Print DK	USA	multicolor dots	6	5½	60% acrylic 40% nylon	machine wash & dry	40 gm	133	2.62	2	—	—	—
Robin Bambino Raindrop DK	USA	shiny thread twist	6	5½	54% acrylic 36% nylon	machine wash & dry	40 gm	117	2.31	2	—	—	—
Robin Bambino with Cotton	USA	worsted twist	7	4½	68% acrylic 32% cotton	machine wash & dry	100 gm	344	7.00	1	3	—	—
Robin Sundance	USA	twist	7	4½	68% acrylic 32% cotton	machine wash	50 gm	172	3.20	—	—	6	—
Saxony II	USA		8	5	100% wool	hand wash	100 gm	200	5.00	—	2-3	3-5	4-6
Stampata	USA		8	5	38% Angora 36% cotton 13% wool 13% nylon	hand wash dry clean	20 gm	75	8.00	—	—	20	—
Rainbow Mills Butterfly Silk Bouclé	USA	hand-dyed	5, 6, 7	4	100% silk	dry clean	100 gm	175	27.00 solids 28.00 variegated	1	2	4	5
Feather Yarn	USA	hand spun feathers on a cotton cord	10½	2	30% feather 70% cotton	dry clean in a net bag	40 gm	32	20.00			for trim	
Paint Box	USA	hand-dyed	5, 6, 7	4 2 strands together	45% cotton 55% rayon	hand wash	100 gm	275	9.75 variegated 9.00 solids	2	3	6	8
Red Heart Clark's "O.N.T." Wondura®	USA	4-ply classic worsted	8	4	100% Orlon acrylic	machine wash & dry	3½ oz.	200	1.60	3	4	6	7
Coats & Clark E-Z Knit	USA	4-ply classic worsted	8	4	100% DuPont acrylic	machine wash & dry	3 oz.	160	1.25	4	5	7	8
Red Heart Caress	USA	4-ply brushed classic worsted	8	4	60% acrylic 40% nylon	machine wash & dry	3 oz.	165	1.75	4	5	7	8
Red Heart Cotton	USA	4-ply smooth	6	4½	100% cotton	machine wash dry flat	2½ oz.	115	1.85	4	5	11	14
Red Heart "Preference"	USA	4-ply classic worsted	8	4	100% Orlon acrylic	machine wash & dry	3½ oz.	200	1.65	3	4	6	7
Red Heart Premier	USA	4-ply classic worsted	8	4	100% premium acrylic	machine wash & dry	3½ oz.	210	1.69	3	4	6	7

*Size 14

Brand and Yarn Name	Where Sold	Type	US Needle Size	Gauge/Tension per Inch	Fiber Content	Cleaning Care	Skein, Hank, Ball, or Cone Weight	Approx. Yardage	Approx. Price	Approx. No. of Skeins for a Small-size Standard Knit Pullover Sweater with Long Sleeves and Crew Neck			
										Man	Woman	Child	Infant
Red Heart "Sparkling" Wintuk	USA	4-ply classic worsted	8	4	60% Wintuk Orlon acrylic 40% nylon	machine wash & dry	3 oz.	170	1.85	8	7	5	4
Red Heart Wintuk	USA	4-ply classic worsted	8	4	100% Wintuk Orlon acrylic	machine wash & dry	3½ oz.	210	1.85	7	6	4	3
Reynolds Capri	USA	—	8	4	60% acrylic 15% mohair 10% wool 15% polyester	—	40 gm	70	—	—	12	—	—
Courant	dis.	—	8	4½	73% rayon 27% linen	—	50 gm	80	—	—	12	—	—
Fleur-de-Lis	USA	—	6	5	22% mohair 22% wool 45% viscose 11% acrylic	—	50 gm	125	—	—	8	—	—
Graffiti	USA	eyelash	8	4	100% cotton	—	50 gm	80	—	—	10	—	—
Highland	USA	smooth classic worsted	8	4½	100% wool	hand wash	100 gm	255	—	—	6	—	—
Highland Heathers	USA	smooth classic worsted	8	4½	100% wool	—	75 gm	195	—	—	7-8	—	—
Katsura	USA	tweed	8	3½	15% mohair 79% wool 6% nylon	—	50 gm	80	—	—	11	—	—
Kitten (Calico)	USA	brushed space-dyed	8	4	84% acrylic 16% wool	—	50 gm	160	—	—	7	—	—
La Madelaine	USA	chenille/metallic	8	4½	44% viscose 32% acrylic 12% nylon 6% Lurex 6% cotton	—	50 gm	100	—	—	10	—	—
Las Brisas	USA	breezy	9	4½	46% cotton 54% viscose	—	40 gm	60	—	—	20	—	—
Linaire	USA	bouclé	6	5	55% linen 25% cotton 20% viscose	—	30 gm	90	—	—	14	—	—
Lopi Light	USA	natural	9	4½	100% Icelandic wool	—	50 gm	120	—	—	9	—	—
Mohair Classique	USA	—	7	5½	52% mohair 48% acrylic	—	50 gm	215	—	—	5	—	—

C

Yarn	Country	Description			Fiber Content	Care	Unit	Yards	Price		Gauge		
Nature Yarn	dis.	vegetable-dyed	6	5½	100% natural	—	50 gm	115	—	—	10	—	—
Opalese	USA	—	9	4	45% viscose 21% wool 15% acrylic 12% mohair 7% nylon	—	50 gm	100	—	—	10	—	—
Pebble Beach	USA	terry	6	5	100% cotton	—	50 gm	135	—	—	10	—	—
Place de Soleil	USA	bouclé terry	6	4	52% cotton 34% viscose 14% polyester	—	50 gm	80	—	—	10	—	—
Portugese Fisherman	USA	scoured or unscoured	8	4½	100% wool	—	100 gm	150	—	—	7	—	—
Raggae	dis.	novelty	8	4½	72% cotton 28% acrylic	wash	40 gm	85	—	—	10	—	—
Reynelle Deluxe	USA	smooth classic worsted	8	4½	100% Orlon	wash	100 gm	240	—	—	4	—	—
Reynaire	dis.	—	8	4½	80% Orlon 20% mohair	—	3 oz.	225	—	—	6	—	—
Rio	USA	string	6	4½	100% cotton	—	50 gm	85	—	—	13	—	—
St. Tropez	USA	contemporary	7	4½	80% kid mohair 20% silk	—	40 gm	110	—	—	8	—	—
Suzie	USA	tweed	6	4½	55% cotton 41% acrylic 4% polyester	—	50 gm	110	—	—	9	—	—
Richard Poppleton Frisco	USA CA GB AU	knits with rio	5	5	60% viscose 36% acrylic 4% polyester	hand wash	50 gm	110	5.60	14	14	10	—
Rio	USA CA GB AU	long brushed	5–8	4	65% acrylic 35% mohair	hand wash	25 gm	62	2.35	10-14	10-14	8-12	—
Rio Deluxe	USA CA GB AU	long brushed	5–8	4	70% acrylic 21% mohair 9% polyester	hand wash	25 gm	60	2.40	10-14	10-14	8-12	—
Sorrento	USA CA GB AU	cotton core viscose ribbon wrap	5	5	58% viscose 42% cotton	hand wash	50 gm	100	3.85	7-9	6-8	5-6	—
Stellar	USA CA GB AU	long brushed mohair with viscose fleck	5–8	4	36% acrylic 30% viscose 24% mohair 10% nylon	hand wash	—	52	2.60	10-14	10-14	8-12	—

Brand and Yarn Name	Where Sold	Type	US Needle Size	Gauge/Tension per Inch	Fiber Content	Cleaning Care	Skein, Hank, Ball, or Cone Weight	Approx. Yardage	Approx. Price	Approx. No. of Skeins for a Small-size Standard Knit Pullover Sweater with Long Sleeves and Crew Neck			
										Man	Woman	Child	Infant
Rio Grande Wool Mill American Columbia	USA	3 single strands	8	5	100% wool	hand wash	4 oz.	131	10.00 dyed 8.75 white	9	7	5	3
American Columbia Kid Mohair	USA	3 single strands	8	5	100% wool	hand wash	4 oz.	119	10.00 dyed 8.00 white	7	5	4	N/A
Montana Targhee Naturals	USA	3 single strands	8	4	100% wool	hand wash	4 oz.	130	8.00	9	6	4	2½
Southwestern Natural	USA	3 single strands	8	4	100% wool	hand wash	4 oz.	125	2.95	9	7	5	N/A
Targhee/Mohair	USA	3 single strands	8	4	100% wool	hand wash	4 oz.	150	9.25	7	5	3	N/A
Samband of Iceland Saga	USA CA	—	7	4½	100% Icelandic wool	hand wash	50 gm	124	2.75	8	7	4	—
Santa Fe Yarn Cabled Wool #875	USA	heavy	9	4	100% wool	dry clean	4 oz.	166	11.80	8	6	2	1
Exotic Cotton #1007	USA	heavy	9	3½	90% cotton 10% rayon	dry clean	4 oz.	125	10.50	8	6	2	1
Pearl Wool #850	USA	heavy	10½	3	100% wool	dry clean	4 oz.	123	10.80	7	5	2	1
Santa Fe Mirage #899	USA	heavy	10½	3½	67% mohair 28% wool 5% nylon	dry clean	50 gm	100	7.60	8	6	2	1
Santa Fe Ribbon #141	USA	heavy	9	4	100% rayon	dry clean	93 gm	150	9.00	8	6	2	1
Schaffhauser Antiqua	USA	textured novelty	4-6	5	56% cotton 44% viscose	machine wash	—	117	3.95	—	10	—	—
Cotobello	USA	smooth	6-8	4½	80% cotton 20% linen	machine wash	50 gm	95	3.55	—	10	—	—
Coton Frotte	dis.	chenille look	4-6	4½	100% cotton	machine wash	50 gm	126	4.55	—	8	—	—
Coton Ribonette	USA	mercerized ribbon	8-10	4	100% cotton	machine wash	50 gm	82	6.45	—	12	—	—
Coton Ribonette Viscose	USA	mercerized cotton/visose blend	7-9	4½	64% cotton 36% viscose	machine wash	—	112	6.70	—	11	—	—
Elysee	USA	elegant classic	6-8	5	25% wool 25% silk 25% alpaca 25% mohair	hand wash	—	135	7.90	—	10	—	—
Irena	dis.	cabled	5-7	5	100% acrylic	machine wash	50 gm	143	2.65	—	7	—	—

C

Name	Country	Description			Fiber	Care	Weight						
La Fileuse	USA	homespun tweed and solid colors	7–9	4	100% wool	machine wash	50 gm	88	3.90	—	10	—	—
La Playa	dis.	twisted	5–6	5	65% cotton 14% linen 13% viscose 8% silk	machine wash	15 gm	105	3.95	—	9	—	—
Laser	USA	shimmering novelty	6–8	4½	60% acrylic 30% nylon 10% wool	machine wash	—	191	3.45	—	6	—	—
Levante	USA	slubby multicolor	4–5	5½	65% cotton 17% viscose 18% polyamide	machine wash	—	149	4.70	—	9	—	—
Mohair Kid 80	USA	fluffy	8–9	4	80% kid mohair 20% acrylic	machine wash	50 gm	163	6.15	—	5	—	—
Nancy	USA	dressy textured novelty	4–6	5	43% cotton 8% silk 32% acrylic 17% viscose	machine wash	50 gm	127	4.15	—	8	—	—
Okay	dis.	cabled	6–8	4½	30% wool 70% acrylic	machine wash	50 gm	138	2.90	—	8	—	—
Salvatore	USA	multitwist multicolor and solid	6–8	5	100% wool	machine wash	50 gm	110	3.95	—	10	—	—
Yes	USA	soft-brushed novelty	5–7	5	10% wool 30% viscose 60% acrylic	machine wash	—	193	2.95	—	6	—	—
Scheepjeswol Bouclé	USA CA GB	shiny worsted	8	3¾	61% wool 39% nylon	hand wash, lukewarm do not bleach do not iron	50 gm	99	4.00	9	7	—	—
Cotton Fantasie	USA CA GB	slubby worsted	8	4	100% cotton	machine wash, 30°C do not iron do not bleach	50 gm	82	4.00	9	8	—	—
Cotton Mohair	USA CA GB	solid with white binding, soft, worsted	10	3½	39% cotton 36% acrylic 13% nylon 12% mohair	hand wash, lukewarm do not iron do not bleach	50 gm	93	5.00	10	8	—	—
Couture	USA CA GB	variegated worsted	10	3¾	100% new wool	hand wash, lukewarm do not iron do not bleach	50 gm	88	5.00	12	10	—	—
Dordogne	USA CA GB	heavy worsted slubby, variegated	9	3½	55% acrylic 40% nylon 5% nylon	machine wash 30°C do not bleach do not iron	50 gm	66	4.00	16	11	—	—

Brand and Yarn Name	Where Sold	Type	US Needle Size	Gauge/Tension per Inch	Fiber Content	Cleaning Care	Skein, Hank, Ball, or Cone Weight	Approx. Yardage	Approx. Price	Approx. No. of Skeins for a Small-size Standard Knit Pullover Sweater with Long Sleeves and Crew Neck			
										Man	Woman	Child	Infant
Fashion Mohair	USA CA GB	solid with variegated binding fluffy worsted	8	4	40% viscose 28% acrylic 15% cotton 12% nylon 5% mohair	hand wash, lukewarm do not iron do not bleach	50 gm	66	4.00	22	15	—	—
Granada	USA CA GB	slightly slubby worsted	4-6	4¾–5½	100% cotton	machine wash, 60°C do not bleach Hot iron	50 gm	110	3.50	15	12	7	—
Linnen Bullent	USA CA GB	shiny slightly slubby worsted	7	5	42% cotton 39% viscose 19% linen	hand wash do not bleach do not iron	50 gm	99	4.00	15	14	—	—
Mohair	USA CA GB	fluffy soft worsted	9-10	3½	67% mohair 28% new wool 5% nylon	hand wash lukewarm cool iron do not bleach	50 gm	110	9.00	—	9	—	—
Nobel Tweed	USA CA GB	soft tweedy worsted	8	4	48% wool 37% acrylic 6% mohair 6% alpaca 3% silk	machine wash 30°C do not iron do not bleach	50 gm	88	5.00	16	11	—	—
Superwash Onde	USA CA GB GB	— —	5-6	4½-5	100% new wool	machine wash & dry, 30°C do not iron do not bleach	50 gm	104	3.50	—	10	—	—
Superwash Onde Fantasie	USA CA GB	slightly variegated worsted	7	4½	100% new wool	machine wash & dry, 30°C do not iron do not bleach	50 gm	104	3.50	14	10	—	—
Superwash Plus	USA CA GB	classic flat worsted	8	4¾	100% new wool	machine wash & dry, 30°C do not iron do not bleach	50 gm	88	3.00	15	13	—	—
Schoeller Anabelle	USA	knubby bouclé solids and tweeds	6	5	55% cotton 23% acrylic 22% viscose	machine wash, mild	50 gm	87	4.09	—	12	9	—
Terra	USA	worsted twisted solids & tweeds 3-ply	10	4	65% acrylic 35% virgin wool	machine wash, mild	50 gm	93	2.85	12	10	8	—
Tina	USA	cotton/flax slubbed 3-ply	4	6	50% cotton 25% viscose 20% flax 5% acrylic	machine wash, mild	50 gm	108	4.09	14	9	5	3

C

Name	Origin	Description	Needle	Gauge	Fiber Content	Care	Put-up	Yds/lb	Price				
Scott's Woolen Mill													
Angelique	USA	glossy, brushed specialty	5–8	4–6	45% kid mohair 35% viscose 20% wool	dry clean	2 oz. skein ½ or 1 lb.	105 skein 850 lb.	7.30 skein 56.00 lb.	12	10	6–8	3
Bijou	USA	brushed with nubs	10½	10=3"	70% acrylic 22% wool 8% polyester	machine wash, gentle	2 oz. sk ½ or 1 lb.	125 skein 1,000 lb.	3.25 skein 24.00 lb.	10	7	5	2
Duchess	USA	fluffy brushed heather	5–9	4–6	20% mohair 20% wool 36% Orlon 24% polyester	machine wash, cold water	2 oz. skein ½ or 1 lb.	150 skein 1,200 lb.	4.50 skein 34.00 lb.	8	6	4	2
Filigree	USA	nubby textured bouclé	5–8	4–6	100% cotton	solid colors: hand wash, cold mixed colors: dry clean	2 oz. skein ½ or 1 lb.	140 skein 1,150 lb.	3.90 skein 29.00 lb.	10	8	6	3
Milan	USA	bouclé	5	5	100% spun rayon	dry clean	2 oz. skein 1 or ½ lb.	95 skein 760 lb.	3.50 26.00	10	8	6	2
Navajo	USA	nubby textured bouclé	5–8	4–6	75% cotton 18% linen 7% nylon	solid colors: hand wash, cold mixed colors: dry clean	2 oz. skein ½ or 1 lb.	130 skein 1,050 lb.	3.90 skein 29.00 lb.	10	8	6	3
Nostalgia	dis.	smooth classic worsted	5–9	4–6	100% wool	solid colors: hand wash, cold mixed colors: dry clean	2 oz. skein ½ or 1 lb.	100 skein 800 lb.	3.20 skein 24.00 lb.	12	10	6–8	4
Romance	USA	specialty blend of a shiny bouclé and a brushed yarn	5–9	4–6	50% wool 50% rayon	solid colors: hand wash, cold mixed colors: dry clean	2 oz. skein ½ or 1 lb.	80 skein 625 lb.	5.25 skein 40.50 lb.	14	12	6–8	5
Tara	USA	mercerized bouclé	5–8	4–6	100% cotton	solid colors: hand wash, cool mixed colors: dry clean	2 oz. skein ½ or 1 lb.	125 skein 1,000 lb.	3.90 skein 29.00 lb.	10	8	6	3
Trifle	dis.	tweedy glossy bouclé	5–9	4–6	100% kid mohair	hand wash, cold water	2 oz. skein ½ or 1 lb.	60 skein 500 lb.	6.25 skein 48.00 lb.	14	12	6–8	5
Serendipity Skeins													
Allure	USA	more soft than hairy hand-dyed	8	4	70% Angora 30% wool	hand wash dry clean	20 gm	99	—	14	9	7	5
Autumn	USA	high sheen slightly hairy hand-dyed	8	4	50% silk 50% mohair	dry clean	2 oz.	100	—	15	9	7	5
Bikini	USA	velvet bouclé hand-dyed	9	5	100% cotton	hand wash dry clean	8 oz.	575	—	3	2	2	1

Brand and Yarn Name	Where Sold	Type	US Needle Size	Gauge/Tension per Inch	Fiber Content	Cleaning Care	Skein, Hank, Ball, or Cone Weight	Approx. Yardage	Approx. Price	Approx. No. of Skeins for a Small-size Standard Knit Pullover Sweater with Long Sleeves and Crew Neck			
										Man	Woman	Child	Infant
Caprice	USA	gutsy cabled cord hand-dyed	8	4	100% cotton	hand wash dry clean	2 oz.	100	—	15	9	7	5
Eclipse	USA	soft, hairy, shiny hand-dyed	8	4	50% baby camel down 50% silk	dry clean	2 oz.	99	—	15	9	7	5
Finesse	USA	soft tabular knit "ribbon" hand-dyed	9	4	100% silk	dry clean	2 oz.	81	—	19	12	8	6
Intrigue	USA	smooth & rough hand-dyed	8	4	80% silk 20% linen	dry clean	3½ oz.	250	—	6	4	2	2
Jubilee	USA	very nubby hand-dyed	8	4	100% cotton	hand wash dry clean	8 oz.	475	—	3	2	2	1
Mosaic	USA	softly brushed hand-dyed	9-10½	4	78% mohair 14% wool 8% nylon	hand wash dry clean	2 oz.	119	—	13	8	6	4
Pin Wheel	USA	creamy bouclé hand-dyed	9-10½	4	74% mohair 13% wool 13% nylon	hand wash dry clean	2 oz.	119	—	13	8	6	4
Savvy	USA	rich, lustrous 2-ply hand-dyed	9	4	100% silk	dry clean	2 oz.	70	—	22	13	10	7
2 to Tango	USA	matte & shiny hand-dyed	8	5	68% rayon 32% cotton	dry clean	8 oz.	515	—	3	2	1	1
Shasha Yarns Little Lamb	USA	knubby	10	6	wool	dry clean	100 gm	120	6.50	—	8	—	—
Piper	USA	classic	8	4½	wool	dry clean	50 gm	68	2.00	—	10–12	—	—
Tweed Jumbo	USA	tweedy-multicolor	10	3½	wool/acrylic	dry clean	100 gm	76	5.00	—	7–8	—	—
Vail	USA	worsted	10	4	wool	dry clean	100 gm / 50 gm	110 / 55	4.00 / 2.00	— / —	7–8 / —	— / —	— / —
Sirdar Aran	USA	—	7	4½	45% acrylic 40% bri-nylon 15% wool	—	40 gm	82	2.36	—	—	1	1
Brushed Tweed	USA	country tweed	8	4	61% acrylic 17% mohair 22% bri-nylon	—	50 gm	79	4.00	—	—	—	—

C

Name	Country	Type	Needle	Gauge	Fiber	Care	Put-up	Yards	Price				
Mosaic	USA	specialty	7	4½	60% acrylic 16% polyamid 12% mohair 12% wool	—	50 gm	110	4.00	—	—	—	—
Nocturne	USA	specialty	8	4	77% mohair 13% wool 10% bri-nylon	—	25 gm	51	4.76	—	—	—	—
Romance	USA	specialty	7	4½	49% acrylic 27% viscose 14% mohair 10% nylon	—	50 gm	144	5.50	—	—	—	—
Sportswool	USA	—	7	4½	100% wool	—	50 gm	87	3.86	—	—	—	—
Softball® Yarn Classic Softball Cotton, Solid Color	USA GB CA HK JP	classic worsted	7	4.5	100% combed cotton	machine wash & dry	3½ oz. 2 lb. cone	154 1,400	5.00 ball 18.80 lb.	7	6	4	3
Classic Softball® Wool Solid Color	USA	classic worsted	7	4.5	100% wool	hand wash dry clean	3½ oz. ball 2 lb. cone	200 1,866	6.50 ball 26.80 lb.	7	6	4	3
Duo	USA	bicolored worsted	7	4.5	100% combed cotton	machine wash & dry	50 gm ball 2 lb. cone	90 1,630	42 doz. 27.80 lb.	7	6	4	3
Duo Woolchine	USA	shiny bicolored worsted	8	4.5	72% wool 22% rayon 5% polyester	dry clean	50 gm ball 2 lb. cone	85 1,553	53.20 doz. 32.80 lb.	7	6	4	3
Shots of Gold	USA	metallic worsted	7	4.5	98% wool 2% Lurex	dry clean	3½ oz. ball 2 lb. cone	170 1,553	8.50 ball 32.80 lb.	7	6	4	3
Triple Play Cotton	USA	contrast wrap worsted	7	4.5	100% combed cotton	machine wash & dry	3½ oz. ball 2 lb. cone	148 1,350	6.50 ball 26.80 lb.	7	6	4	3
Triple Play Wool	USA	contrast wrap worsted	7	4.5	100% wool	hand wash dry clean	3½ oz. ball 2 lb. cone	200 1,646	8.50 ball 32.80 lb.	7	6	4	3
Soie et Soie Alpaca Silk	USA JP	lightweight natural alpaca colors	9–10	5½–6	60% filament silk	hand wash dry clean	40 gm	80 m	—	—	10	—	—
Brushed Silk	USA JP	lightweight	6–7	4½–5	100% filament silk	hand wash dry clean	25 gm	70 m	—	—	10/11	—	—
Silk Bouclé	USA JP	lusterous lightweight	7–8	5–5½	100% filament silk	hand wash dry clean	25 gm	70 m	—	—	11/12	—	—
Silk Ribbon	USA JP	width 8 mm lightweight lustrous	8–9	4–4½	100% filament silk	hand wash dry clean	spool	100 m	—	—	—	—	—
Silk Strand	USA JP	width 8 mm lightweight lustrous	8–9	4–4½	100% filament silk	hand wash dry clean	spool	10 m	—	—	—	—	—

Brand and Yarn Name	Where Sold	Type	US Needle Size	Gauge/Tension per Inch	Fiber Content	Cleaning Care	Skein, Hank, Ball, or Cone Weight	Approx. Yardage	Approx. Price	Approx. No. of Skeins for a Small-size Standard Knit Pullover Sweater with Long Sleeves and Crew Neck			
										Man	Woman	Child	Infant
Spinnerin Deluxe 4-ply	—	worsted	8	4½	100% DuPont acrylic	machine wash & dry, mild cycle	3½ oz.	190	1.79	8	6	4	3
Deluxe 4-ply	—	ombre worsted	8	4½	100% DuPont acrylic	machine wash & dry mild cycle	3 oz.	160	1.79	—	6	4	3
SpringBrook Celeste	USA	puffed rayon spiral	8–9	4	83% rayon 10% mohair 4% acrylic 3% nylon	dry clean	50 gm 1 lb.	75 720	4.25 36.00	—	15	—	—
Devon Creme	USA	3-ply rustic handspun	8–9	4	76% wool 18% nylon 6% silk	dry clean	50 gm 1 lb.	90 840	3.75 31.50	—	13	—	—
Gigi	USA	variegated brushed	8–9	4	32% wool 60% acrylic 8% polyester	machine wash, cold tumble dry	50 gm 1 lb.	95 900	3.40 28.00	—	12	—	—
Harriet	USA	flecked worsted	7–9	4–6	60% wool 40% acrylic	machine wash, cold dry flat	50 gm 1 lb.	120 1,120	2.95 24.00	—	10	—	—
Island	USA	rustic slubby handspun	7–9	4–6	74% rayon 24% cotton 2% silk	dry clean	100 gm 1 lb.	160 750	2.55 8.60	—	8	—	—
Island Print	USA	variegated as above	7–9	4–6	74% rayon 24% cotton 2% silk	dry clean	100 gm 1 lb.	160 750	2.95 10.40	—	8	—	—
Knitting Worsted	USA	heathered	7–9	4–6	85% acrylic 15% wool	machine wash, gentle, cold water tumble dry	100 gm 1 lb.	245 1,120	2.75 15.50	—	5	—	—
Melange	USA	multicolored bouclé	7–9	4–6	83% acrylic 17% polyester	machine wash, gentle, cold water tumble dry	50 gm 1 lb.	150 1,400	2.30 18.00	—	8	—	—
Poodle	USA	bouclé	7–9	4–6	87% acrylic 13% polyester	machine wash, gentle cold water tumble dry	50 gm 1 lb.	120 1,100	2.15 16.50	—	10	—	—
Printemps	USA	bouclé with brushed mohair overwrap	7–9	4–6	31% acrylic 26% mohair 26% wool 17% polyester	dry clean	50 gm 1 lb.	105 1,000	3.25 26.50	—	12	—	—
Savannah	USA	bulky	8–9	4	100% cotton	dry clean	50 gm 1 lb.	60 560	2.55 20.00	—	14	—	—

C

Name	Country	Texture			Fiber	Care	Weight	Length	Price				
Stella	USA	metallic with brushed mohair overwrap	8–9	4	25% metallic 24% mohair 21% wool 17% acrylic 10% polyester	hand wash, cold water dry flat	50 gm / 1 lb.	125 / 1,160	7.10 / 62.00	—	9	—	—
Susan	USA	two tone random bubble	7–9	4–6	87% acrylic 13% polyester	machine wash, gentle, cold water tumble dry	50 gm / 1 lb.	115 / 1,070	2.20 / 17.00	—	11	—	—
Sylvie	USA	fluffy nub	7–9	4–6	44% cotton 15% mohair 15% polyester 11% acrylic 15% wool	dry clean	50 gm / 1 lb.	120 / 1,000	3.60 / 30.00	—	12	—	—
Sunbeam Alaska	CA	chunky	9	4½	60% acrylic 30% wool 10% nylon	hand wash	100 gm	120 m	8.99 (CA$)	—	5	—	—
Aran Bainin	CA	—	8	4½	100% wool	hand wash, 40°C	50 gm	70 m	2.80 (CA$)	—	15	—	—
Aran Bainin Flecks	CA	—	8	4½	100% wool	hand wash	50 gm	70 m	3.00 (CA$)	—	15	—	—
Aran Kemp	CA	—	8	4½	96% wool 4% viscose	hand wash	50 gm	70 m	2.99 (CA$)	—	15	—	—
Aran Oiled	CA	—	8	4½	100% wool	hand wash	50 gm	70 m	2.80 (CA$)	—	15	—	—
Aran Tweed	CA	—	8	4½	100% wool	hand wash	50 gm	70 m	3.99 (CA$)	—	15	—	—
Rumours	CA	mohair	8	4½	79% wool 16% nylon 5% acrylic	hand wash	25 gm	60 m	5.50 (CA$)	—	10	—	—
Sumatra Chunky	CA	chunky	9	3½	63% acrylic 35% nylon 2% polyester	hand wash	50 gm	49 m	4.50 (CA$)	—	13	—	—
Tahki Imports Ambrosia Slim	USA	—	8	4½	100% wool	dry clean	3.5 oz.	220	8.40	—	6	—	—
Amigo	USA	—	5	5	53% cotton 47% linen	dry clean	1.75 oz.	120	3.35	—	8	—	—
Chelsea Silk	USA	—	9	4	65% silk 35% wool	dry clean	1.75 oz.	200	9.00	—	5	—	—
Cotton Dot	USA	—	6–7	5	100% mercerized cotton	dry clean	3.5 oz.	154	7.98	—	6	—	—
Cotton Twist	USA	—	8	5	100% cotton	dry clean	3.5 oz.	190	7.60	—	6	—	—
Designer Tweed	USA	tweed	8	4½	100% wool	dry clean	3.5 oz.	175	6.20	—	6	—	—
Donegal Tweed	USA	tweed	8	4½	100% wool	dry clean	3.5 oz.	175	6.40	—	6	—	—
Laguna	USA	—	7	4½	27% linen 73% viscose	dry clean	3.5 oz.	163	6.40	—	6	—	—

124 *CLASS C   Heavy Worsted Or 4-Ply Weight Yarns*

Brand and Yarn Name	Where Sold	Type	US Needle Size	Gauge/Tension per Inch	Fiber Content	Cleaning Care	Skein, Hank, Ball, or Cone Weight	Approx. Yardage	Approx. Price	Man	Woman	Child	Infant
The Ritz	USA	elegant	8	4½	39% viscose 26% mohair 18% polyamide 10% lambswool 7% polyester	dry clean	1.4 oz.	80	8.98	—	10	—	—
Saki	USA	—	9	4½	75% cotton 25% acrylic	dry clean	1.75 oz.	97	5.50	—	6	—	—
Superkid Mohair	—	fluffy	8	4½	80% superkid mohair 20% acrylic	dry clean	1.4 oz.	100	8.98	—	10	—	—
Windsor Tweed	—	tweed	8	4½	100% wool	dry clean	3.5 oz.	175	6.40	—	6	—	—
Tamm Yarns Rayito Tamm	USA CA AU MX	3-ply medium weight	—	15/3 4-9	75% acrylic 25% poly-nylon	machine wash	454 gm	2,281	14.90	—	1 cone	—	—
Capri Tamm	—	8-strand twisted basket weave	—	26/8 8-10	70% acrylic 30% poly-nylon	machine wash	454 gm	1,636	15.25	—	1 cone	—	—
Tandorri 2-ply Tussah natural color	—	beautifully twisted textured spun wild silk	7	4½	98% silk 2% rayon	dry clean	100 gm	843	—	2 lb.	1½ lb.	—	—
Unger Action	USA CA	—	6	5	100% acrylic	machine wash	50 gm	125	2.25	—	9	—	—
Andorra	USA CA	—	9	4	39% wool 23% mohair 34% acrylic 4% nylon	hand wash dry clean	40 gm	79	3.80	—	8	—	—
Angelspun	USA CA	—	5	5	21% mohair 58% acrylic 21% nylon	dry clean only	50 gm	330	7.00	—	4	—	—
Aries	USA	—	8	4½	45% wool 55% acrylic	machine wash	100 gm	180	3.75	—	5	—	—
Baby Courtelle	USA CA	—	5	5½	100% acrylic	machine wash	50 gm	140	2.00	—	10	—	—
Britania	USA CA	Shetland	6	5½	100% wool	hand wash dry clean	50 gm	140	3.75	—	10	—	—
Bonjour	dis.	—	7	4½	100% acrylic	—	50 gm	155	3.10	—	8	—	—
Cappucino	USA CA	novelty	9	4½	67% wool 22% acrylic 11% rayon	hand wash	50 gm	110	3.20	—	9	—	—

C

Name	Origin	Texture			Fiber	Care	Weight		—		—		—
Cozy	dis.	—	9	4	45% wool 55% acrylic	machine wash	1¾ oz.	82	—	2.70	—	12	—
Darling	dis.	brushed	6	5	20% wool 60% acrylic 20% mohair	machine wash hand wash	40 gm	150	—	3.25	—	10	—
Driftwood	USA CA	semi-bulky	9	4	100% wool	hand wash dry clean	50 gm	103	—	4.50	—	11	—
Fanfare	dis.	—	9	4	58% wool 11% polyester 29% acrylic 2% viscose	hand wash dry clean	50 gm	82	—	5.40	—	9	—
Fleece spun	dis.	knitting worsted	8	5	100% wool	hand wash dry clean	50 gm	110	—	2.90	—	10	—
Fluffy	USA CA	brushed	6	5	100% acrylic	machine wash	50 gm	156	—	2.20 fluffy	—	8	—
Fluffy Tweed	USA CA	brushed	6	5	100% acrylic	machine wash	50 gm	156	—	2.30	—	8	—
Frolic	dis.	tubular cotton braid	10	4	100% cotton braid	hand wash	50 gm	71	—	5.20	—	12	—
Gypsy	USA CA	tubular space-dyed	10	4	50% silk 50% acrylic	hand wash dry clean	50 gm	92	—	9.75	—	12	—
Glicine	USA CA	novelty	8	4½	51% rayon 38% acrylic 11% nylon	dry clean	40 gm	82	—	5.00	—	10	—
Kenya	USA CA	terry	7	4½	96% cotton 4% nylon	hand wash	50 gm	102	—	3.90	—	10	—
Le Tweed	USA CA	—	8	4½	17% wool 56% acrylic 13% viscose 14% polyester	hand wash dry clean	50 gm	110	—	3.60	—	8	—
Magic	dis.	ombré	6	5	100% wool	hand wash dry clean	50 gm	160	—	7.00	—	6	—
Maundi	dis.	knubby	7	4	41% cotton 37% acrylic 17% viscose 5% nylon	hand wash dry clean	50 gm	88	—	4.50	—	11	—
Montage	USA CA	novelty	7	4¼	72% cotton 14% linen 10% rayon 4% acrylic	hand wash	50 gm	82	—	4.75	—	11	—
Morea	USA CA	tubular/ shiny ribbon	10	4	100% rayon	dry clean	50 gm	77	—	4.30	—	14	—
Nubby	dis.	knubby	8	4	100% acrylic	hand wash	50 gm	60	—	2.85	—	11	—

Brand and Yarn Name	Where Sold	Type	US Needle Size	Gauge/Tension per Inch	Fiber Content	Cleaning Care	Skein, Hank, Ball, or Cone Weight	Approx. Yardage	Approx. Price	Approx. No. of Skeins for a Small-size Standard Knit Pullover Sweater with Long Sleeves and Crew Neck			
										Man	Woman	Child	Infant
Pima	USA CA	cotton cable	7	4¾	100% combed mercerized pima cotton	hand wash	50 gm	92	4.25	—	11	—	—
Plantation	USA CA	soft cotton	6	5	100% cotton	hand wash	50 gm	102	2.90	—	10	—	—
Rhapsody	dis.	multicolor	8	4½	50% Angora 44% lambswool 6% nylon	hand wash dry clean	20 gm	60	7.95	—	12	—	—
Riccione	USA CA	nubby	4	5½	75% cotton 25% rayon	hand wash dry clean	50 gm	130	3.20	—	10	—	—
Roly Poly	USA CA	—	6	5	100% acrylic	machine wash	100 gm	255	3.10	—	5	—	—
Roly Poly (Heather Tones)	USA CA	ombré	6	5	100% acrylic	machine wash	100 gm	255	3.25	—	5	—	—
Rygja	USA CA	homespun	5	5½	100% virgin wool	hand wash	100 gm	280	5.20	—	5	—	—
Soiree	dis.	shiny dressy ribbon	8	5	100% silk ribbon	dry clean only	36 gm	92	15.00	—	—	—	—
Twilight	dis.	multicolor	8	4½	70% Angora 44% lambswool 6% nylon	hand wash dry clean	20 gm	66	7.95	—	11	—	—
Utopia	USA CA	worsted	8	4½	100% acrylic	machine wash	3.5 oz. 100 gm	240	2.95	—	5	—	—
Wild Silk	dis.	knubby	6	5	80% silk 20% cotton	hand wash dry clean	50 gm	126	7.00	—	10	—	—
Yum Yum	USA CA	—	6	5	50% Angora 25% lambswool 15% acrylic 10% nylon	hand wash dry clean	20 gm	77	5.40	—	12	—	—
Welcomme Brilliance	USA	smooth	7–8	4	100% viscose	hand wash dry clean	—	105	9.80	—	8	—	—
Crepon	USA	bouclé	7–8	4	100% cotton	hand wash dry clean	—	90	5.00	—	8	—	—
Dievka	USA	ribbon/mohair	7–8	4	45% mohair 36% polyamide 19% acrylic	hand wash dry clean	—	105	9.00	—	8	—	—

C

Name	Country	Description		Fiber	Care	Ball wt.	Yardage	Price			
Eaux Vives	USA	brushed, wiry	7 / 5	30% mohair 27% polyester 20% wool 23% acrylic	hand wash dry clean	—	125	6.50	—	8	—
Flamboyant	USA	tweed	7 / 5¼	55% wool 45% viscose	hand wash dry clean	—	121	6.25	—	10	—
Floraison	USA	nubby multi-colored	7-8 / 4¾	52% viscose 37% cotton 11% polyamid	hand wash dry clean	—	120	10.00	—	9	—
Iris	USA	wiry multi-colored	7 / 5¼	33% polyamid 30% acrylic 25% wool 4% lame 8% viscose	hand wash dry clean	—	77	5.00	—	17	—
Langora	USA	Angora	7-8 / 4½-5	70% Angora 30% lambs wool	hand wash dry clean	20 gm	100	8.00	—	12-13	—
Les Saisons	USA	classic	7-8 / 4½-5	55% acrylic 30% wool 15% mohair	hand wash dry clean	50 gm	150	3.60	—	6-7	—
Reflet	USA	slub/metalic	7 / 5¼	78% viscose 20% mohair 2% polyamid	hand wash dry clean	—	110	9.85	—	10	—
Refuge	USA	brush/multi-colored	7-8 / 4	52% wool 20% mohair 13% polyamid 13% acrylic 2% polyester	hand wash dry clean	—	110	7.65	—	8	—
Shetland et Alpaga 5	USA	Shetland twist	7-8 / 4½-5	90% wool 10% alpaga	machine wash dry clean	50 gm	80	5.40	—	10-11	—
Spiral	USA	wiry	7 / 5	50% cotton 50% viscose	hand wash dry clean	—	140	5.75	—	7	—
Super Mohair	USA	brushed	7-8 / 4½-5	70% kid mohair 30% acrylic	hand wash dry clean	40 gm	135	6.85	—	6-7	—
Triboulet	dis.	textured shiny cotton	7-8 / 4½-5	55% cotton 45% viscose	hand wash dry clean	50 gm	77	4.50	—	14	—
Wendy Amalfi	USA CA GB AU	long brushed	5-7 / 4	65% Courtelle 30% mohair 5% cotton	hand wash	25 gm	63	2.70	14	14	9
Capri	USA CA GB AU	—	4-6 / 5	51% cotton 49% Courtelle acrylic	machine wash	50 gm	115	3.85	6-8	6-8	4-6
Como	USA CA GB AU	ribbon	10-11 / 4.5	100% cotton	hand wash	50 gm	94.5	5.00	8-10	8	6

Brand and Yarn Name	Where Sold	Type	US Needle Size	Gauge/Tension per Inch	Fiber Content	Cleaning Care	Skein, Hank, Ball, or Cone Weight	Approx. Yardage	Approx. Price	Approx. No. of Skeins for a Small-size Standard Knit Pullover Sweater with Long Sleeves and Crew Neck			
										Man	Woman	Child	Infant
Donna	USA CA GB AU	brushed bouclé knits with dolce	4-6	4.5	77% Courtelle acrylic 15% mohair 6% polyester 2% bri-nylon	hand wash	50 gm	119	4.75	8-10	8-10	6-8	—
Donna D'Oro	USA CA GB AU	knits with dolce bouclé with Lurex	4-6	4.5	72% Courtelle acrylic 14% mohair 7% polyester 4% bri-nylon 3% metallic	hand wash	50 gm	114	4.75	8-10	8-10	6-8	—
Elle	USA CA GB AU	brushed Tweed	6-8	4.25	50% nylon 36% wool 14% polyester	hand wash	50 gm	102	4.95	8-10	8-10	6-8	—
Family Choice Aran	USA CA GB AU	—	4-6	4.75	50% Courtelle acrylic 40% bri-nylon 10% wool	machine wash	50 gm	113	2.40	15	14	10	—
Fiori	USA CA GB AU	—	6-8	4	100% cotton	hand wash	50 gm	85	3.95	8	6-8	6	—
Ikon	USA CA GB AU	bouclé with slub	4-6	4.5	69% cotton 16% acrylic 15% polyester	hand wash	50 gm	116	4.25	5-7	5-7	5	—
Kintyre	USA CA GB AU	for fisherman knits	4-6	4.75	100% new wool	hand wash	50 gm	84	2.65	18	16	12	—
Tempo	USA CA GB AU	knits with matina "bright" bouclé	4-6	4.25	46% acrylic 27% wool 15% polyester 12% nylon	hand wash	50 gm	115	4.50	8-10	8-10	6-8	—
White Buffalo Lama	USA CA	—	8	4.5	75% acrylic 25% wool	machine wash	40 gm	87	1.50	6-8	6-8	4-7	—
Whitin Yarns Handsome Harry's Hanks	USA	classic home spun worsted	8-10	5	100% fleece wool	hand wash dry clean	100 gm	190	4.00	—	—	—	—
Wilde Yarns 4-ply Dyed Softie	USA	classic 4-ply	8	4	100% wool	hand wash dry clean	4 oz.	180	4.30	9	7	4	NA
4-ply Natural Softie	USA	classic 4-ply	8	4	100% wool	hand wash dry clean	4 oz.	180	3.80	9	7	4	NA
Yarn by Mills Angora-Silk	USA	hand-spun fluffy	10-10½	3-4	Angora silk	hand wash dry clean	50 gm	85	14.00	8-10	7-9	5	3

C

Name	Origin	Texture	Needle Size	Gauge	Fiber	Care	Put-up	Yards	Price				
Ankara	USA	handspun lustrous multicolor	10½–12	3	51% kid mohair 49% wool	hand wash dry clean	3 oz.	115	15.00	8-10	7-9	5	3
Blue Nile I	USA	handspun variegated color & texture	10–11	3	34% camel down 33% tussah silk 33% wool	hand wash dry clean	3 oz.	115	12.98	8-10	7-9	5	3
Blue Nile II	USA	long fibers tufts of Angora	10–12	3	41% wool 17% camel down 17% tussah silk 17% mohair 8% Angora	hand wash dry clean	3 oz.	115	14.00	8-10	7-9	5	3
Georgia	USA	soft, slightly textured hand spun	9–10½	3–4	50% cultivated silk 50% lambswool	dry clean	50 gm	85	14.00	8-10	7-9	5	3
Kid Mohair	USA	lusturous fuzzy, hand-spun	10–12	3	100% kid mohair	hand wash dry clean	3 oz.	120	16.00	8-10	7-9	5	2-3
Tussah	USA	lustrous variegated hand-dyed	9–11	3	35% tussah silk 35% camel down 30% mohair	dry clean	2 oz.	100	12.00	8-10	7-9	5	2-3
Wool	USA	hand-spun, fleecy	10–12	2½–3½	100% wool	hand wash dry clean	3 oz.	115	9.00	8-10	7-9	5	2-3
Yarn Country/Newton Knits Americana	USA	mercerized	—	5½	100% cotton	wash dry cool	1 lb.	2,200	14.24	—	—	—	—
Chenille	USA	—	8	5	100% rayon	dry clean	1 lb.	1,300	16.00	20 oz.	17 oz.	15 oz.	12 oz.
Frenchy	USA	brushed tweed	8	5	wool/acrylic blend	wash & dry	1 lb.	1,200	24.80	—	—	—	—
Show Time Camel	USA	thick & thin	—	5½	100% Brt Orlon	wash dry flat	1 lb.	1,500	14.24	—	—	—	—

CLASS D — Bulky Weight Yarns

Brand and Yarn Name	Where Sold	Type	US Needle Size	Gauge/Tension per Inch	Fiber Content	Cleaning Care	Skein, Hank, Ball, or Cone Weight	Approx. Yardage	Approx. Price	Approx. No. of Skeins for a Small-size Standard Knit Pullover Sweater with Long Sleeves and Crew Neck			
										Man	Woman	Child	Infant
Aarlan Cinderella	dis.	fluffy with metallic	10–10½	4–3½	65% mohair 27% wool 8% other	hand wash, warm	50 gm	120	7.00	—	5–9	—	—
Sportivo	USA	ball	9–10½	3½	100% wool	hand wash	100 gm	120	6.00	12–14	10–12	8–10	7–9
Symphony	dis.	tweed multicolor	11	3–2½	67% wool 31% mohair 2% nylon	dry clean	100 gm	80	10.00	—	9–12	—	—
Vogue	USA	bulky	8–10	5–4½	88% wool 12% nylon	hand wash	50 gm	92	5.00	12–14	10–12	8–10	6–8
Woodland	dis.	homespun	10–11	4–3½	100% wool	warm water wash	100 gm	130	4.80	—	8–12	—	—
Andean Yarns Alpaquita	USA CA	3-ply dyed	9–10	3½	100% alpaca	hand wash, pure soap dry flat	100 gm	110	10.00	8–9	6–7	4–5	3
Alpaquita	USA CA	3-ply natural	9–10	3½	100% alpaca	hand wash, pure soap dry flat	100 gm	110	9.00	8–9	6–7	4–5	3
Anny Blatt Bright	USA CA AU GB	multicolor soft	8–10	3	52% mohair 35% viscose 13% acrylic	hand wash dry clean	50 gm	55	10.95	20	15	10	5
Broadway	USA CA AU GB	novelty brushed & chenille	7–9	3	47% cotton 32% mohair 11% polyamide 10% Courtelle-Retractable	hand wash dry clean	50 gm	68	10.25	20	15	10	—
Chicago	USA CA AU GB	novelty, brushed & spiral wrapped	7–9	3	50% mohair 24% polyester 20% acrylic 6% polyamide	hand wash dry clean	50 gm	49	13.55	28	20	12	—
City	dis.	novelty tweed multicolored	10½	3	53% mohair 45% wool 27% nylon	hand wash dry clean	50 gm	49	9.25	16	14	8	5

Name		Description			Fiber	Care	Weight	Yardage	Price				
Flair	dis.	soft, thick & thin with nubs in solids & multicolor	11	3	69% wool 29% mohair 2% nylon	hand wash dry clean	100 gm	76	16.50	13	11	5	3
Flirt	—	novelty thick & thin cotton/linen blend	8-10	3½	67% cotton 23% rayon 10% linen	hand wash dry clean	100 gm	118	9.75	9	6-7	3	2
Look	—	novelty woven ribbon	9-10	3½	94% rayon 6% nylon	dry clean	50 gm	60	8.25	15	14	5	3
Mimosa	USA CA AU GB	novelty fabric & singles	8-10	3	36% linen 12% wool 20% polyester 32% polyamide	hand wash dry clean	50 gm	80	11.50	19	13	6	—
Mini-Sport	dis.	bulky-smooth	9	4	100% wool	hand wash dry clean	100 gm	160	7.75	10	8	4	2
Mohair et Soie	—	deluxe, long haired	10	3½	80% mohair 20% silk	dry clean	50 gm	70	9.95	17	14	7	4
News	dis.	multicolor blend of fibers	8-9	3½	50% silk 50% rayon	hand wash dry clean	50 gm	82	6.95	13	11	5	3
New York	USA CA AU GB	novelty, long hair & brushed	7-9	3	47% polyester 42% mohair 6% wool 5% polyamide	hand wash dry clean	50 gm	47	18.50	30	22	10	—
Paris	dis.	novelty ribbon & yarn tog	11	2½	34% mohair 36% rayon 30% nylon	hand wash dry clean	50 gm	38	11.25	18	16	8	5
Serpentine	USA CA AU GB	woven ribbon with metallic trim yarn	9-10½	2½	65% rayon 35% metallic-polyester	hand wash dry clean	—	55	17.25	—	13	—	—
Sport	dis.	bulky classic	10	3½	100% wool	hand wash dry clean	100 gm	125	7.25	11	9	5	3
Tweed	dis.	multicolored soft	10½	3	51% wool 23% acrylic 15% mohair 11% silk	hand wash dry clean	50 gm	60	7.25	15	13	6	4
Argyll Ltd. Bedouin	CA	—	9	4	30% cotton 20% mohair 22% acrylic 20% wool 8% polyester	hand wash, 40c.	50 gm	53 m	5.49 (CA $)	—	10	—	—
Cotton On	CA	—	5	4	64% cotton 31% acrylic 5% nylon	hand wash, 40c.	50 gm	123 m	5.30 (CA $)	—	6	—	—
Cotton On with Viscose	CA	—	5	4	60% cotton 40% viscose	hand wash, 40c.	50 gm	87 m	5.30 (CA $)	—	9	—	—

D

Brand and Yarn Name	Where Sold	Type	US Needle Size	Gauge/Tension per Inch	Fiber Content	Cleaning Care	Skein, Hank, Ball, or Cone Weight	Approx. Yardage	Approx. Price	Approx. No. of Skeins for a Small-size Standard Knit Pullover Sweater with Long Sleeves and Crew Neck			
										Man	Woman	Child	Infant
Siam	CA	—	10	4	43% viscose 33% mohair 14% wool 10% nylon	hand wash, 40°C	50 gm	50 m	9.99 (CA $)	—	13	—	—
Au Ver a Soie Bouclette	USA	novelty bouclé loop	7	4	100% silk	dry clean	100 gm	165	—	—	6	—	—
Aunt Lydia's Rug Yarn Aunt Lydia's Rug Yarn	USA	novelty	10.5	3.5	100% polyester	machine wash & dry	1.37 oz.	60	.89	—	—	—	—
Avocet Yarns Alpaca Mohair	USA CA	mohair	9	4	42% alpaca 42% mohair 16% nylon	hand wash, 40°C	25 gm	50 m	5.99	—	—	—	—
Cactus	USA CA	nubs & curls variegated	10½	3½	54% viscose 28% cotton 15% acrylic 3% polyamide	hand wash, 40°C	50 gm	40 m	8.99	—	—	—	—
Coco	USA CA	silky nubs mohair wrapped	9	3	55% wool 30% acetate 10% viscose 5% acrylic	hand wash, 40°C	50 gm	60 m	6.00	—	—	—	—
Garbo	USA CA	nubby mohair with silky space-dyed ribbon	10½	3½	45% viscose 40% acrylic 15% mohair	hand wash	50 gm	40 m	8.50	—	—	—	—
Bartlettyarns Fisherman	USA	3-ply	10 J	3½	100% wool	hand wash dry clean	4 oz.	145	4.00	9	8	5	3
Fisherman Bulky	USA	bulky (4-ply, unspun)	10½ K	3	100% wool	hand wash dry clean	4 oz.	80	4.10	12	12	6	4
Glen Tweed	USA	3-ply	10 J	3½	100% wool	hand wash dry clean	4 oz.	145	4.00	9	8	5	3
Homespun	USA	3-ply	10 J	3½	100% wool	hand wash dry clean	4 oz.	145	4.50	9	8	5	3
Baruffa Erbe	USA	mohair	11	3	60% kid mohair 20% wool 15% viscose 5% nylon	dry clean	40 gm	88	9.00	—	10	—	—
1 Gennaio	USA	fancy slubbed effect	11	3	45% wool 35% cotton 15% mohair 5% polyamide	hand wash	40 gm	81	4.99	—	10	—	—
8 Maggio	USA	tone on tone	10	3	70% mohair 30% viscose	dry clean	40 gm	88	5.99	—	10	—	—

D

Berger duNord												
Chennille	USA	—	8	3¾	100% cotton	—	50 gm	140	4.95	—	—	—
Cotton 7	USA	—	10	3¼	100% cotton	—	50 gm	55	3.75	—	—	—
Douceur 6	USA	—	10	3¾	85% wool 15% kid mohair	—	100 gm	140	7.95	—	—	—
Fiction	USA	—	9	3¼	38% kid mohair 31% viscose 31% polyester	—	50 gm	89	8.95	—	—	—
Fresque	USA	—	7	4	65% viscose 21% cotton 14% acrylic	—	50 gm	70	7.95	—	—	—
Inspiration	USA	—	8	3½	100% wool	—	100 gm	185	8.95	—	—	—
Kaleidoscope	USA	—	11	2¾	96% wool 4% poly-vis	—	50 gm	80	7.95	—	—	—
Kid Mohair 5	USA	—	9	3¼	80% kid mohair 20% Chiro	—	50 gm	70	8.95	—	—	—
Kid Mohair 7	USA	silky soft	10½	2½	80% kid mohair 20% acrylic	—	50 gm	38	8.95	—	—	—
Kid Tweed	USA	—	11	2¼	62% wool 31% kid mohair 7% acrylic	—	50 gm	30	8.95	—	—	—
Laine o'Islande	USA	—	8	3¼	100% wool	—	100 gm	120	7.00	—	—	—
Landes	USA	—	9	3¾	100% wool	—	50 gm	110	4.50	—	—	—
Lima	USA	—	10	3	78% wool 18% kid mohair 4% Chiro	—	100 gm	110	9.95	—	—	—
Lin o'Hiver	USA	—	8	4	50% wool 48% linen 2% flax	—	50 gm	70	5.50	—	—	—
Mohair and Silk	USA	—	7	3¼	70% kid mohair 30% silk	—	20 gm	55	7.95	—	—	—
Non-Tisse	USA	—	13	—	50% polyester 50% viscose	—	20 gm	55	3.00	—	—	—
Nuage	USA	—	10	3¼	45% kid mohair 44% cotton 11% acrylic	—	50 gm	60	8.95	—	—	—
Pele Mele	USA	—	10	3	100% wool	—	50 gm	55	6.95	—	—	—
Polaire	USA	—	10	3	58% kid mohair 26% wool 16% polyester	—	50 gm	87	8.95	—	—	—
Rabane	USA	—	10½	3¼	100% polyester	—	50 gm	122	4.50	—	—	—

Brand and Yarn Name	Where Sold	Type	US Needle Size	Gauge/Tension per Inch	Fiber Content	Cleaning Care	Skein, Hank, Ball, or Cone Weight	Approx. Yardage	Approx. Price	Approx. No. of Skeins for a Small-size Standard Knit Pullover Sweater with Long Sleeves and Crew Neck			
										Man	Woman	Child	Infant
Shetland	USA	—	8	4	100% Shetland wool	—	50 gm	110	3.95	—	—	—	—
Sideral	USA	—	10	2¾	58% mohair 15% wool 27% polyester	—	50 gm	80	8.95	—	—	—	—
Silkid	USA	—	10	3	52% kid mohair 35% viscose 13% acrylic	—	50 gm	55	8.95	—	—	—	—
Sport	USA	—	8	4	100% wool	—	100 gm	125	7.00	—	—	—	—
Tweed	USA	—	8	3½	100% wool	—	100 gm	185	8.95	—	—	—	—
Bernat Bimini	USA	terry bouclé	8	4	100% cotton	hand wash	50 gm	92	3.95	12	10	6	—
Celebrity	USA	brushed basic	10	3½	75% acrylic 25% wool	machine wash	50 gm	80	2.95	14	12	7	—
Celebrity Ombres	USA	brushed basic	10	3	75% acrylic 25% wool	machine wash	50 gm	80	3.50	14	12	7	—
Creme de Tweed	USA	tweed roving	9	3½	60% wool 40% cotton	hand wash	50 gm	75	3.95	15	12	8	—
Mesa	USA	"kemp" accents	8	4	51% wool 45% acrylic 4% viscose	hand wash	50 gm	119	3.95	10	9	5	—
Myriade	USA	variegated twisted roving	8	4	57% wool 43% acrylic	hand wash	50 gm	100	4.25	11	9	6	—
Pebblespun	USA	brushed slub novelty	9	3½	70% wool 22% mohair 8% nylon	hand wash	50 gm	87	7.95	13	11	7	—
Renaissance	USA	brushed metallic	9	3½	40% mohair 29% acrylic 17% metallic polyester 14% wool	hand wash	40 gm	77	6.50	—	12	—	—
Venetian	USA	brushed with nub	8	4	67% acrylic 18% mohair 15% nylon	hand wash	50 gm	115	4.95	10	8	5	—
Venetian Frost	USA	brushed with nub	8	4	55% acrylic 29% bright nylon 16% mohair	hand wash	50 gm	115	5.25	10	8	5	—
Berroco Bijou	dis.	fluffy with colored strand	10 K hook	3½	20% mohair 40% acrylic 34% acetate 6% nylon	—	50 gm 1 lb. 4 lb.	65 600 2,400	4.65	12	10	—	—

D

Yarn	Origin	Texture	Hook/Needle	Gauge	Fiber Content	Care	Weight	Yards	Price				
Floriad	USA	ribbon & fluff	10½ K hook	3½	15% mohair 45% viscose 40% acrylic	—	50 gm / 1 lb. / 7–10 lb.	44 / 400 / —	6.65	—	—	—	—
Montevideo	dis.	homespun	10½ K hook	3½	100% wool	—	100 gm	85	10.20	—	8	—	—
Olé	USA	ombré twist	9 J hook	4	100% wool	—	100 gm / 1 lb. / 6–8 lb.	132 / 600 / —	9.70	7	6	7	—
Tiffany	USA	fluffy looped	8 I hook	4	77% wool 23% viscose	—	50 gm / 1 lb. / 4–6 lb.	110 / 1,000 / —	4.40	—	11	—	—
Zoom Zoom Plus	dis.	fluffy nubby tweed	11 J hook	2½	45% wool 42% acrylic 13% viscose	—	50 gm / 1 lb. / 3–4 lb.	44 / 400 / —	4.15	—	8	—	—
Bouquet Arctic Spun	USA CA	bulky classic	10	3½	100% acrylic	machine wash & dry	100 gm	80	3.15	14	12	7	—
Celebrity	dis.	brushed	10–10½	3–3½	70% acrylic 30% wool	machine wash & dry	50 gm	77	2.25	—	8	5	—
Floss	USA CA	brushed mohair	10	3½	75% mohair 10% wool 10% acrylic 5% nylon	hand wash dry clean	25 gm	60	2.95	—	10	7	—
Icicle	USA CA	classic with sparkle	10	3¾	75% acrylic 25% nylon	machine wash & dry	50 gm	90	2.35	16	14	10	—
Malibu	USA CA	chunky classic	9–10	3½–4	70% acrylic 30% wool	machine wash & dry	50 gm	95	1.95	11	9	6	—
Monterey	USA CA	classic	10	3¾	100% superwash wool	machine wash & dry	50 gm	65	2.55	18	16	14	—
Polar	USA CA	bulky classic	10	3½	60% acrylic 40% wool	machine wash & dry	100 gm	86	3.55	13	11	6	—
Rio	USA CA	classic with nubs	10	3¾	56% acrylic 36% wool 8% acrylic nubs	machine wash & dry	50 gm	80	2.35	17	15	13	—
Brentwood Yarns Carousel	USA	fluffy/bump	11	3/1	wool & rayon	hand wash	hank/cone	70 / 700	6.50/63.00	15	13	9	5
Brown Sheep Co. Lambs Pride	USA CA	bulky worsted	10½	3	85% wool 15% mohair	hand wash	4 oz.	125	4.00	10	8	4	—
Brunswick Amadeus	USA CA AU	fleecy	10½	11 sts = 3"	43% rayon 27% wool 14% acrylic 9% polyester 7% nylon	hand wash dry clean	40 gm	82	—	—	10	—	—
Aspen	dis.	smooth	10	3½	100% wool	dry clean only	100 gm	105	—	11	8	8	NR

Brand and Yarn Name	Where Sold	Type	US Needle Size	Gauge/Tension per Inch	Fiber Content	Cleaning Care	Skein, Hank, Ball, or Cone Weight	Approx. Yardage	Approx. Price	Approx. No. of Skeins for a Small-size Standard Knit Pullover Sweater with Long Sleeves and Crew Neck			
										Man	Woman	Child	Infant
Crystal	USA CA AU	smooth	10½	3½	100% pure virgin wool	hand wash dry clean	50 gm	60	—	11	9	7	—
Lochwind	USA CA AU	smooth	10	3½	100% acrylic	machine wash & dry	100 gm	105	—	11	8	8	NR
Monterey	USA CA AU	smooth mohair	10	3½	45% cotton 30% acrylic 22% mohair 3% nylon	hand wash dry clean	50 gm	105	—	11	8	8	—
Paper Lace	USA CA AU	feathered gauzy	10½	15 sts = 4"	73% nylon 27% polyester	hand wash machine wash, delicate	25 gm	95	—	—	12	—	—
Quickmist	USA CA AU	fleecy	10	3½	100% acrylic (brushed)	hand wash machine wash & dry, delicate	50 gm	80	—	11	9	7	—
Quicknit Breeze	USA CA AU	knobby	8	15 sts = 4"	84% cotton 16% polyester	machine wash	50 gm	75	—	13	9	—	—
Rugger	USA CA AU	smooth	10½	3½	80% acrylic 20% wool	machine wash & dry, delicate	50 gm	70	—	11	9	7	NR
Snowflake	USA CA AU	knobby	10½	3½	100% wool	hand wash dry clean	50 gm	60	—	11	9	7	—
Sunsplash	USA CA AU	knobby	6	4	58% cotton 20% acrylic 22% polyester	machine wash	40 gm	85	—	—	12	—	—
Thistledown	USA CA AU	fleecy	10	4	42% alpaca 42% mohair 16% nylon	hand wash dry away from heat	40 gm	90	—	15	11	9	—
Vail	USA CA AU	smooth	10	3½	100% wool	dry clean only	100 gm	115	—	11	8	8	NR
Video	USA CA AU	knobby	10½	3½	38% cotton 16% kid mohair 23% acrylic 19% nylon 4% wool	hand wash dry clean	50 gm	72	—	—	12	—	—
Bucilla Four Seasons	dis.	bulky	10½	3	100% acrylic	machine wash & dry	3½ oz.	118	2.10	9	7	4	2
Busse Country Wool	USA	bulky tweed	11	3	100% pure new wool	hand wash, cold	100 gm	110	7.30	9	7	—	—
Platin	USA	fashionable slub texture	10	3½	100% cotton	hand wash, cold	50 gm	55	3.75	22	20	—	—

D

Name	Origin	Texture	Needle	Needle	Fiber Content	Care	Weight						
Caron Bulky Bouclé	USA	bulky novelty	11	2.5	100% Orlon	machine wash warm	3 oz.	93	1.89	13	10	7	4
Cotton Terry	USA	knobby novelty	7	4	90% cotton 10% polyester	hand wash	1.75 oz.	84	1.69	15	11	NA	NA
Rug & Craft yarn	USA	novelty	10½	3½	100% Dacron	machine wash & dry	1.6 oz.	70	89	—	—	—	—
Chanteleine Baccarat	USA	brushed jazzy	9-10	3½-4	38% acrylic 31% wool 21% mohair 10% bright nylon	hand wash	50 gm	82	5.70	NR	8-9	—	NR
Bidjin	dis.	smooth classic	10	3½-4	70% acrylic 30% wool	hand wash	50 gm	60	2.25	15+	13-14	9	NR
Blondine	dis.	mohair brushed tweed	10½-11	3-3½	57% mohair 15% wool 12% rayon 6% polyester	hand wash	50 gm	82	6.60	10	8	NR	NR
Cathy	USA	ribbon/tape high texture	9-11	3-4	80% acrylic 20% linen	hand wash dry clean	50 gm	75	5.80	10-12	9-10	NR	NR
Cevennes	USA	brushed printed jazzy	11-13	3	56% mohair 32% acrylic 8% nylon 4% wool	hand wash	50 gm	60	8.25	15	12	—	NR
Floride	USA	nubby texture	10	3½-4	68% cotton 22% acrylic 10% rayon	hand wash	50 gm	87	4.60	13	11	5	NR
Gael	dis.	smooth classic	10	3½-4	60% superwash wool 40% acrylic	machine wash	50 gm	54	2.90	16+	13-14	9	NR
Goliath	USA	smooth classic	9-10	4	100% superwash wool	machine wash	50 gm	73	3.75	13-14	12-14	6-7	NR
Marlene	USA	brushed metallic mix	10½-11	3-3½	66% kid mohair 28% acrylic 4% rayon 2% metallic	hand wash	50 gm	82	8.50	—	9-10	—	NR
Medici Silk	dis.	bouclé	9-10	3½-4	100% silk	hand wash dry clean	50 gm	103	7.90	9	7	—	—
Michka	dis.	roughly textured look, tweed	9-10	3½-4	45% wool 17% alpaca 38% acrylic	hand wash	50 gm	88	4.85	13	10	6	NR
Mylene	USA	soft wool with novelty shiny wrap	8-10	3½	50% wool 45% rayon 5% polyester	hand wash	50 gm	77	4.85	15	12	—	NR
Papagaye	USA	bright multiprint rayon tube	9-10	4-4½	94% rayon 4% nylon	hand wash	50 gm	66	7.50	NR	10-12	—	NR

Brand and Yarn Name	Where Sold	Type	US Needle Size	Gauge/Tension per Inch	Fiber Content	Cleaning Care	Skein, Hank, Ball, or Cone Weight	Approx. Yardage	Approx. Price	Approx. No. of Skeins for a Small-size Standard Knit Pullover Sweater with Long Sleeves and Crew Neck			
										Man	Woman	Child	Infant
Siderale	USA	glitzy brushed metallic	11–13	3–3½	58% mohair 27% viscose 10% nylon 5% metallic	hand wash	50 gm	77	9.90	—	8-9	—	NR
Sophie	USA	brushed textured	9–11	3–3½	42% wool 20% mohair 30% cotton 8% polyester	hand wash	50 gm	66	5.70	12-15	10-11	—	NR
Sophie	USA	highly textured novelty yarn brushed	9–11	3–3½	42% wool 20% mohair 30% cotton 8% polyester	hand wash	50 gm	66	5.70	12-13	10-11	NR	NR
Tricadie	dis.	knit tube	10	3½-4	70% acrylic 30% cotton	hand wash	50 gm	95	5.50	13	10	6	4
Tricotine	USA	rayon tube	9–10	4-4½	94% rayon 6% nylon	hand wash	50 gm	66	6.90	—	10-12	—	—
Charity Hill Farm Charity Hill Farm	USA	bulky classic woolen-spun 3-ply	10	3	100% pure wool	hand wash	4 oz.	145	4.89	7-8	5-6	4-5	2-3
Chat Botte Alexandrie	USA CA AU	multi/ novelty	7	4	55% mohair 30% acrylic 15% lambswool	hand wash dry clean	50 gm	61	10.00	17	15	7	NR
Folie Douce	USA CA AU	knubby	7	3¼	96% wool 4% nylon	hand wash dry clean	100 gm	63	12.00	12	10	6	4
Himalaya	USA CA AU	multi/ novelty	9	3½	57% wool 40% acrylic 3% nylon	hand wash dry clean	50 gm	63	6.00	17	15	7	NR
Hivernale	USA CA AU	tubular/ novelty	10½	3	100% wool	hand wash dry clean	100 gm	84	11.60	10	8	5	NR
Melody	USA CA AU	novelty	9	3½	60% rayon 40% wool	hand wash dry clean	40 gm	40	6.50	NR	15	10	NR
Ysalie	USA CA AU	fleecy	10½	3	100% wool	hand wash dry clean	40 gm	44	4.20	17	14	10	NR
Zelande	USA CA AU	classic	6	3½	100% wool	hand wash dry clean	100 gm	120	7.60	9	7	5	3
Chester Farms Chester Farms 2-ply	—	natural	9–10	4½-4	100% wool	hand wash dry clean	4 oz. 1 lb.	210 840	5.45 8.40	6-8 2	4-6 2	2-3 1	2 1
China Silk Co., Inc. Gossamer	USA CA AU GB	¼" woven web mesh tape	9	4	100% silk	dry clean	100 gm 1 lb.	220 1,000	31.00	7	6	4	3

D

Name		Description	Needle	Gauge	Fiber	Care	Put-up	Yards	Price				
Kimono	USA CA AU BR	textured nubby	9	4	100% silk	dry clean	90 gm / 1 lb.	90 / 450	25.00	7	6	4	3
Lotus	USA CA AU BR	¼" braided ribbon	10	4	100% silk	dry clean	100 gm / 1 lb.	115 / 514	28.50	7	6	4	3
Rickshaw	USA CA AU BR	textured fancy	9	4	100% silk	dry clean	100 gm / 1 lb.	130 / 585	30.00	7	6	4	3
Classic Elite Yarns, Inc. Boston	USA	smooth, 2-ply	6	4½	100% wool	hand wash	50 gm	99	3.50	—	12	—	—
Cascade	USA	brushed multicolor	9	4	37% cotton 31% mohair 22% wool 5% polyester	dry clean	1½ oz.	72	5.95	—	14	—	—
Fanfare	USA	thick & thin	10½	3½	100% wool	hand wash	100 gm	160	7.95	—	6	—	—
Impulse	USA	thick & thin novelty slub	10½	3½	90% silk 10% wool rayon/nylon binder	dry clean	50 gm	57	8.95	—	15	—	—
Jazzmo	USA	metallic mohair	10½	3½	55% mohair 18% Lurex 10% wool 10% nylon 8% acetate	dry clean	1½ oz.	75	6.95	—	13	—	—
La Gran	USA	brushed	10½	3	74% mohair 13% wool 13% nylon	dry clean	1½ oz	92	5.25	—	10	—	—
Newport	USA CA	cabled 4-ply	9	4	100% pima mercerized cotton	hand wash	50 gm	70	3.95	—	15	—	—
Riviera	USA, CA	2-ply soft	9	4	100% cotton	hand wash	50 gm	74	2.95	—	15	—	—
Sharon	USA	bouclé	10½	3	74% mohair 13% wool 13% nylon	dry clean	1½ oz.	92	4.95	—	10	—	—
Sydney	USA	chenille and brushed mohair	10	3	50% rayon 40% mohair 5% wool 5% nylon	dry clean	50 gm	65	5.95	—	15	—	—
Columbia-Minerva Himalaya	USA	fluffy	8 / 1	4 / 2½	70% So-lara acrylic 20% nylon 10% mohair	machine wash & dry	50 gm	93	1.99	9	7	3	3
Sorrelle	USA	fluffy	8 / 1	4 / 2½	50% cotton flake 33% So-lara acrylic 10% nylon 5% mohair 2% metallic	hand wash	50 gm	93	1.99	10	8	5	4

Brand and Yarn Name	Where Sold	Type	US Needle Size	Gauge/ Tension per Inch	Fiber Content	Cleaning Care	Skein, Hank, Ball, or Cone Weight	Approx. Yardage	Approx. Price	Approx. No. of Skeins for a Small-size Standard Knit Pullover Sweater with Long Sleeves and Crew Neck			
										Man	Woman	Child	Infant
Windspun	USA	smooth	10 I	3½ 3	99% So-lara acrylic 1% nylon	machine wash & dry	85 gm	135	1.69	9	7	4	3
Condon's Yarns Bulky	USA	—	9	3	100% wool	hand wash	—	150	2.10	9	7	6	—
Copley Camargue Chunky	USA BR	fashion basic	10	3¾	58% acrylic 25% nylon 17% wool	hand wash machine wash, gentle 40°C dry flat dry clean	50 gm	83	2.59	11	9	6	3
Lugano	USA	brushed multicolor bouclé	11	3	38% cotton 10% kid mohair 44% wool 8% nylon	hand wash, 30°C dry flat dry clean	1.6 oz.	70	5.95	10	8	5	3
Masquerade®	USA	glittery high-fashion bouclé	10½	3½	34% viscose 28% acrylic 12% nylon 10% mohair 6% Lurex 10% wool	hand wash, 30°C dry flat dry clean	1.6 oz.	75	6.95	12	10	6	3
Serenade®	USA	mohair-like brushed softness with silken rayon	10½	3½	50% acrylic 29% rayon 14% wool 7% nylon	hand wash, 30°C dry flat dry clean	50 gm	83	4.50	11	9	6	3
Sundazzler®	USA BR	vibrant color ribbon effect with cotton slub	11	3½	55% viscose 45% cotton	hand wash, lukewarm water dry flat dry clean	50 gm	66	5.95	14	12	7	3
Cotton Clouds Aurora Cloud	USA	novelty fluffy-loopy	8	3	100% cotton	machine wash & dry	10 oz.	375	16.00	5	3	2	1
Cloudburst	USA	fluffy chenille 3-cut	10	3½	100% cotton	machine wash & dry	16 oz.	250	16.00	4	3	2	1
Creative Parisienne	—	glossy textured bouclé	—	—	95% acrylic 5% nylon	machine wash	1 lb.	1,100	20.00	—	—	—	—
Crystal Palace BeBop	USA	bulky lots of texture	11–13	2½–3	59% acrylic 25% mohair 16% wool	hand wash	50 gm	44	6.20	16–20	15	—	—
Carnival	USA	bulky 3-ply	10½–11	3½	100% wool	hand wash	100 gm	110	4.30	10–15	7–8	4–6	—

D

Name		Country	Texture	Needle	Gauge	Fiber Content	Care	Weight	Yards	Price	10-13	8-9	6-7	3-4
City Linen		USA	subtle texture	6-7	4½	35% cotton 35% rayon 30% linen	hand wash	50 gm	99	3.40	10-13	8-9	6-7	3-4
Glimmer		USA	pigtail ville multicolor jazzy	10½-11	3-3½	59% acrylic 25% wool 16% polyester	dry clean	50 gm	86	6.90	—	9-10	—	—
Luxor		USA	lustrous 2-ply	9-10	4	100% Egyptian cotton	hand wash	50 gm	55	4.80	11-15	9-10	—	—
Moonshine		USA	brushed exotic color metallic	10½-11	3½	36% wool 26% mohair 21% nylon 11% viscose 6% metallic polyester	hand wash	50 gm	142	11.50	—	6-7	—	—
Roman Holiday (Solids/printed colors)		USA	novelty	9-10	4-4½	50/50 cotton & rayon	hand wash	50 gm	76	4.60/5.00	11-15	9-10	—	—
Thumper		USA	brushed fuzzy tweedy	10½-11	3	40% Angora 40% lambswool 20% nylon	dry clean	50 gm	93	11.90	—	9-10	—	—
Di. Vé Antonella		USA	basic	10	3.5	50% wool 50% acrylic	machine wash	50 gm	92	2.60	—	10	—	—
Corale		USA	basic with sheen	8	4	30% wool 44% acrylic 26% viscose	hand wash	50 gm	93	3.75	—	10	—	—
Donna		USA	mohair with metallic	10	3.5	68% wool 18% mohair 14% metallic	dry clean	50 gm	120	4.50	—	10	—	—
Festival		USA	multi-colored	9	3.5	50% wool 35% acrylic 8% polyamide 7% mohair	dry clean	50 gm	99	3.50	—	10	—	—
Fiocco Di Neve		USA	slubbed	11	3.5	100% wool	hand wash	50 gm	50	3.25	—	12	—	—
Gioia Garzata		USA	toned mohair	9	3.5	40% acetate 35% wool 15% acrylic 5% mohair 5% nylon	dry clean	50 gm	93	3.99	—	8	—	—
Preludio		USA	wrapped	9	3.5	30% wool 28% rayon 19% nylon 15% acrylic 8% mohair	hand wash	50 gm	99	3.50	—	10	—	—
Waltzer		USA	flecked	9	4	50% wool 50% acrylic	hand wash	50 gm	71	3.25	—	8	—	—
Dorothee Bis Alias		USA	—	10½	3¾	60% alpaca 25% kid mohair 15% wool	—	40 gm	64	12.40	—	12	—	—

Brand and Yarn Name	Where Sold	Type	US Needle Size	Gauge/Tension per Inch	Fiber Content	Cleaning Care	Skein, Hank, Ball, or Cone Weight	Approx. Yardage	Approx. Price	Approx. No. of Skeins for a Small-size Standard Knit Pullover Sweater with Long Sleeves and Crew Neck			
										Man	Woman	Child	Infant
Bise Bise	USA	—	10½	3¼	65% wool 28% kid mohair 7% acrylic	—	50 gm	47	8.00	—	13–15	—	—
Borneo	USA	—	10½	3	100% viscose	—	50 gm	77	4.80	—	10–14	—	—
Brume	USA	—	11	3	43% mohair 42% acrylic 15% polyester	—	50 gm	83	8.00	—	8	—	—
Exotic Chine	USA	—	9	4¼	100% cotton	—	50 gm	81	3.50	—	10	—	—
Fancy	USA	—	10½	3	100% acrylic	—	100 gm	93	11.00	—	6–7	—	—
Fastueuse	USA	—	10½	3½	60% alpaca 25% kid mohair 15% wool	—	20 gm	32	7.00	—	18–22	—	—
Mohair and Soie	USA	—	10½	3	70% kid mohair 30% silk	—	50 gm	74	13.00	—	10	—	—
Nitro	USA	—	10½	3	100% wool	—	50 gm	70	5.00	—	12–14	—	—
Patchwork	USA	—	10½	3½	100% wool	—	100 gm	137	9.00	—	5–7	—	—
Pillard	USA	—	11	3½	98% wool 2% viscose	—	50 gm	50	4.00	—	15	—	—
Puce	USA	—	10½	3½	59% wool 31% viscose 10% cotton	—	50 gm	60	6.00	—	12–13	—	—
Scratch	USA	—	10½	3½	64% acrylic 32% mohair 2% wool 2% polyamide	—	50 gm	36	9.50	—	18–20	—	—
Suede	USA	—	10½	3½	30% acrylic 27% polyester 23% cotton 20% nylon	—	50 gm	72	19.00	—	10–12	—	—
Super Fancy	USA	—	10½	3	100% acrylic	—	100 gm	93	12.00	—	6–7	—	—
Tac	USA	—	10½	3½	31% mohair 31% wool 27% acrylic 11% polyester	—	50 gm	66	8.00	—	10–11	—	—
Tweed	USA	—	11	3	100% wool	—	50 gm	60	6.00	—	12–14	—	—
Dyed in the Wool Cotton Bouclé	USA	hand painted	9	4	52% cotton 48% rayon	dry clean	8 oz.	264	20.00	5	4	2–3	1
Cotton Bouclé	USA	companion solid	9	4	52% cotton 48% rayon	dry clean	8 oz.	264	12.00	5	4	2–3	1

Company / Yarn	Origin	Type	Needle	Gauge	Fiber	Care	Put-up	Yds/m	Price				
Homespun	USA	hand painted	10	3½	100% merino wool	hand wash dry clean	35 oz.	1,225	105.00	1	1	—	—
Homespun	USA	companion solid	10	3½	100% merino wool	hand wash dry clean	35 oz.	1,225	105.00	1	1	—	—
Mohair	USA	hand painted	10½	3	78% mohair 13% wool 9% nylon	hand wash dry clean	11 oz.	1,100	85.00	1	1	—	—
Shoelaces™	USA	variegated ribbon	9	4	100% cotton	hand wash	24 oz.	1,200	80.00	1	1	—	—
Erdal Yarns Fettucini	USA	ribbon	13	3½	100% acrylic	—	50 gm / 1 lb.	65 / 580	3.00 / 24.00	— / —	15 / —	— / —	— / —
Frappe	USA	—	10½	3	85% cotton 15% rayon	—	50 gm / 1½ lb.	55 / 500	2.55 / 15.00	— / —	14 / —	— / —	— / —
Mirtillo	USA	—	10	4	59% acrylic 17% mohair 13% cotton 11% nylon	—	50 gm / 1½ lb.	88 / 800	3.00 / 23.00	— / —	12 / —	— / —	— / —
Moda Joven 2055	USA	—	10	4	50% rayon 17% mohair 6% wool 21% acrylic 5% nylon	—	50 gm	87 mts	3.60	—	15	—	—
Moda Joven 2060	USA	—	10½	2½	76% acrylic 14% wool 10% nylon	—	50 gm	45 mts	2.75	—	15	—	—
Moda Joven 2087	USA	—	15	2½	72% acrylic 22% polyester 6% mohair	—	50 gm	30 mts	3.50	—	—	—	—
Moda Joven 2212	USA	—	15	2½	72% acrylic 22% polyester 6% mohair	—	50 gm	30 mts	4.00	—	—	—	—
Estelle Yarns Chrysalis	CA	Viscose nubs and mohair	13	2½	51% viscose 34% mohair 8% wool 7% polyamide	hand wash, 40°C	50 gm also available on cone (2,000 gm)	40 m	12.99	—	12	—	—
Fiesta Yarns LaBoheme	—	hand-dyed novelty	10	4	mohair and rayon bouclé	hand wash dry clean	1 lb. skein / ½ lb. skein / 2 oz.	675 / 337 / 85	84.00 / 42.00 / 10.50	—	—	—	—
Rio Grande	—	hand-dyed novelty	9	3½–4	100% rayon	hand wash dry clean	1 lb. skein / ½ lb. skein / 2 oz.	500 / 250 / 63	60.00 / 30.00 / 8.50	2	1½	—	1
Flere Troder, USA Flere Troder (5 strands)	USA	basic	10	4–3½	100% acrylic	hand wash machine wash	1 lb.	5,200	—	—	—	—	—

D

Brand and Yarn Name	Where Sold	Type	US Needle Size	Gauge/Tension per Inch	Fiber Content	Cleaning Care	Skein, Hank, Ball, or Cone Weight	Approx. Yardage	Approx. Price	Approx. No. of Skeins for a Small-size Standard Knit Pullover Sweater with Long Sleeves and Crew Neck			
										Man	Woman	Child	Infant
Froehlich Bergschaff	USA	thick & thin	8–9	5	100% mountain sheep's wool	hand wash, warm water machine wash, delicate, wool cycle	100 gm	192	7.25	—	—	—	—
Chihuahua	USA	novelty shine	6–7	5–6	64% cotton 36% triacetate	hand wash dry clean	50 gm	97	4.80	—	—	—	—
Mufflone	USA	super bulky	12–15	2½–3½	100% mountain sheep's wool	hand wash dry clean	100 gm	58	9.00	—	—	—	—
Nastrella	USA	slinky ribbon	8–10	—	100% viscose	hand wash dry clean	50 gm	88	5.25	—	—	—	—
Nastrino	USA	knit ribbon	8–10	—	100% cotton	hand wash dry clean	50 gm	88	5.80	—	—	—	—
Oriente	USA	ribbon & nub	6–8	6	51% viscose 38% acrylic 11% nylon	hand wash dry clean	50 gm	105	7.80	—	—	—	—
Swiss Chalet	USA	thick & thin come & go colors hand-spun variegated	8–9	4½–5	100% wool	hand wash, warm water dry clean	100 gm	176	10.20	—	—	—	—
Gemini ½" Dazzle Ribbon	USA	dressy ribbon with gold	11	3½	100% rayon	dry clean	—	100	15.00	—	6–8	—	—
½" Solid Ribbon	USA	dressy ribbon	11	3½	100% rayon	dry clean	—	100	12.00	—	6–8	—	—
½" Multicolor Ribbon	USA	dressy ribbon	11	3½	100% rayon	dry clean	—	100	16.00	—	6–8	—	—
Fur Fantastic	USA	100% soft rabbit fur	13	3	rabbit fur	dry clean	—	30	4.66	—	30 yds trim	—	—
Galaxy	USA	fuzzy multicolor mohair	11	3	70% mohair 22% acrylic 8% nylon	hand wash	—	138	9.00	—	8–10	—	—
Harlekin-soft	USA	multicolor tweedy	10½	3½	100% wool	hand wash	—	185	9.00	—	8–10	—	—
Mongolia	dis. USA	looped yarn	11	3	36% wool 34% acrylic 20% mohair 10% polyamide	dry clean	—	35	15.00	—	8–10	—	—
Shadow Ribbon	USA	½" dressy ribbon tye-dyed	11	3½	100% rayon	dry clean	—	100	15.00	—	6–8	—	—

D

Name	Origin	Description	Needle	Gauge	Fiber Content	Care	Unit Size	Yards	Price				
Trend	USA	fluffy	9	4	38% acrylic 46% nylon 16% mohair	hand wash	40 gm	165	6.00	—	—	—	—
Winter Garden	USA	cotton & paper	10	3½	63% cotton 10% acrylic 27% nylon	hand wash	50 gm	60	9.00	—	—	—	—
Gerald H. Whitaker, Inc. BMS Riverline	—	brushed mohair bulky	4-5 mm	4	78% mohair 13% wool 9% nylon	hand wash with care dry flat	50 gm / 400 gm	108 / —	6.50 ball 115.00 kgm 52.25 lb.	7-8	6-7	4-5	2-3
Giovanni Amora	USA	brushed	10½	3	100% acrylic	hand wash machine wash	50 gm	—	—	—	9	—	—
Avanti	USA	tweed	10½	4	93% acrylic 3% mohair 4% polyamide	hand wash machine wash	50 gm	—	—	—	11	—	—
Primavera	USA	ribbon	10	4-4½	100% cotton	hand wash machine wash	50 gm	—	—	—	11	—	—
Grandor Chenille 3	USA	chenille	10	3½	95% cotton 5% nylon	hand wash	1 oz.	17	.70	—	—	—	—
Heavy Gimp	USA	soft textured	10	4	100% cotton	hand wash	1 oz.	19	1.50	—	—	—	—
Mohair Loop	USA	large loops (for decorative highlight)	10	3-4	95% mohair 5% wool	hand wash	1 oz.	7	2.29	—	—	—	—
Slub	USA	thick & thin (smooth)	9	5	100% wool	hand wash	1 oz.	19	1.55	—	—	—	—
Slub Gimp	USA	bulky textured	10	4	100% wool	hand wash	1 oz.	10	1.80	—	—	—	—
Spiral Gimp	USA	bulky textured	10	4	100% cotton	hand wash	1 oz.	20	1.50	—	—	—	—
Sumatra Chunky	USA dis.	bulky brushed	10½	3½	63% acrylic 35% nylon 2% polyester	machine wash	50 gm	54	3.20	14	12	NA	NA
Grignasco Griflock	USA	mohair-type fuzzy tweed	10	3.25	66% wool 33% mohair 1% viscose	hand wash, warm water	100 gm	131	6.90	8	6	4	2
Grijockey	USA	classic solid bulky	10	3.25	50% wool 50% acrylic	hand wash, warm water	100 gm	142	3.95	7	6	4	2
Gripull	USA	mohair-type fuzzy/splashes & knobs of color	11	3	40% mohair 27% polyamide 18% polyester 15% wool	hand wash, cool	50 gm	66	8.95	16	12	8	4
Halcyon Yarn Halcyon Geo	USA	outdoorsy homespun type, heather	10	3½	100% wool	hand wash dry clean	approx. 4 oz.	120 yd	—	8	6	4	N/A

Brand and Yarn Name	Where Sold	Type	US Needle Size	Gauge/Tension per Inch	Fiber Content	Cleaning Care	Skein, Hank, Ball, or Cone Weight	Approx. Yardage	Approx. Price	Approx. No. of Skeins for a Small-size Standard Knit Pullover Sweater with Long Sleeves and Crew Neck			
										Man	Woman	Child	Infant
Harrisville Designs HD Designer	USA	bulky, solid & heather colors in 60 shades	10	3½	100% virgin wool	hand wash in tepid water with soap or mild detergent dry clean	100 gm skein 8 oz. cone	110 250	4.50 7.70	9	7	5	2-3
Hayfield of England Brushed Chunky	USA CA GB	brushed	10½	3½	50% acrylic 50% nylon	machine wash	100 gm	161	4.50	6	4	—	—
Click	USA CA GB	thick & thin multitone	10½	3	53% cotton 27% acrylic 12% nylon 8% mohair	hand wash	50 gm	68	4.20	12	11	—	—
Hawaii Chunky	USA CA GB	nubby	10½	3½	50% acrylic 50% nylon	machine wash	50 gm	71	3.40	11	9	—	—
Premier Brushed Chunky	USA CA GB	brushed multitone	10½	3½	50% acrylic 50% nylon	machine wash	100 gm	161	5.25	6	4	—	—
Top Nop Chunky	USA CA GB	nubby multitone	10½	3	50% acrylic 50% nylon	machine wash	100 gm	148	5.20	7	5	—	—
Heirloom Monterey	USA CA	novelty	10 machine knit bulky 1-3	4 4½	100% Orlon	machine wash dry clean	1 lb.	500	14.95	—	—	—	—
Newport	USA CA	novelty	10 machine knit bulky 1-3	4 4½	78% Orlon 22% rayon	machine wash dry clean	1 lb.	1,300	21.95	—	—	—	—
Hovland Chenille	DE GB	Chenille	5-6	3½	acrylic	hand wash	50 gm	60	3.25	—	14	—	—
Natur	NO	rough® twist	10	3½	100% wool	careful hand wash	50 gm	55	2.35	24	21	13	—
Ironstone English spun	USA	smooth classic worsted	—	3½	100% wool	dry clean	1 lb.	160	15.60	2	1½	—	—
Felicia	USA	slub	9	4 double	71% cotton 29% rayon	hand wash	100 gm	142	4.50	—	5	—	—
Flake	USA	mercerized	9 double	6 4	100% cotton	hand wash	100 gm	328	4.50	6	5	4	—
Funky	USA	smooth	9	3½	100% wool	hand wash	100 gm	110	5.00	—	6	—	—
FY 2	USA	bouclé	13	2½	96% wool 4% nylon	dry clean	2 oz.	26	4.00	8	6	—	—
FY 3	USA	slub	11	2½	96% wool 4% nylon	dry clean	2 oz.	50	4.00	12	10	—	—

Name	Country	Texture			Fiber Content	Care	Unit						
FY 5	USA	bouclé	10½	4	99% wool 1% nylon	dry clean	2 oz.	120	4.00	10	8	—	—
FY 6	USA	brushed	—	4	99% wool 1% nylon	dry clean	2 oz.	120	4.50	10	8	—	—
Glitter	USA	slubbed	10	3½	54% wool 36% polyester 10% nylon	hand wash	50 gm	105	5.30	—	8	—	—
Hot Stuff	USA	fluffy	9	3½–4	70% mohair 30% acrylic	dry clean	50 gm	105	5.30	—	8	—	—
Island Wool	USA	smooth	11	3½–4	100% wool	dry clean	100 gm	110	5.00	—	5	—	—
Moon Dust	USA	brushed	10	3½	62% mohair 25% nylon 13% wool	—	5 gm	105	5.30	—	8	—	—
NS 119	USA	slub	—	3½	97% wool 3% nylon	dry clean	2 oz.	39	3.70	—	15	—	—
N 37	USA	slub	—	3½–4	93% wool 7% nylon	dry clean	2 oz.	62	3.75	—	7	—	—
NS 55	USA	slub	—	4	97% wool 3% nylon	dry clean	2 oz.	65	3.75	—	7	—	—
NS-MB	USA	brushed	9	4	78% mohair 13% wool 8% nylon	dry clean	50 gm	105	5.50	—	8	—	—
NS-ML	USA	bouclé	—	4	78% mohair 13% wool 8% nylon	dry clean	2 oz.	120	6.00	—	8	—	—
NZN	USA	worsted	—	4	100% wool	dry clean	100 gm	166	4.00	—	7	—	—
Papicoco	USA	slubby	9	4	100% cotton	hand wash	50 gm	72	3.60	—	7	—	—
Rockpool	USA	brushed	10	3½	78% mohair 13% wool 9% nylon	—	—	—	—	—	—	—	—
Rose Quartz	USA	brushed	10	3½	62% mohair 22% nylon 9% wool 7% acrylic	dry clean	50 gm	105	5.30	—	8	—	—
Silk Wing	USA	smooth	8	4–5	70% silk 19% wool 11% ramie	dry clean	50 gm	122	8.00	—	8	—	—
Silk Wool	dis.	—	—	4	60% wool 40% silk	dry clean	100 gr	166	3.25	—	6	—	—
Spunky	USA	smooth	9	3½	100% wool	hand wash	100 gm	110	5.00	—	6	—	—
Zodiac	USA	—	10	3½	44% cotton 28% mohair 15% nylon 13% wool	—	50 gm	105	5.30	—	8	—	—

D

Brand and Yarn Name	Where Sold	Type	US Needle Size	Gauge/Tension per Inch	Fiber Content	Cleaning Care	Skein, Hank, Ball, or Cone Weight	Approx. Yardage	Approx. Price	Approx. No. of Skeins for a Small-size Standard Knit Pullover Sweater with Long Sleeves and Crew Neck			
										Man	Woman	Child	Infant
Jack Frost Designer 12	USA	worsted	10	4	100% DuPont Comfort 12	wash	50 gm	111	1.89	9	7	5	2
Jaeger Jaeger Contessa	dis.	bouclé stained glass coloration	10½	3	65% acrylic 35% wool	hand wash dry flat	50 gm	53	—	16	13	9	4
Jaeger Gabrielle	dis.	brushed	10	3¾	75% acrylic 25% wool	hand wash dry flat	50 gm	78	—	14	11	7	3
Jaeger Ribbon Mist	USA CA	ribbon with brushed	10	4	61% viscose 22% acrylic 16% mohair 1% nylon	hand wash dry flat	50 gm	71	—	14	11	7	3
Jaeger Mohair Cotton	USA	brushed slub	9	3¾	46% mohair 44% cotton 10% nylon	hand wash dry flat	25 gm	41	—	16	13	8	3
Joseph Galler, Inc. Atlanta	dis. USA	silky soft	9–10	3½–4	100% double mercerized cotton	hand wash	50 gm	58	3.80	24	20	16	—
"Belangor"	USA	luxurious & fluffy	9–10	4½	100% Angora	hand wash	10 gm	33	6.50	—	24	16	—
Harmonieuse	USA FR	rich yarn in blended colors	10–11	2½–3	60% wool 40% mohair	hand wash dry clean	75 gm	67	8.80	12	10	8	—
LaPaz	USA SW	soft, tweedy thick & thin	10	4½–4	100% alpaca	hand wash	40 gm	97	5.00	14	12	8	—
Louisiane	USA	space-dyed knubby cotton	9–10	4	100% cotton	hand wash machine wash	50 gm	80	4.20	—	12	9	—
Majestic-Mohair	USA	brushed	10–10½	3	78% mohair 14% wool 8% nylon	hand wash	40 gm	70	4.80	12	8	7	—
Marbre	USA	soft heathery tweed	9–10	3½	100% wool	hand wash dry clean	50 gm	79	5.00	18–20	16	10	—
Nordland	USA dis.	Iceland type yarn	10–11	4–3	100% wool	hand wash dry clean	3½ oz.	110	NA	12	10	8	—
Ping Pong	USA	soft heather with flecks	10	3½–3	100% wool	hand wash dry clean	50 gm	63	7.00	20	16	12	—
Romance	USA dis.	textured Persian lamb	10	4	52% acrylic 23% wool 21% nylon 4% mohair	hand wash dry clean	50 gm	72	NA	14	12	10	—

D

Yarn	Country	Description	US	Metric	Fiber	Care	Weight		Price				
Swiss-Mohair	USA	luxurious multicolored brushed	10	3	80% mohair 15% rayon 5% nylon	hand wash	40 gm	68	6.40	12	10	8	—
Katia Angoretta	USA	—	7	4	50% acrylic 50% nylon	—	25 gm	82	2.50	—	12	—	—
Arlequin	USA	—	10½	3	64% cotton 15% acrylic 12% nylon 9% rayon	—	50 gm	44	5.50	—	15	—	—
Artesana	USA	—	10½	2¾	100% wool	—	100 gm	137	6.00	—	6	—	—
Bahia	USA	—	10	3½	100% cotton	—	50 gm	57	4.00	—	15	—	—
Baltica	USA	—	10	4	92% wool 8% viscose	—	50 gm	82	4.25	—	10-12	—	—
Brandy	USA	—	8	4	35% wool 30% acrylic 23% alpaca 12% viscose	—	50 gm	79	5.00	—	11-13	—	—
Cosaco	USA	—	10½	3	50% wool 34% acrylic 10% mohair 4% nylon 2% polyester	—	50 gm	58	5.00	—	12-16	—	—
Crack	USA	—	11	3½	43% acrylic 25% nylon 18% wool 14% mohair	—	50 gm	61	8.00	—	13-15	—	—
Ebano	USA	—	9	3½	57% linen 43% acrylic 5% polyester	—	50 gm	59	4.50	—	12-14	—	—
Fastuosa	USA	—	9	3½	48% acrylic 21% wool 15% mohair 11% nylon 5% polyester	—	50 gm	111	7.50	—	9	—	—
Kena	USA	—	7	4	40% wool 30% alpaca 30% acrylic	—	50 gm	82	5.00	—	11-13	—	—
Mosaico	USA	—	—	3¾	72% acrylic 17% nylon 11% mohair	—	50 gm	105	4.50	—	9	—	—
Nocturno	USA	—	8	4	28% acrylic 25% wool 18% mohair 18% nylon 11% polyester	—	50 gm	153	6.50	—	7	—	—
Nostalgia	USA	—	8	4	75% acrylic 15% nylon 10% mohair	—	50 gm	91	4.75	—	10	—	—

Brand and Yarn Name	Where Sold	Type	US Needle Size	Gauge/Tension per Inch	Fiber Content	Cleaning Care	Skein, Hank, Ball, or Cone Weight	Approx. Yardage	Approx. Price	Approx. No. of Skeins for a Small-size Standard Knit Pullover Sweater with Long Sleeves and Crew Neck			
										Man	Woman	Child	Infant
Ole	USA	—	11	2½	100% polyethylene	—	50 gm	125	9.50	—	6	—	—
Salvaje	USA	—	11	3	40% mohair 32% acrylic 28% wool	—	50 gm	60	6.90	—	14-16	—	—
Talisman	USA	—	10½	3	57% wool 22% nylon 12% acrylic 9% mohair	—	50 gm	60	6.00	—	13-15	—	—
Knitting Fever King Tut (solid colors)	USA	—	9	4	100% cotton	—	40 gm	66	4.00	—	10-13	—	—
King Tut (multicolors)	USA	—	9	4	100% cotton	—	40 gm	66	4.50	—	10-13	—	—
Lace	USA	—	8	4	84% rayon 16% polyamide	—	40 gm	176	6.50	—	5	—	—
Satin	USA	—	8	4	100% rayon	—	40 gm	70	4.00	—	9-11	—	—
Shadows	USA	—	9	4	54% cotton 40% rayon 6% nylon	—	40 gm	52	5.00	—	14-16	—	—
Whispers	USA	—	9	4	100% rayon	—	50 gm	83	4.50	—	8-10	—	—
Lanas Margarita Anatolia	dis.	fake fur	11	2	53% acrylic 36% wool 7% polyester 4% rayon	hand wash	100 gm	74	7.50	—	6	—	—
Big Bouclé	dis.	bouclé	9	3½	46% acrylic 52% wool 2% nylon	hand wash	50 gm	66	3.99	—	10	—	—
Flama	dis.	thick-thin novelty	11	3	16% acrylic 10% mohair 2% nylon 72% wool	hand wash	100 gm	95	8.50	—	8	—	—
Fluky	USA ES FR IT DE GB	novelty slub	11	3	28% acrylic 24% mohair 31% nylon 17% wool	hand wash	50 gm	65	7.00	—	10	—	—
Galaxy	USA ES FR IT DE GB	novelty	10	3½	33% mohair 22% acrylic 21% polyester 14% nylon 10% rayon	hand wash	50 gm	136	6.50	—	7	—	—
Islandia	dis.	classic bulky	10½	3	60% acrylic 40% wool	hand wash	100 gm	133	5.99	—	6	—	—

D

Name	Country	Description	Needle	Gauge	Fiber content	Care	Ball	Yards	Price				
Kurdan	dis.	bulky bouclé	11	2	89% acrylic 3% wool 8% nylon	hand wash	100 gm	60	6.80	—	10	—	—
Lucille	USA ES FR IT DE GB	novelty	9	3.5	14% mohair 65% acrylic 13% nylon 5% polyester 3% rayon	hand wash	50 gm	79	6.00	—	10	—	—
Partenon	USA ES FR IT DE GB	classic	11	3	40% wool 60% acrylic	machine wash	100 gm	158	6.40	12	10	8	6
Scandal	dis.	thick & thin with slub	10	10 sts = 3"	90% cotton 10% nylon	hand wash	100 gm	117	7.00	—	8	—	—
Scott	USA ES FR IT DE GB	bulky tweed	10	3½	21% acrylic 31% nylon 33% mohair 15% wool	hand wash	50 gm	87	7.10	—	11	—	—
Lane Borgosesia Dream	USA	variegated effect	8	4	26% kid mohair 21% wool 20% silk 33% acrylic	dry clean	50 gm	93	5.99	—	10	—	—
Hockey Brillant	USA	multicolored brushed	11	3.5	65% wool 20% nylon 15% mohair	dry clean	40 gm	100	4.99	—	10	—	—
Lancilotto	USA	multicolored bouclé	9	3.5	50% wool 35% acrylic 10% mohair 5% polyester	hand wash	50 gm	82	4.50	—	10	—	—
Loden	USA	brushed classic	9	4	85% Shetland wool 15% mohair	hand wash dry clean	40 gm	78	4.50	—	12	—	—
Selvaggio	USA	brushed effect	11	3	70% wool 20% mohair 10% nylon	dry clean	40 gm	98	3.99	—	10	—	—
4 Staggioni	USA	fisherman	8	4	100% wool	hand wash	100 gm	147	5.99	—	7	—	—
Lion Brand Bulky Knit	USA dis.	—	10	3½	100% Orlon	hand wash	114 gm	140	—	—	—	—	—
Jiffy	USA	brushed mohair look	—	—	100% acrylic	machine wash & dry	85 gm	136	—	—	—	—	—
Molaine (Solids & prints)	USA	brushed mohair look	H or J	3 sts	100% virgin acrylic	machine wash & dry	40 gm	132	—	—	—	—	—
Sushi	USA	novelty slub with ribbon effect	10½	2½	53% cotton 47% nylon	hand wash	40 gm 1.4 oz.	52	—	—	24	—	—
Lisle Neon	USA	rayon lace	9	3	100% rayon	hand wash cold	4, 8 & 16 oz.	275 lb.	4 oz. hand-dyed 15.00 4 oz. natural 11.00	6-7	6-7	5-6	3-4

Brand and Yarn Name	Where Sold	Type	US Needle Size	Gauge/Tension per Inch	Fiber Content	Cleaning Care	Skein, Hank, Ball, or Cone Weight	Approx. Yardage	Approx. Price	Approx. No. of Skeins for a Small-size Standard Knit Pullover Sweater with Long Sleeves and Crew Neck			
										Man	Woman	Child	Infant
Lundgren Rya Lundgren Rya	USA	heavy rya 2-ply	8 2¾" steel rug needle	5	100% wool	hand wash mild soap	3-4 oz.	100	4.00	—	—	—	—
Manos DeUruguay Manos DeUruguay	USA	thick & thin hand-spun hand-dyed	9	4	100% wool	dry clean	100 gm 3½ oz.	155	8.50	8	7 med.	3	2
Mark Yarns Carnival	USA	nubby multi-colored	10½-11	3½	47% rayon 40% cotton 8% linen 5% polyamide	hand wash, cold dry clean	—	43	6.00	—	12	—	—
Malibu	USA	tricotene	10½-11	3½	94% viscose 6% nylon	hand wash dry clean	50 gm	66	6.00	—	10-11	—	—
Princess Angora	USA	Angora	9-10	4	100% Angora	hand wash in iced water dry clean	—	29	6.75	—	30	—	—
Melrose Angel Hair	USA	fluffy	9	3½-4	50% nylon 50% acrylic	—	50 gm	165	2.80	—	—	—	—
Eyelash	USA	novelty 2-tone	6	4¼	85% rayon 15% nylon	hand wash	50 gm	180	7.00	—	—	—	—
Funspun	USA	—	19	3	100% wool	—	8 oz.	80	14.00	—	—	—	—
Memory Eight	USA	winter cotton	10	4	98% cotton 2% stretch fiber	—	50 gm	80	3.50	—	—	—	—
Metallic Eyelash	USA	novelty metallic	6	4¼	29% metallic 56% rayon 15% nylon	—	50 gm	160	10.00	—	—	—	—
Rhapsody Mohair	USA	fluffy	10	3½-4	78% mohair 13% wool 9% nylon	—	40 gm	90	7.50	—	—	—	—
Woolbrite	USA	—	9-10	3½-4	82% wool 18% rayon	—	50 gm	65	5.00	—	—	—	—
Yummy	USA	fluffy iridescent	9-10	3½-4	25% kid mohair 38% nylon 37% acrylic	—	50 gm	110	3.90	—	—	—	—
Merino Angora	USA	cloud-like	8	4	100% Angora	—	10 gm	35	9.75	—	—	—	—
Bijou	USA	speciality	9	3½	83% wool 8% viscose 6% nylon 3% metal plastic	—	50 gm	77	8.00	—	—	—	—

Name	Origin	Type			Fiber content		Ball weight	Yards	Price				
Chahut	USA	fleecy	9–13	2½	78% mohair 11% wool 9% nylon 2% polyester	—	50 gm	51	10.00	—	—	—	—
Ecrin	USA	soft	7	4	50% kid mohair 20% baby alpaca 20% cashmere 10% silk	—	20 gm	55	10.00	—	—	—	—
Fascination	USA	shiny novelty	6–7	4	100% nylon	—	50 gm	120	6.00	—	—	—	—
Florac	USA	multicolor tweed	10½	3½	56% wool 36% kid mohair 8% acrylic	—	50 gm	45	8.00	—	—	—	—
Furlana	USA	textured ribbon	9–13	3–4	100% wool	—	50 gm	52	11.20	—	—	—	—
Futuria	USA	chenille-cellophane	7	4	100% nylon	—	20 gm	33	7.75	—	—	—	—
Hourrah	USA	specialty	13	2½	46% acetate 31% mohair	—	50 gm	35	15.00	—	—	—	—
Lana	USA	ribbon	8–10	4	100% wool	—	50 gm	72	10.80	—	—	—	—
Melo	USA	felted with ribbon	9–10½	3	44% nylon 39% acrylic 10% viscose 7% wool	—	50 gm	66	10.80	—	—	—	—
Noix-de-Coco	USA	flagged novelty	9	4	67% rayon 18% polyamide 15% acrylic	—	15 gm	93	15.00	—	—	—	—
Palace	USA	novelty	7	4	41% mohair 37% rayon 12% cotton 10% acrylic	—	40 gm	55	9.50	—	—	—	—
Paille	USA	metallic chenille	9	4	51% wool 38% metalized polyester 11% nylon	—	20 gm	110	7.50	—	—	—	—
Palais Royale	USA	fluffy, metallic tweed	9	3½	27% wool 21% mohair 20% viscose 11% acrylic 8% polyester	—	50 gm	85	14.00	—	—	—	—
Rocaille	USA	fleecy novelty	8–9	4	51% cotton 40% mohair 9% nylon	—	50 gm	66	8.50	—	—	—	—
Seri Norie	USA	multicolor with pigtail	7–8	4	51% kid mohair 30% acrylic 19% cotton	—	50 gm	96	8.50	—	—	—	—
Sport Picand	USA	smooth, classic worsted	6–7	4	100% wool	—	50 gm	83	4.40	—	—	—	—

D

Brand and Yarn Name	Where Sold	Type	US Needle Size	Gauge/Tension per Inch	Fiber Content	Cleaning Care	Skein, Hank, Ball, or Cone Weight	Approx. Yardage	Approx. Price	Approx. No. of Skeins for a Small-size Standard Knit Pullover Sweater with Long Sleeves and Crew Neck			
										Man	Woman	Child	Infant
Streky Tweed	USA	brushed multicolor	9–10½	3½	43% acetate 37% mohair 7.5% acrylic 6.5% wool 5.5% polyester	—	50 gm	77	4.20	—	—	—	—
Ticker Tape	USA	½" ribbon	9–13	—	100% acetate	—	—	100	12.00	—	—	—	—
Voyou	USA	novelty	8	4	80% wool 20% acrylic	—	50 gm	88	8.00	—	—	—	—
Nomis Excellence Bulky	USA	smooth	11	3	100% acrylic	machine wash & dry	100 gm	120	—	8	6	4	2
Nomotta Dolly	USA	brushed tubular	9	4	50% mohair 50% acrylic	hand wash do not bleach do not iron dry clean	50 gm	98	4.95	12	10	—	—
Hi-Fi	USA	nubby	7	4	35% new wool 26% cotton 24% acrylic 15% modal	hand wash do not bleach do not iron dry clean	50 gm	98	4.95	16	14	—	—
Multi-Show	USA	fluffy textured multicolor	8	4	67% acrylic 17% mohair 12% wool 4% viscose	machine wash, gentle do not bleach do not iron dry clean	50 gm	93	4.50	—	10	—	—
Noro Amagi	USA	—	10½	3½	90% wool 10% cashmere	—	50 gm	116	14.00	—	8	—	—
Asahi	USA	—	11	3	100% wool		50 gm	53	9.00	—	9–11	—	—
Asuka	USA	—	10½	3	58% wool 37% Angora 5% nylon	—	50 gm	94	13.50	—	8–10	—	—
Azumi	USA	—	10½	3½	55% silk 25% Angora 20% wool	—	50 gm	120	18.00	—	7–9	—	—
Bebe	USA	—	11	3	73% cotton 27% linen	—	50 gm	46	9.50	—	12–14	—	—
Ginga	USA	—	10	3½	39% alpaca 35% silk 13% mohair 13% wool	—	50 gm	57	12.00	—	10–12	—	—
Ginrei	USA	—	10	3½	58% mohair 21% wool 11% nylon 10% polyester	—	50 gm	85	14.00	—	8–10	—	—

Name	Country				Fiber							
Hakucho G	USA	feathers	—	—	64% feathers 36% silk	—		5½	—	—	—	—
Hakucho H	USA	feathers	—	—	70% feathers 30% silk	—		5½	—	—	—	—
Hakucho I	USA	feathers	—	—	35% feathers 50% wool 15% silk	—		5½	—	—	—	—
Hakucho K	USA	feathers	—	—	34% feathers 40% wool 26% silk	—		5½	—	—	—	—
Hanataba	USA	—	11	3	77% mohair 19% wool 4% nylon	—	40 gm	97	9.00	8-9	—	—
Haruna	USA	—	11	3	62% mohair 38% wool	—	50 gm	121	16.00	7-9	—	—
Hinageshi	USA	—	10½	3	52% rayon 31% cotton 15% linen 2% nylon	—	50 gm	50	9.00	10-12	—	—
Hokuto	USA	—	9	3	57% viscose 30% mohair 13% wool	—	50 gm	45	12.00	14-16	—	—
Ibuki	USA	—	11	2½	64% mohair 36% wool	—	50 gm	45	20.00	10	—	—
Izumi	USA	—	9	4	40% silk 35% cotton 25% linen	—	50 gm	120	9.50	8-10	—	—
Kasuga	USA	—	11	2½	100% wool	—	50 gm	44	8.50	10	—	—
Kasumi	USA	—	10½	3½	60% wool 40% Angora	—	50 gm	110	16.50	9	—	—
Katorea	USA	—	10½	3	50% cotton 50% linen	—	50 gm	45	8.50	8-12	—	—
Kiku	USA	—	10½	3½	83% cotton 16% silk 1% nylon	—	50 gm	83	9.00	8	—	—
Kosumosu	USA	—	10½	3½	70% wool 30% silk	—	50 gm	77	9.50	8-10	—	—
Matsu	USA	—	9	4¼	60% silk 40% cashmere	—	25 gm	62	12.50	10-14	—	—
Mizuho	USA	—	8	4¼	39% linen 30% acrylic 21% polyester 10% nylon	—	50 gm	110	9.50	5-6	—	—
Moegi	USA	—	9	4	90% wool 10% cashmere	—	50 gm	115	13.50	10	—	—

D

Brand and Yarn Name	Where Sold	Type	US Needle Size	Gauge/Tension per Inch	Fiber Content	Cleaning Care	Skein, Hank, Ball, or Cone Weight	Approx. Yardage	Approx. Price	Approx. No. of Skeins for a Small-size Standard Knit Pullover Sweater with Long Sleeves and Crew Neck			
										Man	Woman	Child	Infant
Nadeshiko	USA	–	11	3	40% Angora 39% wool 21% silk	–	50 gm	72	19.00	–	10	–	–
Nagareha	USA	–	13	2½	55% silk 30% acrylic 15% wool	–	50 gm	48	9.00	–	14–16	–	–
Nijyo	USA	–	10½	3	60% silk 28% cotton 12% nylon	–	50 gm	55	11.00	–	8–11	–	–
Nanohana	USA	–	9	4	100% viscose	–	50 gm	102	9.80	–	8–10	–	–
Nishiki	USA	–	10	4	100% silk	–	50 gm	74	19.00	–	10–12	–	–
Sakura	USA	–	10	3¾	70% wool 30% Angora	–	50 gm	120	13.50	–	8–10	–	–
Sarubia	USA	–	10½	3½	60% silk 40% mohair	–	50 gm	88	15.00	–	10	–	–
Shabon	USA	–	10½	3½	70% cotton 30% rayon	–	50 gm	85	10.50	–	8–11	–	–
Shinano	USA	–	9	4	80% wool 20% silk	–	50 gm	115	9.00	–	8–10	–	–
Suzuran	USA	–	10½	3	100% wool	–	50 gm	88	9.50	–	10	–	–
Tsubaki	USA	–	10½	3½	65% wool 35% silk	–	50 gm	83	11.00	–	8–10	–	–
Wakaba	USA	–	11	3	100% cotton	–	40 gm	72	10.50	–	8–10	–	–
Wakasa	USA	–	9	4	70% wool 30% silk	–	50 gm	120	9.00	–	8–10	–	–
Yamato	USA	–	10½	3½	79% wool 21% silk	–	50 gm	96	9.00	–	9	–	–
Yuri	USA	–	9	4	56% cotton 41% silk 3% nylon	–	50 gm	110	9.00	–	8–10	–	–
Yuzuru	USA	–	9	4	100% viscose	–	50 gm	102	8.50	–	8–10	–	–
Ole Oaxala American Harvest	USA	1-ply fluffy	11	3.5	100% wool	hand wash dry clean	100 gm	132	4.40	10	9	6	4
Patons Beehive Shetland-Style Chunky	USA CA GB	basic	10	3¾	75% acrylic 25% wool	machine wash dry flat	50 gm	89	–	15	12	6	3

D

Name	Country	Type	US	Gauge	Fiber content	Care	Ball	Yards	Price				
Beehive Shetland Chunky with Mountain Wool	USA CA	basic	10	3¾	50% acrylic 25% nylon 25% wool	machine wash dry flat	50 gm	82	—	15	12	6	3
Chunky Twirl	USA CA GB	pigtail	10	3¾	56% acrylic 17% wool 17% nylon 10% cotton	machine wash dry flat	50 gm	81	—	15	12	6	3
Country Life	USA CA	slub	10	3¾	66% acrylic 34% cotton	machine wash & dry	50 gm	76	—	15	12	6	3
Diana	USA CA GB	brushed	10	3¾	70% acrylic 30% nylon	machine wash & dry	50 gm	81	—	15	12	6	3
Firefly	USA	brushed fancy	10	3¾	45.5% viscose 29% acrylic 17.5% wool 4.5% mohair 3.5% nylon	hand wash dry flat	50 gm	76	—	15	12	6	3
Focus on Cotton	dis.	brushed fancy	9	3¾	30% cotton 30% mohair 30% acrylic 10% nylon	hand wash dry flat	25 gm	55	—	15	12	7	3
Mohair Focus	dis.	brushed	9	3¾	54% acrylic 42% mohair 4% nylon	hand wash dry flat	25 gm	63	—	14	11	7	3
Moorland Chunky	USA CA GB	smooth classic	10	3¾	100% wool	hand wash dry flat	50 gm	69	—	15	12	6	3
Princess	USA	brushed fleck	9	3¾	59% acrylic 17.5% mohair 12.5% nylon 11% wool	hand wash dry flat	50 gm	97	—	14	11	5	3
Siberia	USA GB	brushed multicolor	9	3¾	77.5% acrylic 12% cotton 8.5% mohair 2% nylon	hand wash dry flat	50 gm	102	—	15	12	7	3
Solo Chunky	USA CA GB	brushed	10	3¾	56% acrylic 24% wool 20% mohair	hand wash dry flat	50 gm	81	—	15	12	7	4
Viking	dis.	smooth roving	10	3½	100% wool	hand wash dry flat	100 gm	110	—	9	7	6	3
Perendale Quicknit	USA	bulky	10	3½	100% Perendale wool	wash with pure soap dry flat	100 gm	120	5.20	8	6	4	3
Pernelle Espiegle	USA	nubby	10½–11	3½	41% viscose 25% acrylic 16% mohair 18% cotton	hand wash dry clean	—	60	4.95	—	10	—	—
Maxi Bouquets	USA	classic	10½–11	3½	51% wool 49% acrylic	machine wash dry clean	50 gm	50	2.70	—	12–13	—	—

Brand and Yarn Name	Where Sold	Type	US Needle Size	Gauge/ Tension per Inch	Fiber Content	Cleaning Care	Skein, Hank, Ball, or Cone Weight	Approx. Yardage	Approx. Price	Approx. No. of Skeins for a Small-size Standard Knit Pullover Sweater with Long Sleeves and Crew Neck			
										Man	Woman	Child	Infant
Phentex Galleria Angorel	USA CA	3-ply	10	4st-6R= 1po.	100% brushed acrylic	machine wash, cold machine dry, gentle	50 gm	80	1.19	—	—	—	—
Can Can	USA CA	2-ply	10	4st-6R= 1po.	92% acrylic 6% polyester 2% polyamide	machine wash, cold machine dry, gentle	50 gm	90	1.29	—	—	—	—
Chunky	USA CA	2-ply	10.5	6st-11R= 2po.	100% acrylic	machine wash, cold machine dry, gentle	85 gm	125	1.39	—	—	—	—
Cotton Charade	USA CA	3-ply	6	5st-7R= 1po.	57% cotton 38% viscose 5% polyamide	machine wash, cold machine dry, gentle	40 gm	55	2.95	—	—	—	—
Cotton Renata	USA CA	3-ply	8	4st-10R= 1po.	49% cotton 48% acrylic 3% polyester	machine wash, cold machine dry, gentle	50 gm	85	1.69	—	—	—	—
Cotton Tahiti	USA CA	3-ply	8	4st-8R= 1po.	59% cotton 30% acrylic 11% polyester	machine wash, cold machine dry, gentle	40 gm	75	3.25	—	—	—	—
Bouclé Machine Knit	USA CA	2-ply	10	4st-6R= 1po.	92% acrylic 6% polyester 2% polyamide	machine wash, cold machine dry, gentle	1 lb.	815	10.95	—	—	—	—
Bulky Machine Knit	USA CA	2-ply	10.5	6st-11R= 2po.	100% acrylic	machine wash, cold machine dry, gentle	1 lb.	665	8.95	—	—	—	—
Tiffany	USA CA	3-ply	9	4st-9R= 1po.	34% viscose 30% acrylic 30% wool 6% polyester	machine wash, cold machine dry, gentle	40 gm	60	2.95	—	—	—	—
Phildar Aurore	dis.	mohair blend	10	3	36% mohair 24% wool 19% polyamide 18% acrylic 3% polyester	hand wash	50 gm	83	4.95	—	8	—	—
Bagherra	dis.	classic	10	3	100% acrylic	machine wash	100 gm	113	3.10	—	7	—	—
Elegance	USA	novelty	11	3.25	41% mohair 3% wool 40% acetate 16% metalicized polyester	hand wash	40 gm	56	7.50	—	14	—	—

Name	Country	Type	Needle	Gauge	Fiber Content	Care	Ball Wt.	Yds	Price		No.		
Falbadouce	USA	mohair blend	10	3.25	32% wool 25% kid mohair 22% nylon 18% acrylic 3% polyester	hand wash	40 gm	66	4.50	—	10	—	—
Geolite	USA	novelty	10	3.5	41% viscose 19% polyester 17% kid mohair 8% nylon 8% wool 7% acrylic	hand wash	50 gm	94	6.25	—	9	—	—
Imprime	USA	novelty	9	4.25	80% wool 20% nylon	hand wash	50 gm	60	4.75	—	15	—	—
Kadischa	USA	wool blend	10	3.25	75% acrylic 25% wool	machine wash	50 gm	50	1.99	—	13	—	—
Kid Flamme	dis.	fancy mohair	11	3	35% mohair 32% wool 31% acrylic 2% polyester	hand wash	50 gm	52	4.95	—	14	—	—
Legende	dis.	fancy bouclé	9	3.5	48% wool 48% acrylic 4% polyester	hand wash	50 gm	87	3.75	—	7	—	—
Marjory	dis.	fancy mohair	10-11	3	58% mohair 27% wool 15% acrylic	hand wash	40 gm	49	5.50	—	12	—	—
Ondiaflamme	dis.	fancy bouclé	10	3	47% acrylic 24% cotton 22% wool 5% mohair 2% polyester	machine wash hand wash	50 gm	48	3.25	—	16	—	—
Phildar Tweed	dis.	fancy tweed	9	4	58% wool 29% acrylic 11% polyester 2% viscose	hand wash	50 gm	82	4.50	—	9	—	—
Phil Star	USA	novelty	11	3.25	29% kid mohair 28% nylon 22% polyester 12% wool 9% acrylic	hand wash	50 gm	87	6.50	—	8	—	—
Poile Flamme	USA	novelty	11	3.25	37% cotton 32% polyester 16% acrylic 6% nylon 6% nylon 3% kid mohair	machine wash	50 gm	78	4.50	—	9	—	—
Preciosa	dis.	mohair & wool	10-11	3	38% mohair 62% wool	hand wash	40 gm	52	5.95	—	12	—	—
Reine Wool	—	wool meche	11-13	3	100% wool	hand wash	100 gm hanks	77	4.50	—	9	—	—

D

Brand and Yarn Name	Where Sold	Type	US Needle Size	Gauge/Tension per Inch	Fiber Content	Cleaning Care	Skein, Hank, Ball, or Cone Weight	Approx. Yardage	Approx. Price	Approx. No. of Skeins for a Small-size Standard Knit Pullover Sweater with Long Sleeves and Crew Neck			
										Man	Woman	Child	Infant
Shoot	dis.	classic	9	4	75% acrylic 25% wool	machine wash hand wash	50 gm	83	2.30	—	10	—	—
Steeple	dis.	fancy alpaca	9	4	30% alpaca 30% wool 29% acrylic 11% polyester	hand wash	50 gm	79	5.25	—	10	—	—
Top Secret	USA	novelty	11	3.50	23% mohair 22% wool 22% cotton 33% viscose	hand wash	50 gm	62	7.25	—	13	—	—
Vizir	dis.	mohair blend	10	3	36% mohair 24% wool 19% polyamide 18% acrylic 3% polyester	hand wash	50 gm	90	4.75	—	8	—	—
Pingouin Aubade	USA FR	novelty	10	4	36% wool 31% acrylic 20% polyester 13% mohair	hand wash	50 gm	99	—	—	—	—	—
Biais de Coton	USA FR	bias fabric strip	15	12/4	100% cotton	hand wash dry clean	50 gm	55	5.95	—	12°	—	—
Bouclette Imprimee	dis.	2-ply bouclé	7	14/4	53% wool 46% acrylic 1% polyamide	hand wash dry clean	50 gm	60	—	—	13°	—	—
Brigantin	dis.	fuzzy variegated blend with "bobbles"	10	14/4	75% wool 15% polyamide 10% mohair	hand wash dry clean	50 gm	40	7.95	—	15°	—	—
Contrastes	USA FR	novelty thick & thin	8	3½	64% viscose 25% mohair 11% wool	dry clean only	50 gm	80	—	—	—	—	—
Esprit d'Angora	USA FR	soft	6	4¼	60% polyamide 30% acrylic 10% Angora	hand wash	20 gm	81	—	—	—	—	—
Fourrure	dis.	rabbit fur strip	to crochet	—	100 coney fur	dry clean only	—	33	3.95	—	—	—	—
Iceberg	USA FR	3-ply heather	10	12/4	55% acrylic 45% wool	machine wash dry clean	50 gm	50	2.75	—	14°	—	—
Impressions	USA FR	bouclé	7	4	57% polyester 41% acrylic 2% polyamide	machine wash	50 gm	82	—	—	—	—	—

D

Name	US/FR	Description			Fiber	Care	Unit	Yards	Price		Size 14°		
Intrigue	USA FR	fancy variegated stranded	8	4¼	42% polyamide 25% wool 18% acrylic 15% mohair	hand wash	50 gm	99	—	—	—	—	—
Meche Bouclee	dis.	bouclé	13	8/4	100% wool	hand wash dry clean	100 gm	33	—	—	12°	—	—
Meche Bouclee Imprimee	dis.	bouclé variegated	13	8/4	100% wool	hand wash dry clean	100 gm	31	4.95	—	12°	—	—
Meche Cendree	dis.	loosely twisted heather blend	9	15/4	100% wool	hand wash dry clean	100 gm	110	—	—	7°	—	—
Menestrel	dis.	—	9	13/4	30% mohair 27% acrylic 25% cotton 15% wool 3% polyester	hand wash dry clean	50 gm	80	4.95	—	—	—	—
Mille et Une Nuits	USA FR	fluffy with metallic	8	4	37% wool 30% mohair 25% acrylic 5% polyester 3% polyamide	hand wash	50 gm	137	—	—	—	—	—
1920	USA FR	novelty	6	4¼	85% viscose 15% polyamide	hand wash	50 gm	82	—	—	—	—	—
Paprika	dis.	variegated bouclé	9	12/4	57% acrylic 35% wool 8% polyester	hand wash dry clean	50 gm	40	—	—	17°	—	—
Pingoland	dis.	3-ply heather	10	12/4	75% acrylic 25% wool	machine wash dry clean	50 gm	50	1.69	—	14°	—	—
Reflets d'Or	dis.	3-ply variegated with metallic strand	8	14/4	62% acrylic 27% wool 11% other	hand wash dry clean	50 gm	60	—	—	12°	—	—
Ritoumelle	USA FR	bumpy	7	4¼	55% cotton 45% viscose	hand wash	50 gm	60	—	—	—	—	—
Shetland et Lin	USA FR	soft classic	9	4	70% wool 30% flax	hand wash	50 gm	80	—	—	—	—	—
Sorbet	USA FR	soft worsted	9	3½	50% acrylic 30% polyamide 10% mohair 10% wool	hand wash	50 gm	110	—	—	—	—	—
Super Chenille	dis.	—	10½	8/4	59% viscose 49% acrylic	dry clean only	100 gm	65	—	—	10°	—	—
Tweede Rustique	dis.	2-ply heather blend	10	13/4	63% wool 22% acrylic 15% mohair	hand wash dry clean	50 gm	55	3.95	—	13°	—	—

°Size 14

Brand and Yarn Name	Where Sold	Type	US Needle Size	Gauge/Tension per Inch	Fiber Content	Cleaning Care	Skein, Hank, Ball, or Cone Weight	Approx. Yardage	Approx. Price	Approx. No. of Skeins for a Small-size Standard Knit Pullover Sweater with Long Sleeves and Crew Neck			
										Man	Woman	Child	Infant
Typhon	USA FR	loosely spun fuzzy	10	15/4	60% acrylic 20% wool 20% mohair	hand wash dry clean	50 gm	55	3.95	—	12*	—	—
Plymouth Apollo	USA	thick & thin	10	3½	100% wool	hand wash	4 oz.	125	6.00	10	8	6	—
Emu Daisy	USA	slubs & nubs	10	4	100% acrylic	hand wash	50 gm	62	3.20	—	11	8	—
Indicieta Roving Yarn	USA	roving	11	3	100% Peruvian alpaca	hand wash	100 gm	120	8.00	9	7	—	—
Naturewoole	dis.	novine	10½	3	100% wool	hand wash	100 gm	110	4.60	10	8	5	—
Puff	USA	slub	11	3	100% wool	hand wash	100 gm	125	7.50	9	7	—	—
Robin Charade	USA	knubby multicolor	11	2½	69% acrylic 11% nylon 11% mohair 9% wool	hand wash	50 gm	46	6.40	—	11	6	—
Robin Intrigue	USA	variegated mohair blend	9	3½	76% acrylic 12% mohair 12% nylon	hand wash	50 gm	107	5.00	—	8	6	—
Robin Landscape Chunky	USA	bulky smooth	10	4	75% acrylic 25% wool	hand wash lukewarm	50 gm	88	3.00	13	11	6	—
Robin Mardi Gras	USA	knubby bulky	10	4	73% wool 21% acrylic 6% nylon	hand wash lukewarm	50 gm	61	5.60	—	11	—	—
Robin Mysterie	USA	bulky mohair blend	9	3½	40% mohair 60% acrylic	hand wash	20–25 gm	55	3.20	—	11	—	—
Robin Mysterie w/Lurex	USA	mohair blend silver thread	9	3½	40% mohair 60% acrylic	hand wash	20–25 gm	55	3.40	—	11	—	—
Robin Soft 'n' Easy Chunky	USA	fluffy blend	11	3	60% acrylic 40% nylon	machine wash	100 gm	155	5.00	—	6	4	—
Saxony II	USA	heather	13	3	100% wool	hand wash	100 gm	200	5.00	4	3	2	—
Rainbow Mills Butterfly Silk	USA	hand-dyed solids and variegated	9, 10, 11	7/2	100% silk	dry clean	4 oz.	115	33.00 variegated 32.00 in solids	9	7	4	2
Candy	USA	hand-dyed hand-spun	13, 15, 17	2	50% wool 30% mohair curl 20% rayon binder	dry clean	100 gm	60	31.00	6–7	5–6	3–4	2–3

D

Name	Source	Texture	Needle Size	Gauge	Fiber Content	Care	Put-up	Yards	Price				
Paint Box	—	hand-dyed	9, 10½, 11	3 3 strands	60% cotton 40% rayon	hand wash	100 gm	275	9.75 variegated 9.00 solids	8	8	3	2
Persian Cord	USA	curled chenille	13–15	8st=5"	acrylic & Lurex	dry clean	500 gm bag	160	70.00	—	3 bags	—	—
Red Heart® Red Heart Brushed Bulky	USA	2-ply brushed	10	3½	100% Orlon acrylic	machine wash & dry	3 oz.	125	1.69	12	10	8	5
Red Heart Bulky	USA	2-ply smooth	10	3½	100% Orlon acrylic	machine wash & dry	3 oz.	120	1.59	12	10	8	5
Red Heart Heavy Rug Yarn	USA	3-ply smooth	10	3⅓	100% Dacron polyester	machine wash & dry	1.4 oz. folded skein	60	0.85	—	—	—	—
Reynolds Barcelona	dis.	multicolor slub	10½	3	45% wool 45% acrylic 10% polyester	—	50 gm	60	—	—	10	—	—
Coquette	USA	frothy	10	3½	40% cotton 24% wool 13% acrylic 9% mohair 8% polyester 6% nylon	—	50 gm	90	—	—	11	—	—
Fantasie	dis.	hi-fashion	10½	3	47% mohair 37% cotton 14% viscose 7% polyester	—	40 gm	45	—	—	15	—	—
Firenze	USA	ribbon/chenille	7	4	—	—	50 gm	125	—	—	12	—	—
Ice Wool	USA	heather	10	3½	100% Icelandic wool	—	50 gm	86	—	—	9–10	—	—
Jezebel	dis.	luxury	9	3½	52% silk 46% viscose 2% Lurex	—	50 gm	80	—	—	12	—	—
Jolie	dis.	—	10½	3	100% wool	—	50 gm	65	—	—	8	—	—
Kurlie Lamb	USA	—	7	3½	100% wool	—	50 gm	90	—	—	9	—	—
Lopi	USA	water repellant	10	3½	100% Icelandic wool	—	100 gm	110	—	—	8	—	—
Lopi Tweed	USA	tweed	10	3½	100% Icelandic wool	—	100 gm	120	—	—	8	—	—
Menton	USA	wool/metallic blend	10½	3	—	—	50 gm	45	—	—	10	—	—
Monte Carlo	USA	—	10½	3	alpaca & cotton	—	50 gm	50	—	—	10	—	—
Nuance	USA	bulky	10	4	acrylic & Angora	wash	50 gm	70	—	—	12	—	—

*Size 14

Brand and Yarn Name	Where Sold	Type	US Needle Size	Gauge/ Tension per Inch	Fiber Content	Cleaning Care	Skein, Hank, Ball, or Cone Weight	Approx. Yardage	Approx. Price	Approx. No. of Skeins for a Small-size Standard Knit Pullover Sweater with Long Sleeves and Crew Neck			
										Man	Woman	Child	Infant
Portugese Fisherman Bulky	USA	scoured	10	3½	100% wool	—	100 gm	70	—	—	11	—	—
Scherherazade	USA	exotic	10½	3	34% wool 32% mohair 20% viscose 11% polyester 3% Lurex	—	50 gm	45	—	—	12	—	—
Taboo	USA	—	9	3½	—	—	50 gm	115	—	—	9	—	—
Tipperary Tweed	USA	tweed	9	3½	100% Irish wool	—	100 gm	145	—	—	6	—	—
Toulon	USA	contemporary	9	4	65% wool 35% Angora	—	30 gm	85	—	—	10	—	—
Samband of Iceland Samband Laua	USA CA	—	10	3½	100% Icelandic wool	hand wash	100 gm	120	4.75	11	9	4	—
Samband Tweed	USA CA	twisted	8	4	100% Icelandic wool	hand wash	50 gm	110	2.95	9	8	4	—
Schaffhauser Boutique	dis.	fluffy multi-color novelty	9–10½	3½	58% wool 17% mohair 25% acrylic	hand wash	50 gm	96	5.15	—	9	—	—
Flaminia	USA	slubbed thick & thin multicolor novelty	10½	3½	100% wool	machine wash	100 gm	132	7.90	—	7	—	—
Gallery	USA	fluffy novelty	9–10½	3½	53% mohair 23% viscose 13% cotton 13% acrylic	machine wash	—	97	5.95	—	8	—	—
Hollywood	USA	light textured novelty	6–7	4½	58% cotton 42% silk	hand wash	—	137	5.95	—	8	—	—
King	USA	multicolor and solid classic	10–10½	3½	100% wool	machine wash	50 gm	55	3.55	—	13	—	—
La Maille	USA	variegated solid and tone-on-tone colors heathery	9–10	3/2	90% wool 10% alpaca	hand wash	50 gm	83	3.80	—	11	—	—
Laser	USA	shimmering novelty	6–8	4½	60% acrylic 30% nylon 10% wool	machine wash	—	191	3.45	—	6	—	—

D

Name	Origin	Description	Needle	Gauge	Fiber Content	Care	Put-up	Yardage	Price				
Plaza	USA	multi-colored bouclé	7–9	4	68% wool 14% viscose 18% acrylic	machine wash	—	97	4.75	—	10	—	—
Rigoletto	USA	elegant thick & thin	8–10	4	67% wool 33% silk	hand wash	—	98	6.95	—	12	—	—
Stefanie	dis.	soft-brushed tweed novelty	10–10½	3	35% wool 22% mohair 20% cotton 23% acrylic	machine wash	50 gm	60	5.50	—	11	—	—
Scheepjeswol Flamme Colori	USA CA GB	super bulky variegated	10	2½	100% new wool	hand wash only lukewarm do not bleach do not iron	100 gm	72	8.00	9	7	—	9
Schoeller Gabi	USA	fluffy	9	3	60% mohair 30% acrylic 10% wool	machine wash cold dry flat	50 gm	97	7.79	14	12	9	14
La Plata	USA	worsted	6	5½	50% acrylic 30% wool 10% alpaca 10% linen	machine wash	50 gm	141	4.49	—	8	—	—
Terra Jarre	USA	worsted	9	4½	55% acrylic 37½% wool 7½% viscose	machine wash	50 gm	93	3.59	—	14	—	—
Scotts Woolen Mills Charisma Now	dis.	specialty textured multicolor bulky	10–13	2–3	⅓ tussah silk ⅔ rayon	dry clean	2 oz. skein ½ or 1 lb. cone	40 330	6.25 48.00	18–20	16	10–14	8
Eider Down	dis.	rustic bulky homespun look	10–13	2–3½	100% cotton	solid colors: machine wash, cold mixed colors: dry clean	2 oz. skein ½ or 1 lb. cone	55 450	1.95 14.00	16	14	10–12	6
Flutter	USA	thick & thin	8	4	64% cotton 26% rayon 6% linen 4% nylon	hand wash	2 oz. skein 1 lb. or ½ lb. cone	67 540	3.25 24.00	8	6	4	2
Joy	dis.	classic thick & thin	9–13	2–4	100% wool	solid colors: hand wash, cold mixed colors: dry clean	2 oz. skein ½ or 1 lb. cone	55 450	3.30 24.50	16	14	10–12	6
Reverie	USA	wool bouclé	10	3½	85% wool 15% nylon	hand wash	2 oz. skein 1 or ½ lb. cone	56 450	3.90 29.00	16	12	10	4
Romance	USA	specialty blend of shiny bouclé brushed yarn	10–13	2–3½	50% wool 50% rayon	solid colors: hand wash, cold mixed colors: dry clean	2 oz. skein ½ or 1 lb. cone	80 625	5.25 40.50	13	11	5–7	4

Brand and Yarn Name	Where Sold	Type	US Needle Size	Gauge/ Tension per Inch	Fiber Content	Cleaning Care	Skein, Hank, Ball, or Cone Weight	Approx. Yardage	Approx. Price	Man	Woman	Child	Infant
Silhouette	USA	thick & thin rayon wrapped	10	3½	53% wool 25% rayon 22% acrylic	hand wash dry clean	2 oz. skein 1 or ½ lb. cone	52 / 420	3.75 / 28.00	16	12	10	5
Trifle	dis.	multicolored tweed bouclé	9–13	2–4	100% kid mohair	hand wash, cold; dry clean	2 oz. skein ½ or 1 lb. cone	60 / 500	6.25 / 48.00	13	11	5–7	4
Velvet	dis.	fleecy chenille	9–13	2–4	100% wool	solid colors: hand wash, cold; mixed colors: dry clean	2 oz. skein ½ or 1 lb. cone	55 / 450	5.20 / 39.80	16	14	10–12	6
Serendipity Skeins Debut	USA	silken interlacement hand-dyed	10½	3½	100% silk	dry clean	3½ oz.	94	—	13	6	5	3
Mirage	USA	lofty, softy hand-dyed	10½	3	100% alpaca	hand wash dry clean	3½ oz.	120	—	10	5	4	3
Silk Ltd. Silk Feather Yarn	USA JP	8 different colors	8	4	100% silk	dry clean only	bobbin 8 oz.	210	34.07	3	2	2	1
Sirdar Chunky	USA	country	10	3½	45% acrylic 40% bri-nylon 15% wool	—	50 gm	73	3.30	—	—	—	—
Flambo	USA	specialty	10	3½	85% acrylic 15% polyamide	—	100 gm	165	5.00	—	—	—	—
Gemini Brushed Chunky	USA	specialty	10	3½	50% bri-nylon	—	100 gm	146	5.00	—	—	—	—
Gemini Gemstone	USA	specialty	10	3½	66% acrylic 34% nylon	—	100 gm	147	5.50	—	—	—	—
Leisuretime Chunky	USA	blend	10½	3½	90% wool 10% acrylic	—	50 gm	70	4.00	—	—	—	—
Nomad Chunky	USA	specialty	10	3½	70% wool 17% cotton 10% mohair		50 gm	58	3.60	—	—	—	—
Spring Brook Buzz	USA	thick & thin flecked	10–13	2–3	58% wool 39% acrylic 3% polyester	machine wash, gentle, cold water dry flat	50 gm 1 lb.	75 / 700	2.85 / 23.00	—	14	—	—
Celeste	USA	puffed rayon spiral with brushed look	10–10½	3	83% rayon 10% mohair 4% acrylic 3% nylon	dry clean	50 gm 1 lb.	75 / 720	4.25 / 36.00	—	15	—	—

Approx. No. of Skeins for a Small-size Standard Knit Pullover Sweater with Long Sleeves and Crew Neck

Name	Origin	Description	Needle		Fiber Content	Care	Weight	Yards	Price				
Devon Creme	USA	3-ply rustic hand-spun	10–10½	3	76% wool 18% nylon 6% silk	dry clean	50 gm 1 lb.	90 840	3.75 31.50	—	13	—	—
Diamond Soufflé	USA	brushed mohair with loops	10–13	2–3	50% rayon 35% mohair 13% acrylic 2% nylon	dry clean	50 gm 1 lb.	50 500	5.00 43.00	—	20	—	—
Gigi	USA	variegated brushed wool	10–10½	3	32% wool 60% acrylic 8% polyester	machine wash, cold tumble dry	50 gm 1 lb.	95 900	3.40 28.00	—	12	—	—
Meteor	USA	airy, bubbled with nubs	10–10½	3	42% wool 32% rayon 15% polyester 9% linen 2% nylon	hand wash cold wash dry flat	50 gm 1 lb.	40 400	4.30 36.00	—	15	—	—
Savannah	USA	bulky, combed cotton	10–10½	3	100% cotton	dry clean	50 gm 1 lb.	60 560	2.55 20.00	—	14	—	—
Stella	USA	brushed overwrap with metallic	10–10½	3	25% metallic 24% mohair 24% wool 17% acrylic 10% polyester	hand wash, cold dry flat	50 gm 1 lb.	125 1,160	7.10 62.00	—	9	—	—
Sunbeam Paris "Haze"	CA	mohair	9	4	78% mohair 13% wool 9% nylon	hand wash	25 gm	50	4.75 (CA $)	—	14	—	—
Paris Mohair "Pearls"	CA	mohair	9	4	60% mohair 23% acrylic 13% nylon 4% metalized	hand wash	25 gm	47	4.75 (CA $)	—	—	—	—
Paris Mohair "Sheens"	CA	mohair	9	4	78% mohair 13% wool 9% nylon	hand wash	25 gm	50 m	4.25 (CA $)	—	14	—	—
Paris "Splash"	CA	mohair	9	4	53% mohair 27% nylon 13% wool 7% acrylic	hand wash	25 gm	52.5	4.75 (CA $)	—	14	—	—
Sumatra Solid Shades	CA	mohair	8	4	67% acrylic 33% nylon	hand wash	25 gm	49	2.40 (CA $)	—	11	—	—
Sumatra Space-Dyed	CA	mohair	8	4	67% acrylic 33% nylon	hand wash	25 gm	49	2.99 (CA $)	—	11	—	—
Tahki Imports Cabaret	USA	—	10	3½	72% mohair 28% polyamide	dry clean	1.75 oz.	97	9.00	—	8	—	—
Creole	USA	—	10	4	100% cotton	dry clean	3.5 oz.	109	6.40	—	6	—	—
Morocco	USA FR	—	10	3½	45% wool 15% mohair 15% polyamide 25% acrylic	dry clean	1.75 oz.	82	4.70	—	10	—	—

D

Brand and Yarn Name	Where Sold	Type	US Needle Size	Gauge/Tension per Inch	Fiber Content	Cleaning Care	Skein, Hank, Ball, or Cone Weight	Approx. Yardage	Approx. Price	Approx. No. of Skeins for a Small-size Standard Knit Pullover Sweater with Long Sleeves and Crew Neck			
										Man	Woman	Child	Infant
Soho Bulky Tweed	GB	tweed	10½	3	100% wool	dry clean	3.5 oz.	110	6.40	—	6	—	—
Tamm Yarns Peluche Tamm	USA MX CA AU	chunky	—	(16/3) 3–5	80% acrylic 20% poly-nylon	short spin	454 gm	1,091	16.40	—	1 cone	—	—
Tish and Amy Originals Rag Straight	USA	flat	13–15	3	polyester/cotton	machine wash & dry (colorfast)	4 oz.	100	6.00	10	7	4	—
Tish's Twine	USA	smooth	13–15	2½	100% polyester	machine wash & dry	3 oz.	50	3.00	10	8	—	—
Unger Amour	dis.	—	10	3½	75% mohair 15% wool 10% nylon	hand wash dry clean	50 gm	105	8.00	—	7	—	—
Bali	dis.	—	10	3½	55% wool 45% acrylic	—	50 gm	65	2.90	—	10	—	—
Fizz	USA CA	pigtail novelty	10½	3½	63% viscose 23% acrylic 8% wool 4% nylon	dry clean	50 gm	60	8.50	—	13	—	—
Patina	USA CA	soft metallic	9	3¾	73% wool 24% metallic 3% nylon	hand wash dry clean	20 gm	49	5.50	—	—	—	—
Primrose	USA CA	novelty	9	4	93% wool 7% mohair	hand wash	50 gm	77	5.80	—	11	—	—
Skol	dis.	Skol	10	3½	100% wool	hand wash dry clean	50 gm	85	3.40	—	10	—	—
Venetta	USA CA	mohair novelty	10½	3	24% mohair 21% wool 40% viscose 10% cotton 5% acrylic	hand wash dry clean	50 gm	62	7.50	—	14	—	—
Whimsey	USA CA	mohair	10	3½	70% mohair 30% wool	hand wash	40 gm	105	4.80	—	10	—	—
Welcomme Diamante	dis.	tubular ribbon	10½–11	3½	100% cotton	hand wash dry clean	50 gm	87	4.50	—	9–10	—	—
Kibor	USA	brushed/wiry multicolor	10½–11	3½	54% mohair 27% acetate 16% polyamide 3% acrylic	hand wash dry clean	—	100	13.95	—	6	—	—
Kid Mohair et Soie	USA	brushed	10½–11	3½	88% kid mohair 12% silk	hand wash dry clean	20 gm	45	6.00	—	14–15	—	—

Name		Description			Fiber	Care							
Maxi Mohair	USA	brushed	10½-11	3½	70% kid mohair 30% acrylic	hand wash dry clean	50 gm	55	8.25	—	11-12	—	—
Shetland et Alpaga 6	dis.	Shetland twist	10½-11	3½	90% wool 10% alpaga	machine wash dry clean	50 gm	50	5.40	—	12-13	—	—
Tivoli	USA	dressy	10½-11	3½	88% polyamide 12% acrylic	hand wash dry clean	50 gm	74	7.20	—	10-11	—	—
Tournesol	dis.	slub homespun	10½-11	3½	50% silk 40% acrylic 10% wool	hand wash dry clean	50 gm	70	6.25	—	9-10	—	—
Tweed Brilliant	dis.	textured dressy	10½-11	3½	57% wool 43% viscose	hand wash dry clean	50 gm	50	8.65	—	13-14	—	—
Virevolte	USA	bulky chenille	11	2½	59% viscose 41% acrylic	dry clean	100 gm	65	9.00	—	7-8	—	—
Voltige	USA	wiry/multi-color	10½-11	3½	64% wool 36% acrylic	hand wash dry clean	—	105	11.50	—	7	—	—
Wendy Matisse	USA CA GB AU	brushed bouclé knits with monet	9-10½	3	64% Courtelle acrylic 23% wool 9% bri-nylon 4% polyester	hand wash	50 gm	60	3.95	8-10	12	14	—
Monaco	USA CA GB AU	brushed	6-8	4.25	50% wool 50% Courtelle acrylic	hand wash	50 gm	90	2.99	8	10	10	—
Monet	USA CA GB AU	brushed	8-10	3.25	50% bri-nylon 50% Courtelle acrylic	hand wash	50 gm	69.5	2.80	5	8	8	—
Monet	USA CA GB AU	brushed	8-10	3.25	50% Courtelle acrylic 50% bri-nylon	hand wash	100 gm	139	4.95	3-5	4-6	4-6	—
Sarto	USA CA GB AU	knits with sharma	8-10	4	80% wool 20% bri-nylon	hand wash	50 gm	95	3.15	6	9	10	—
Sharma	USA CA GB AU	knits with sarto roving with bouclé rayon wrap	8-10	3.5	60% wool 35% acrylic 5% nylon	hand wash	50 gm	73	4.60	8	10	12	—
Shetland Chunky	USA CA GB AU	—	8-10	3.5	100% pure new wool	machine wash	50 gm	57	2.99	10	12	14	—

D

Brand and Yarn Name	Where Sold	Type	US Needle Size	Gauge/Tension per Inch	Fiber Content	Cleaning Care	Skein, Hank, Ball, or Cone Weight	Approx. Yardage	Approx. Price	Approx. No. of Skeins for a Small-size Standard Knit Pullover Sweater with Long Sleeves and Crew Neck			
										Man	Woman	Child	Infant
Yes	USA CA GB AU	long brushed mohair/slub	8-10	3.75	70% mohair 16½% acrylic 13½% bri-nylon	hand wash	50 gm	102	6.95	4-6	4-6	—	—
White Buffalo Elena	USA CA	Icelandic-type yarn	10	3.5	100% wool	hand wash dry clean	100 gm	109	3.85	7-9	7-9	5-7	—
Elena Plus	USA CA	Icelandic-type yarn	10	3.5	75% acrylic 25% wool	machine wash	75 gm	109	2.55	7-9	7-9	5-7	—
Whitin Yarns Handsome Harry's Hanks	USA	classic homespun worsted	8-10	5	100% fleece wool	hand wash dry clean	100 gm	190	4.00	—	—	—	—
Wilde Yarns Natural Berber 2-ply	USA	classic tweed	10½	3½	100% wool	hand wash dry clean	1 lb. cone	480	8.40	3	2	NA	NA
Pebbles	USA	nubby bouclé	10-10½	2½-3	100% wool	hand wash dry clean	2 oz. skein 8 oz. cone	51	3.50 13.00	16	12	N/A	N/A
Top-Dyed Berber 2-ply	USA	classic tweed	10½	3½	100% wool	hand wash dry clean	8 oz. cone	240	6.50	5	4	NA	NA
Tumbleweed	USA	brushed loop	8-9	3-3½	100% wool	hand wash dry clean	2 oz. skein 8 oz. cone	94	3.25 12.00	10	7	NA	NA
Yarn by Mills Angora-Silk	USA	fluffy soft long fiber luxurious hand-spun	10-12	3-4	Angora silk	hand wash dry clean	50 gm	85	14.00	8-10	7-9	5	3
Ankara	USA	multicolor fluffy soft lustrous hand-spun	10½-12	3	51% kid mohair 49% wool	hand wash dry clean	3 oz.	115	15.00	8-10	7-9	5	3
Blue Nile I	USA	hand-spun soft, variegated color & texture all natural	10-12	3	34% camel down 33% tussah silk 33% wool	hand wash dry clean	3 oz.	115	12.98	8-10	7-9	5	3
Blue Nile II	USA	soft variegated natural long fiber with tufts of Angora	10-12	3	41% wool 17% camel down 17% tussah silk 17% mohair 8% Angora	hand wash dry clean	3 oz.	115	14.00	8-10	7-9	5	3
Georgia	USA	luxurious slightly textured, hand-spun	9-10½	3-4	50% cultivated silk 50% lambswool	dry clean	50 gm	85	14.00	8-10	7-9	5	3

D

Name	Origin	Description			Fiber	Care	Weight							
Kid Mohair	USA	lustrous very soft fuzzy hand-spun	10-13	2-3	100% kid mohair	hand wash dry clean	3 oz.	120	16.00	8-10	7-9	5	3
Tussah	USA	silky soft lustrous variegated hand-dyed	9-11	2-3½	35% tussah silk 35% camel down 30% mohair	hand wash dry clean	2 oz.	100	12.00	8-10	7-9	5	3
Wool	USA	first quality New Zealand Romney long fiber hand-spun fleecy	10-12	2½-3½	100% wool	hand wash dry clean	3 oz.	115	9.00	8-10	7-9	5	3
Yarn Country/ Newton Knits Exotic	—	nubby dressy	—	4½-5	25% rayon 25% cotton 25% acrylic 25% polyester	machine wash & dry	1 lb.	800	—	—	—	—	—
Yarns Galore Terry	USA	fleecy	11	3	100% cotton	hand wash dry flat dry clean	4 oz.	140	6.95	12	10	5	3½
Terry Blend	USA	fleecy	11	3	85% acrylic 15% polyester	hand wash dry flat dry clean	4 oz.	212	6.95	11	8	4	3

Specialty Yarns

CLASS E

Brand and Yarn Name	Where Sold	Type	US Needle Size	Gauge/ Tension per Inch	Fiber Content	Cleaning Care	Skein, Hank, Ball, or Cone Weight	Approx. Yardage	Approx. Price	Approx. No. of Skeins for a Small-size Standard Knit Pullover Sweater with Long Sleeves and Crew Neck			
										Man	Woman	Child	Infant
Anny Blatt Boa	dis.	maribou feathers	—	—	99% feathers 1% cotton	—	40 gm	2.2	9.75	—	—	—	—
Castox	dis.	unsheared beaver	13–15	1½	fur	dry clean	45 gm	16	49.50	—	—	—	—
Diva	dis.	long-haired fur-like	15	1½	96% mohair 2% wool 2% nylon	hand wash dry clean	50 gm	19	11.00	22	19	9	3
Paradis	dis.	novelty, very textured with nubs	11–13	2½	50% mohair 40% rayon 9% wool 1% nylon	hand wash dry clean	50 gm	32	8.50	19	16	8	4
Bartlettyarns Fisherman Bulky	USA	bulky (4-ply, unspun)	10½ K	3	100% wool	hand wash dry clean	4 oz.	80	4.10	12	12	6	4
Quick Knit	USA	4-ply	11 K	2¾	100% wool	hand wash dry clean	4 oz.	75	4.50	12	12	6	4
Rug Yarn	USA	4-ply	11 K	2¾	100% wool	hand wash dry clean	4 oz.	75	4.50	NA	NA	NA	NA
Navajo (Primitive)	USA	1-ply	10 J	3½	100% wool	hand wash dry clean	1 lb.	560	17.00	2 lb.	2 lb.	1 lb.	1 lb.
Bernat Musetta	USA	brushed	10	3	48% wool 36% mohair 16% acrylic	hand wash	50 gm	80	6.50	—	9	—	—
Scandia	USA	thick & thin	11	3	78% wool 17% polyester 5% acrylic	hand wash	50 gm	68	3.95	15	11	7	—
Bouquet Noel	dis.	specialty	11	2½	100% acrylic	machine wash & dry	50 gm	20	2.19	—	—	—	—
Siwash	USA CA	carded wool	11	2½	100% wool	hand wash dry clean	200 gm	70	6.25	8	6	4	—
Chinook of Australia Chinook	USA AU	6-strand	10	2½	100% wool	hand wash	8 oz.	133	7.95	9	8	6	—

E

Product	Origin	Description	Needle	Gauge	Fiber Content	Care	Put-up	Yds	Price				
Condon's Yarns Unspun	USA	—	10	3.25	100% wool	hand wash	—	100	1.70	10	8	6	—
Erdal Yarns Caterpillar	USA	solid	15	1½	100% acrylic	hand wash machine wash	4 oz. 1 lb.	25 100	4.50 18.00	—	10 2	—	—
Caterpillar	USA	variegated	15	1½	100% acrylic	hand wash machine wash	4 oz. 1 lb.	25 100	5.75 23.00	—	10 2	—	—
Caterpillar	USA	Lurex	15	1½	100% acrylic	hand wash machine wash	4 oz. 1 lb.	25 100	6.00 24.00	—	10 2	—	—
Fiesta Yarns Moki	USA	hand-dyed novelty	10	3	51% rayon 49% wool	dry clean	2 oz. 8 oz.	480 yds. per lb.	48.00	—	1½ tube 2 lb.	—	—
Froehlich Chihuahua	USA	novelty shine	6–7	5–6	64% cotton 36% triacetate	hand wash dry clean	50 gm	99	4.80	—	—	—	—
Mufflone	USA	super bulky	12–15	2½–3½	100% mountain sheep's wool	hand wash dry clean	100 gm	58	9.00	—	—	—	—
Nastrella	USA	slinky ribbon knit	8–10	—	100% viscose	hand wash dry clean	50 gm	88	5.25	—	—	—	—
Nastrino	USA	ribbon	8–10	—	100% cotton	hand wash dry clean	50 gm	88	5.80	—	—	—	—
Oriente	USA	ribbon nub	6–10	—	51% viscose 38% acrylic 11% nylon	hand wash dry clean	50 gm	105	7.80	—	—	—	—
Grandor Slub Loop Twist	USA	heavy bulky specialty	14	2	100% wool	hand wash	2 oz.	18	3.00	NA	NA	NA	NA
Halcyon Yarn Elastic Yarn	USA	fine elastic for ribbings etc.	—	—	—	—	approx. 1 oz.	100	—	—	—	—	—
Halcyon Rug Wool	USA	3-ply rug yarn for rugs & throws	11–13	2–3	100% wool	hand wash dry clean	approx. 4 oz.	65	—	NA	NA	NA	NA
Lundgren Rya Lundgren Rya	USA	heavy rya 2-ply	8 2¾ steel rug needle	5	100% wool	hand wash mild soap	3–4 oz.	100	4.00	—	—	—	—
Merino Asphalte	USA	textured multicolor	10	2	97% wool 2% viscose 1% nylon	—	50 gm	35	5.00	—	—	—	—
Delire	USA	multicolor nubby	10½	2	78% viscose 19% wool 3% nylon	—	50 gm	66	10.00	—	—	—	—
Ecume	USA	novelty	15–17	2	63% acrylic 35% mohair 2% nylon	—	50 gm	42	10.00	—	—	—	—

Brand and Yarn Name	Where Sold	Type	US Needle Size	Gauge/Tension per Inch	Fiber Content	Cleaning Care	Skein, Hank, Ball, or Cone Weight	Approx. Yardage	Approx. Price	Approx. No. of Skeins for a Small-size Standard Knit Pullover Sweater with Long Sleeves and Crew Neck			
										Man	Woman	Child	Infant
Ouragan	USA	novelty	13	2½	47% viscose 41% mohair 10% wool 2% nylon	—	50 gm	45	14.40	—	—	—	—
Passion	USA	novelty ribbon	9–15	2	53% viscose 47% nylon	—	50 gm	128	14.00	—	—	—	—
Patchi	USA	fur	15–17	1½	69% acrylic 31% cotton	—	100 gm	33	18.00 22.00	—	—	—	—
Strip	USA	fleecy multicolor	9–13	2½	90% kid mohair 8% wool 2% polyester	—	50 gm	51	10.00	—	—	—	—
Phildar Epopee	dis.	fancy meche	13	2.5	69% wool 31% acrylic	hand wash	100 gm	45	6.25	—	11	—	—
Ladina	dis.	fancy mohair	13	2.5	91% mohair 4% wool 5% nylon	hand wash	40 gm	54	5.75	—	12	—	—
Suggestion	dis.	super fancy	13–15	2	32% acrylic 22% mohair 21% polyamide 11% cotton 3% polyester	hand wash	100 gm	45	6.50	—	15	—	—
Rainbow Mills Candy	USA	hand-dyed hand-spun	15–17	7 sts = 4"	50% wool 30% mohair curl 20% rayon binder	dry clean	100 gm	60	31.00	6–7	5–6	3–4	2–3
Teddy Bear	USA	extra plush mohair hand-dyed	17–19	5 st = 4"	95% mohair 3% wool 2% nylon	dry clean do not block	180 gm	40	19.00 solids 20.00 variegated	8–10	8–10	5	2–3
Reynolds Artisan	USA	thick & thin country spun	10½	2½	100% wool	—	100 gm	80	—	—	7	—	—
Bairritz	USA	contemporary	9	2½	52% kid mohair 48% wool	—	50 gm	45	—	—	10	—	—
Chamonix	dis.	—	11	2½	31% mohair 38% rayon 31% acrylic	—	50 gm	40	—	—	15	—	—
Gardena	dis.	brushed multicolor	11	2½	80% wool 20% acrylic	—	50 gm	50	—	—	15	—	—
Marseilles	USA	—	9	2½	83% wool 17% rayon	—	50 gm	50	—	—	12	—	—

Name	Origin	Texture	Needle	Gauge	Fiber Content	Care	Put-up	Yards	Price				
Rodeo	dis.	—	13	2	66% acrylic 34% wool	—	100 gm	60	—	—	10	—	—
Santa Fe Yarn Fleece Handspun #302	USA	super	15	—	100% wool	dry clean	4 oz.	varies	16.00	—	—	—	—
Serendipity Skeins Cumulus	USA	lofty, light double bouclé hand-dyed	15–17	2	100% wool	hand wash dry clean	8 oz.	150	—	6	2	2	1
Flying Colors	USA	tickle your fancy hand-dyed	—	—	feathers	hand wash dry clean	continuous strand	35	—	—	—	—	—
Plumage	USA	wrap in drama hand-dyed	—	—	feather boa	hand wash dry clean	—	2	—	—	—	—	—
Wave	USA	undulating thick & thin hand-dyed	15–17	2	100% wool	hand wash dry clean	8 oz.	125	—	7	2	2	1
Spring Brook Meteor	USA	airy, bubbled with nubs	11–13	2	42% wool 32% rayon 15% polyester 9% linen 2% nylon	hand wash, cold dry flat	50 gm 1 lb.	40 400	4.30 36.00	—	15	—	—
Tahki Imports Jumbo Tweed	USA FR	tweed	13	2½	100% wool	dry clean	3.5 oz.	108	10.80	—	8	—	—
Tish & Amy Tish's Twine	USA	smooth	13–15	2½	100% polyester	machine wash & dry	3 oz.	50	3.00	10	8	—	—
Unger Aurora	USA CA	mohair/ pigtail	13	2½	51% mohair 45% acrylic 4% nylon	dry clean	50 gm	55	12.50	—	11	—	—
Aurora II	USA CA	mohair/ pigtail	11	2½	54% mohair 43% acrylic 3% nylon	dry clean	50 gm	66	12.50	—	10	—	—
Caprice	dis.	—	10½	3	50% wool 50% acrylic	hand wash dry clean	—	51	5.60	—	8	—	—
Cheetah	dis.	—	10½	3	75% wool 15% acrylic 10% nylon	hand wash dry clean	50 gm	70	4.90	—	8	—	—
Crackerjack	USA CA	novelty mohair	13	2	52% mohair 34% acrylic 8% wool 6% nylon	hand wash	50 gm	60	9.60	—	12	—	—
Derby	dis.	—	10½	3	54% acrylic 37.5% wool 8.5% rayon	hand wash dry clean	50 gm	58	3.00	—	11	—	—
Potpourri	USA CA	tweed novelty	10½	2½	72% acrylic 17% wool 11% mohair	hand wash	50 gm	55	3.80	—	14	—	—

E

Brand and Yarn Name	Where Sold	Type	US Needle Size	Gauge/Tension per Inch	Fiber Content	Cleaning Care	Skein, Hank, Ball, or Cone Weight	Approx. Yardage	Approx. Price	Approx. No. of Skeins for a Small-size Standard Knit Pullover Sweater with Long Sleeves and Crew Neck			
										Man	Woman	Child	Infant
Ruffles	USA CA	novelty	13	2	43% mohair 36% viscose 13% nylon 8% acrylic	hand wash dry clean	50 gm	55	10.40	—	13	—	—
Viola	dis.	—	10	11 = 3"	45% wool 40% acrylic 15% nylon	hand wash dry clean	50 gm	70	5.60	—	10	—	—
Welcomme Cariatides	USA	multicolored slub	11-13	2½	48% acrylic 30% mohair 21% wool 1% polyamide	machine wash dry clean	50 gm	53	7.50	—	10-11	—	—
Megamohair	USA	brushed multicolor	15	2½	95% mohair 5% polyamide	hand wash dry clean	50 gm	28	13.00	—	9-10	—	—
Noir et Blank	USA	multicolored slub	15	2½	40% viscose 30% mohair 27% wool 3% polyamide	hand wash dry clean	50 gm	31	11.25	—	12-13	—	—
Shetland et Alpaga 6	USA	Shetland twist	10½-11	3½	90% wool 10% alpaga	machine wash dry clean	50 gm	50	5.40	—	12-13	—	—
Stilb	USA	large slub brushed	11-13	3	48% acrylic 36% mohair 7% polyamide 6% viscose 3% polyester	hand wash dry clean	—	94	13.95	—	8	—	—
Wallaby	USA	fur	13-15	2½	100% wallaby fur	dry clean	17 yd. container	17	3.25 yd.	—	—	—	—
Wendy Lima	USA CA GB AU	brushed	8-10	2.75	75% acrylic 25% wool	hand wash	50 gm	54.5	3.25	10	10	7	—
White Buffalo Frosty	USA CA	—	11	2.75	75% acrylic 25% wool	machine wash	100 gm	68	3.30	15-18	15-18	10-12	—
White Buffalo Unspun	USA CA	for traditional west coast Cdn. Indian sweaters	11	2.75	100% wool	hand wash dry clean	8 oz. 227 gm	122	7.30	8-10	8-10	6-8	—
White Buffalo Spun	USA CA	for traditional west coast Cdn. Indian sweaters	11	2.75	100% wool	hand wash dry clean	8 oz. 227 gm	122	7.80	8-10	8-10	6-8	—
Wilde Yarns Heavyweight	USA	smooth bulky	12	2	100% wool	hand wash dry clean	8 oz.	80	6.00	5	4	NA	NA

Appendix A: Conversion Charts

OUNCES AND GRAMS

Ounces to Grams	Yards to Meters	Grams to Ounces	Meters to Yards
1 = 28.4	1 = .91	25 = ⅞	25 = 27.34
2 = 56.7	10 = 9.14	40 = 1⅖	50 = 54.68
3 = 85.0	50 = 45.5	50 = 1¾	75 = 82.02
4 = 113.4	75 = 68.25	100 = 3½	100 = 109.36
	100 = 91.44		

KNITTING NEEDLE SIZES

United States (US)	0	1	2	3	4	5	6	7	8	9	10	10½	11	13	15
Great Britain (GB)	14	13	12	11	10	9	8	7	6	5	4	2	1	00	0000
Metric (MM)	2	2¼	2¾	3	3¼	3¾	4	4½	5	5½	6	7	7½	9	11

CROCHET HOOK SIZES

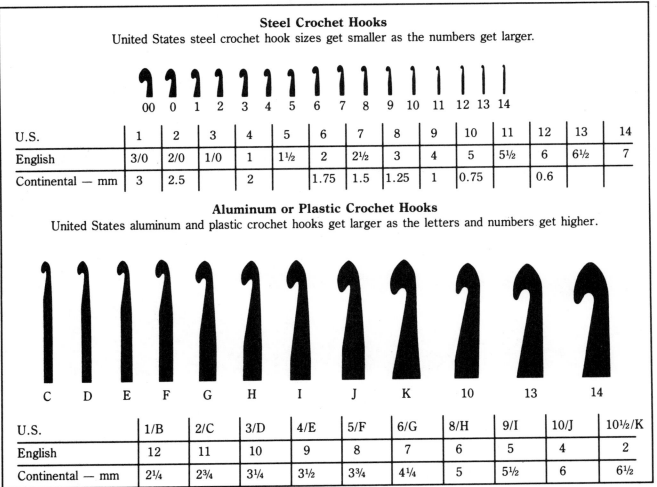

Steel Crochet Hooks
United States steel crochet hook sizes get smaller as the numbers get larger.

U.S.	1	2	3	4	5	6	7	8	9	10	11	12	13	14
English	3/0	2/0	1/0	1	1½	2	2½	3	4	5	5½	6	6½	7
Continental — mm	3	2.5		2		1.75	1.5	1.25	1	0.75		0.6		

Aluminum or Plastic Crochet Hooks
United States aluminum and plastic crochet hooks get larger as the letters and numbers get higher.

U.S.	1/B	2/C	3/D	4/E	5/F	6/G	8/H	9/I	10/J	10½/K
English	12	11	10	9	8	7	6	5	4	2
Continental — mm	2¼	2¾	3¼	3½	3¾	4¼	5	5½	6	6½

WASHING TEMPERATURES

30°C = 86°F	40°C = 104°F	50°C = 122°F	60°C = 140°F	100°C = 212°F
Cooler than body temperature	Slighty above body temperature warm to touch.	Very hot to the touch	Too hot to touch	Boiling

Appendix B: Standard Body Measurements

The charts that follow give the **body measurements** upon which most contemporary patterns are based. Choose that size nearest the actual tape measure reading. Sleeves can always be made shorter or longer. Body length can be adjusted. The chest measure is determined by the number of stiches cast on or by the length of the starting chain, so start with the instructions which have a chest measurement closest to the intended wearer's.

These are minimum body measurements to be used as guidelines for sizing knit and crochet garments. They are not meant, in all cases, to be used as is. Ease for fit and design characteristics must be added. They are based on the voluntary standards of the National Bureau of Standards and are "average." It is still advisable to include in instructions "or to length desired" to allow for individual fit.

BABY

	Newborn 5 to 10 lbs.	6 Month 11 to 18 lbs.	12 Month 19 to 24 lbs.
Chest	to 18″	to 20″	to 22″
Waist	18	19	20
Hip	19	20	21
Back Waist Length	6⅛	6⅞	7½
Across Back	7¼	7¾	8¼
Shoulder	2	2¼	2½
Neck	3¼	3¼	3¼
Sleeve Length to Underarm	6	6½	7½
Armhole Depth	3¼	3½	3¾
Upper Arm Circumference	6½	7	7¼
Wrist Circumference	5	5⅛	5⅛
Head	15	15	16

CHILDREN

	C-2	C-3	C-4	C-5	C-6	C-7	C-8	C-10	C-12
Chest	21	22	23	24	25	26	27	28½	30
Waist	20	20½	21	21½	22	22½	23	24	25
Hip	22	23	24	25	26	27	28	30	32
Back Waist Length	8½	9	9½	10	10½	11½	12½	14	15
Across Back	8¾	9¼	9½	9¾	10¼	10¾	11	11½	12
Shoulder	2¾	3	3	3⅛	3⅜	3½	3⅝	3¾	4
Neck	3¼	3¼	3½	3½	3½	3¾	3¾	4	4
Sleeve Length to Underarm	8½	9½	10½	11	11½	12	12½	13½	15
Armhole Depth	4¼	4¾	5½	5½	6	6	6¼	6½	7
Upper Arm Circumference	7½	7¾	8	8¼	8½	8¾	9	9⅜	9¾
Wrist Circumference	5¼	5¼	5½	5½	5½	5¾	5¾	6	6
Head	17	18							

MISSES

	6	8	10	12	14	16	18
Bust	30½	31½	32½	34	36	38	40
Waist	23	24	25	26½	28	30	32
Hip	32½	33½	34½	36	38	40	42
Back Waist Length	15½	15¾	16	16¼	16½	16¾	17
Across Back	13½	13½	14	14½	15	15½	16
Shoulder	4¾	4¾	5	5	5	5¼	5¼
Neck	4	4	4	4½	5	5	5½
Sleeve Length to Underarm	16¾	16¾	17	17½	17¾	18	18¼
Armhole Depth	7	7	7½	7½	7½	8	8
Upper Arm Circumference	9¾	9¾	10¼	10½	11	11½	12
Wrist Circumference	6	6	6¼	6¼	6½	6½	6½

WOMEN

	38	40	42	44	46	48	50
Bust	42	44	46	48	50	52	54
Waist	35	37	39	41½	44	46½	49
Hip	44	46	48	50	52	54	56
Back Waist Length	17¼	17⅜	17½	17⅝	17¾	17⅞	18
Across Back	16½	17	17½	18	18	18½	18½
Shoulder	5½	5½	5¾	5¾	6	6¼	6¼
Neck	5½	6	6	6	6	6	6
Sleeve Length to Underarm	18¼	18¼	18¼	18¼	18¼	18¼	18¼
Armhole Depth	8¼	8¼	8¼	8½	8½	8¾	8¾
Upper Arm Circumference	13	13½	14	15	15¾	16½	17
Wrist Circumference	6¾	7	7¼	7½	7¾	8	8

MEN

	34	36	38	40	42	44	46	48
Chest	34	36	38	40	42	44	46	48
Waist	28	30	32	34	36	39	42	44
Hip	35	37	39	41	43	45	47	49
Across Back	15½	16	16½	17	17½	18	18½	19
Shoulder	5	5¼	5½	5½	5½	6	6	6
Neck: Shirt Size	14	14½	15	15½	16	16½	17	17½
Length to Armhole	14	14½	15	15½	16	16	16½	17
Armhole Depth	8	8½	9	9½	10	10½	11	11½
Sleeve to Underarm	17½	18	18½	19	19½	20	20	20½
Back Length	22	23	24	25	26	26½	27½	28½

Source: The committee for National Knit and Crochet Standards Simplified Instructions

Appendix C: Manufacturers And Distributors

"Help!" you are sometimes driven to cry. "If I make red and green and white stripes, will the colors run when I wash it?" "Can I carefully hand wash this silk?" "Why am I getting a corkscrew effect?" "Will dry cleaning take the lanolin out of this unscoured wool?"

Sometimes there is lots of information that we need to know that is not printed on the yarn label. And let's face it, we can't keep all the facts about all of the yarns in our heads. There will even be occasions when your local, friendly, and usually very knowledgable retailer won't know the answers to all your questions. Then it will be time to contact the consumer affairs/public relations department of the manufacturer/distributor of the yarn in question.

"This yarn is full of knots, flaws and imperfections and is impossible to work with."

In any system, even under the best of conditions, quality control procedures can break down. No spinner deliberately makes bad yarn. He knows that he wouldn't stay in business if he did. Moreover, the spinner wants to know about it if imperfect yarn is somehow slipping through to the consumer. Let the yarn company know so it can be prevented from happening again.

"Is there a retailer in my area who sells your yarn?"

The manufacturers and distributors listed here will not sell directly to the consumer, but they can direct you to a yarn supplier in your area who retails their product.

If your favorite manufacturer and his yarns are not listed in the *Universal Yarn Finder,* it is not because I didn't try. Every yarn company in the United States and Canada was asked repeatedly by mail and by phone to contribute information about their yarns. If some companies are missing, it was their choice to refuse to give information about their yarns.

Aarlan (USA)
128 Smith Place
Cambridge MA 02138
(800) 343-5080

Aarlan (Canada)
5800 St. Dennis Street, No. 303
Montreal, Ont. H2S 3L5
(514) 274-9475

Andean Yarns
54 Industrial Way
Wilmington MA 01887
(617) 657-7680

Anny Blatt (USA)
Laines Anny Blatt
24770 Crestview Court
Farmington Hills MI 48018
(313) 474-2942

Anny Blatt (Canada)
Diamond Yarns, Inc.
6797 St. Laurence Blvd.
Montreal, Ont. PQ H3L 2N1

Argyll Ltd.
Estelle Designs & Sales Ltd.
38 Continental Place
Scarborough, Ont. M1R 2T4
(800) 387-5167

Astra
Uki Company
541 West 37th Street
New York NY 10018
(800) 221-2795

Au Ver a Soie
Kreinik Manufacturing Co.
PO Box 1996
Parkersburg WV 26101
(800) 624-1928

Aunt Lydia's Rug Yarn
Caron International
Avenue E and First Street
Rochelle NY 61068
(800) 435-2938

Aurora Designs
RFD Box 158
Marlborough NH 03455
(603) 827-3464

Avocet Yarns (USA)
Beth Imports, Inc.
4675 Pickering Road
Birmingham MI 48010
(313) 851-1930

Avocet Yarns (Canada)
Estelle Designs & Sales
38 Continental Place
Scarborough, Ont. M1R 2T4
(800) 387-5167

Balger
Kreinik Manufacturing Co.
PO Box 1996
Parkersburg WV 26101
(800) 624-1928

Bartlettyarns, Inc.
Box 36
Harmony ME 04942
(207) 683-2341

Baruffa
Lane Borgosesia USA Ltd.
RD2, Fields Lane
North Salem NY 10560
(914) 277-8424

Berger du Nord (USA)
Brookman & Sons
12075 NW 39th Street
Coral Springs FL 33065
(800) 327-2770

Berger du Nord (Canada)
Diamond Yarn Co.
153 Ridgeland Avenue, Unit 11
Toronto, Ont. M6A 2Y6
(416) 789-7264

Bernat (USA)
Bernat Yarn & Craft Corp.
Depot and Mendon Streets
Uxbridge MA 01569
(617) 278-2414

Bernat (Canada)
48 Milner Avenue
Scarborough, Ont. M1S 3P8

Berroco
Stanley Berroco
Elmdale Road
Uxbridge MA 01569
(800) 343-4948

Bouquet Yarns
Spinrite Yarns
Box 40
Listowel, Ont. N4W 3H3
(519) 291-3780

Brentwood Yarns
13739 Ventura Blvd.
Sherman Oaks CA 91423
(800) 872-8729

Brown Sheep Co., Inc.
Route 1
Mitchell NB 69357
(308) 635-2198

Brunswick Yarns (USA)
PO Box 276

Pickens SC 29671
(803) 878-6375

Brunswick Yarns (Canada)
S.R. Kertzer
257 Adelaide St. West
Torronto, Ont. M5H 1Y1
(416) 483-5208

Bucilla Company (USA)
150 Meadowland Parkway
Secaucus NJ 07094
(201) 330-9100

Bucilla Yarn (CANADA)
Lamplough Cully
751 Victoria Sq., Suite 206
Montreal, Que. H2Y 2J3
(514) 842-8616

Busse Yarn (USA)
Joan Toggit Ltd.
35 Fairfield Place
West Caldwell NJ 07006
(800) 922-0808

Busse Yarn (Canada)
Gerald Whitaker & Company
12 Keefer Road
St. Catharines, Ont. L2M 7N9
(416) 937-1730

Candide Yarns
Box 407
Woodbury CT 06798
(203) 263-3213

Caron
Caron International
Avenue E and First Street
Rochelle NY 61068
(800) 435-2938

Chanteleine
Crystal Palace Yarns
3006 San Pablo Avenue
Berkeley CA 94702
(800) 227-0323

Charity Hill Farm
Rte. 32, Box 68
Gilbertville MA 01031
(413) 477-6031

Chat Botte
The Armen Corporation
PO Box 8348
Asheville NC 28814
(704) 667-9902

Chester Farms
Route 1
Raphine VA 24472
(703) 377-6633

China Silk Co. Inc.
RD # 5, Box 848-A
Newton NJ 07860
(201) 579-3257

Chinook of Australia
Shepherd Wools, Inc.
PO Box 2027
Blaine WA 98230
(206) 332-8144

Christopher Farms
Maine Maid
13 Bow Street
Freeport ME 04032
(207) 865-9202

Classic Elite Yarns (USA)
12 Perkins Street
Lowell MA 01854
(800) 343-0308

Classic Elite Yarns (Canada)
Gerald H. Whitaker
12 Keefer Road
St. Catharines, Ont. L2M 7N9

Columbia-Minerva
McBess Industries
Box 1240
East Virginia Avenue
Bessemer City NC 28016
(704) 732-0713

Condon's Yarns
Wm. Condon & Sons, Inc.
PO Box 129
Charlottetown, P.E.I. C1A 7K3

Copley USA, Inc.
383 Main Avenue
Norwalk CT 06851
(203) 847-6038

Cotton Clouds
2, Desert Hills # 16
Safford AZ 85546
(602) 428-7000

Country Spun
Box 117
Loganville PA 17342
(717) 428-1162

Creative Yarn
New Jersey Yarn Mills
PO Box 57
Fairview NJ 07022
(201) 943-7529

Crystal Palace Yarns
3006 San Pablo Avenue
Berkeley CA 94702
(800) 227-0323

Di. Ve
RD 2
North Salem NY 10560
(914) 277-8424

DMC (USA)
DMC Corporation
107 Trumbull Street

Elizabeth NJ 07206
(201) 351-4550

DMC (Canada)
Domcord Belding
617 Denison Street
Markham, Ont. L3R 1B8

Dorothee Bis
Knitting Fever, Inc.
180 Babylon Turnpike
Roosevelt NY 11575
(800) 654-3457

Drop Spindle
417 East Central
Santa Maria CA 93454
(805) 922-1295

Dyed in the Wool Ltd.
252 West 37th Street
New York NY 10018
(212) 563-6669

Erdal
Erdal Yarns Ltd.
303 Fifth Avenue, Room 1109
New York NY 10016
(212) 725-0162

Esslinger Wool
Craft World, Inc.
PO Box 779
New Windsor MD 21776
(800) 638-6454

Estelle Yarns
Estelle Designs & Sales Ltd.
38 Continental Place
Scarborough, Ont. M1R 2T4
(800) 387-5167

Fiesta Yarns
PO Box 2548
Corrales NM 87048
(505) 982-9206

Flere Troder, USA
Delaine Worsted Mills
PO Box 951
Gastonia NC 28053
(800) 872-9276

Froehlich Yarns
Renaissance Yarns
PO Box 937
Norwalk CT 06856
(203) 852-8823

Gemini Innovations
720 E. Jericho Turnpike
Huntington Station NY 11746
(516) 549-5650

Giovanni
National Yarn Crafts
183 Madison Avenue
New York NY 10016
(800) 334-0721

Grandor Yarn
Grandor Industries
716 E. Valley Parkway, # 48
Escondido CA 92025
(619) 743-2345

Grignasco
Bell Yarn Company, Inc.
10 Box Street
Brooklyn NY 11222
(718) 389-1904

Halcyon Yarns
12 School Street
Bath ME 04530
(800) 341-0282

Harrisville Designs
Harrisville NH 03450
(603) 827-3332

Hayfield
Shephard Wools, Inc.
PO Box 2027
Blaine WA 98230
(206) 332-8144

Heirloom Yarns
PO Box 239
Rochelle IL 61068
(800) 435-2938

Hovland
Scandinavian House Imports
PO Box 99268
Tacoma WA 98499
(206) 475-3714

Ironstone Wearhouse
PO Box 365
Uxbridge MA 01569
(800) 343-4914

Jack Frost Yarns
Gottlieb Brothers
866 United Nations Plaza
New York NY 10017
(212) 935-5000

Jaeger (USA)
Susan Bates, Inc.
212 Middlesex Avenue
Chester CT 06412
(203) 526-5381

Jaeger (Canada)
Patons & Baldwins
1001 Roselawn Avenue
Toronto, Ont. M6B 1B8
(416) 782-4481

Jaggerspun
Water Street
Springvale ME 04083
(207) 324-4455

Joseph Galler Yarns, Inc. (USA)
27 West 20th Street

New York NY 10011
(212) 620-7190

Joseph Galler Yarns (Canada)
C & H Yarn Enterprises
2320 Truscott Drive
Mississauga, Ont. L5J 2B2

Katia
Knitting Fever, Inc.
180 Babylon Turnpike
Roosevelt NY 11575
(800) 645-3457

Knitting Fever, Inc. (USA)
180 Babylon Turnpike
Roosevelt NY 11575
(800) 645-3457

Knitting Fever (Canada)
Diamond Yarns, Inc.
9697 St. Laurence Blvd.
Montreal PQ H3L 2N1
(514) 384-8726

Lana Moro Yarns, Inc.
260 Fifth Avenue
New York NY 10001
(800) 221-4731

Lanas Margarita, Inc.
Box R, 9 Central Avenue
Island Heights NJ 08732
(201) 929-3232

Lane Borgosesia USA Ltd.
R.D. #2, Fields Lane
North Salem NY 10560
(914) 277-8424

Lee Ward, Inc.
1200 Saint Charles Street
Elgin IL 60120
(312) 888-5789

Lily Craft Products
B. Blumenthal, Inc.
140 Kero Road
Carlstadt NJ 07072
(201) 935-6220

Lion Brand Yarn Co.
1270 Broadway
New York NY 10001
(212) 243-8995

Lisle Yarns
1201 East First Street
Austin TX 78702
(512) 472-1760

Lo-Ran
Dal-Craft, Inc.
PO Box 61
Tucker GA 30084
(404) 939-2894

Lundgren Rya, Inc.
1602 Concord Street

Saxonville MA 01701
(617) 877-2491

Lynn Ellen Yarns, Inc.
Uki, Incorporated
541 West 37th Street
New York NY 10018
(800) 221-2795

Macauslan Yarns
668 Old Toll Road
Madison CT 06443
(203) 421-3084

Malina Company
150 Meadowland Parkway
Secaucus NJ 07094
(201) 330-9100

Manos de Uruguay
Simpson Southwick Co.
421 Hudson Street
New York NY 10014
(212) 620-0053

Mark Yarns
Mark Distributors, Inc.
5239 Commerce Avenue
Moorpark CA 93020
(800) 423-5466

Mary Lue's Inc.
101 West Broadway
St. Peter MN 56082
(507) 931-3702

Mayflower
Scheepjeswool USA, Inc.
155 Lafeyette Avenue North
White Plains NY 10603
(914) 997-8181

Melrose Yarn Company, Inc.
1305 Utica Avenue
Brooklyn NY 11203
(718) 629-0200

Merino Wool Company
230 Fifth Avenue
New York NY 10001
(212) 686-0050

Millor
Knitcraft, Inc.
909 West Lexington
Independence MO 64050
(816) 461-1248

Natura
National Yarn Crafts
183 Madison Avenue
New York NY 10016
(800) 334-0721

Nature Spun Yarns
101 27th Avenue SE
Minneapolis MN 55414
(800) 328-5506

Nomotta Yarns (USA)
Leisure Arts, Inc.
PO Box 5595
Little Rock AR 72215
(800) 643-8030

Nomotta Yarns (Canada)
5800 St. Dennis Street, # 303
Montreal, Ont. H2S 3L5
(514) 274-9475

Nomis Yarn Company
146 Tosca Drive CS-40
Stoughton MA 02072
(617) 344-2673

Noro Yarn
Knitting Fever, Inc.
180 Babylon Turnpike
Roosevelt NY 11575
(800) 645-3457

Offray Knitting Ribbon
Offray & Son, Inc.
Box 601, Route 24
Chester NJ 07930
(201) 879-4700

Ole-Oaxaca Loom Exports
851 Hamilton Avenue
Menlo Park CA 94025
(415) 322-0109

Patons & Baldwins (USA)
Susan Bates, Inc.
212 Middlesex Avenue
Chester CT 06412
(203) 526-5381

Patons & Baldwins (Canada)
1001 Roselawn Ave.
Toronto, Ont. M6B 1B8
(416) 782-4481

Peer Gynt
Norsk Engros USA, Inc.
Box 229
Decorah IA 52101
(319) 382-9431

Peer Gynt
Scandinavian House Imports
PO Box 99268
Tacoma WA 98499
(206) 475-3714

Perendale
Kiwi Imports, Inc.
54 Industrial Way
Wilmington MA 01887
(800) 531-6325

Pernelle
Mark Distributors, Inc.
5239 Commerce Avenue
Moorpark CA 93020
(800) 423-5466

Phentex
Phentex Galleria
6375 Picard
St. Hyacinthe, QC J2S 1H3
(514) 866-4488

Phildar, Inc. (USA)
6438 Dawson Blvd.
Norcross GA 30093
(404) 448-7511

Ping Ling
Kreinik Manufacturing Co.
PO Box 1996
Parkersburg WV 26101
(800) 624-1928

Pingouin
PO Box 100, Highway 45
Jamestown SC 29453
(800) 845-2291

Plymouth Yarn Company, Inc.
500 Lafayette Street
Bristol PA 19007
(215) 788-0459

Rainbow Yarn
Rainbow Mills
5539 Fair Oaks Street
Pittsburgh PA 15217
(412) 422-7012

Red Heart Yarn
Coats & Clark, Inc.
PO Box 6044
Norwalk CT 06852
(800) 241-5997

Reynolds Yarns, Inc.
PO Box 1176
15 Oser Avenue
Hauppauge NY 11788
(516) 582-9330

Reynolds Yarns (Canada)
5800 St. Dennis Street, No. 303
Montreal, ONT H2S 3L5
(514) 274-9475

Richard Poppleton
White Buffalo Mills, Inc.
6365 Kestral Road
Mississauga, Ont. L5T 1S4

Rio Grande Wool Mill
PO Box B
Tres Piedras NM 87577
(505) 758-1818

Rowan Yarns
Estelle Designs & Sales Ltd.
38 Continental Place
Scarborough, Ont. M1R 2T4
(800) 387-5167

Samband of Iceland
Shepherd Wools, Inc.
PO Box 2027

Blaine WA 98230
(206) 332-8144

Santa Fe Yarns
1570 Pacheco Street, Ste. C-1
Santa Fe NM 87501
(505) 982-4798

Schaffhauser Wool (USA)
Qualitat Ltd.
3489 N W Yeon, Bldg. # 3
Portland OR 97210
(503) 222-3022

Schaffhauser Wool (Canada)
White Knitting Products
1470 Birchmount Road
Scarborough, Ont. M1P 2G1

Scheepjeswool USA, Inc.
155 Lafeyette Avenue North
White Plains NY 10603
(914) 997-8181

Scheepjeswool (Canada) Ltd.
400 B Montee de Liesse
Montreal, Que. H4T 1NB
(514) 735-1119

Schoeller Wool
Craft World, Inc.
PO Box 779
New Windsor MD 21776
(800) 638-6454

Scott's Woolen Mill, Inc.
PO Box 1204
528 Jefferson Ave.
Bristol PA 19007
(800) 225-4661

Serendipity Skeins
The Sheepish Grin
40 Fairfield Road
Kingston NJ 08528
(609) 924-9276

Shasha Yarns
Yarnville, Inc.
230 Ferris Avenue
White Plains NY 10603
(914) 997-5653

Silk, Ltd.
350 N. Orleans St., Ste. 1350
Chicago IL 60654
(312) 329-1678

Sirdar Yarns
Kendex Corporation
PO Box 4347
Westlake Village CA 91359
(800) 468-8807

Skinner® Ultrasuede®
Conshohocken Cotton Co.
Ford Bridge Road
Conshohocken PA 19428
(215) 825-4270

Softball Yarn (USA)
Conshohocken Cotton Co.
Ford Bridge Road
Conshohocken PA 19428
(215) 825-4270

Softball Yarn (Canada)
Southern Cross Yarns
49 Spadina Avenue
Toronto, Ont. M5V 2J1
(416) 593-8988

Soie et Soie
Things Japanese
11460 109th Avenue, NE
Kirkland WA 98033
(206) 821-2287

Solberg Yarns
Nor-Min Corporation
405 Washington Street
Brainerd MN 56401
(218) 828-4332

Spinnerin Yarns
Craft World, Inc.
PO Box 779
New Windsor MD 21776
(800) 638-6454

Spring Brook Yarn
Ware Novelty Spinner
Box 630, East Street
Ware MA 01082
(413) 967-4572

Stardust Yarns
Henry Seligman Company
2337 McDonald Avenue
Brooklyn NY 11223
(718) 336-6262

Sunbeam Yarns
Estelle Designs & Sales Ltd.
38 Continental Place
Scarborough, Ont. M1R 2T4
(800) 387-5167

Susan Bates (USA)
212 Middlesex Avenue
Chester CT 06412
(203) 526-5381

Susan Bates (Canada)
Patons & Baldwins
1001 Roselawn Avenue
Toronto, Ont. M6B 1B8

Swiss Straw
Artis, Inc.
Box A
Solvang CA 93463
(805) 688-7339

Tahki (USA)
Tahki Imports, Inc.
92 Kennedy Street

Hackensack NJ 07601
(201) 489-9505

Tahki (Canada)
Gerald Whitaker & Company
12 Keefer Road
St. Catharines, Ont. L2M 7N9
(416) 937-1730

Tamm Yarns
Jary, Inc.
8562 Katy Freeway
Suite 154
Houston TX 77024
(713) 465-2515

Tandorri
Kreinik Manufacturing Co.
PO Box 1996
Parkersburg WV 26101
(800) 624-1928

Tish and Amy
Tish & Amy Originals, Inc.
5306 10th Avenue, East
Tuscaloosa AL 35405
(205) 758-1351

Unger Yarn (USA)
William Unger & Company
230 Fifth Avenue
New York NY 10001
(800) 223-7526

Unger Yarn (Canada)
Bell Tootal, Inc.
PO Box 999
Arthur, Ont. N06 1A0

Welcomme (USA)
Laninter Corporation
P.O. Box 300
Highway 45
Jamestown, S.C. 29453
(800) 845-2291

Welcomme & Parnelle (Canada)
Craftsmen Distributors Ltd.
4166 Halifax Street
Burnaby, B.C. V5C 3X2

Wendy Yarn
White Buffalo Mills
6365 Kestral Road
Mississauga, Ont. L5T 1S4

White Buffalo Mills
Peace Bridge Plaza
Suite 211
Buffalo NY 14213
(416) 673-7676

Whitin Yarns
PO Box 937
Norwalk CT 06856
(203) 852-8823

Wilde Yarns
John Wilde & Brothers, Inc.

3737 Main Street
Philadelphia PA 19127
(215) 482-8800
Yarn Country
Newton's Knits
3969 East LaPalma
Anaheim CA 92807
(714) 632-9860

Yarns by Mills
Box 28
Wallback WV 25282
(304) 587-2561
Yarns Galore
5711 Kennedy Blvd.
North Bergen NJ 07047
(201) 869-6300

Glossary

Acrilan®. Registered trademark for acrylic fiber manufactured by Monsanto.

Acrylic. A man-made fiber in which the fiber-forming substance is a long chain synthetic polymer composed of at least 85% by weight of acrylonitrile units. It is noted for its bulk, loft, warmth, and wool-like aesthetics in knit fabrics.

Alpaca. An animal, domesticated in Peru, that has fine, long, wooly hair. Fleece from an alpaca.

Alpaga. Alternate spelling of "alpaca."

Ball. A way in which yarn is "put-up" in specified amounts for retail sale. Often used for small amounts of yarn.

Bouclé. A type of yarn that has small nubs or loops spaced at regular intervals. It results in a lovely fabric that looks like crepe.

Bri-nylon. An abbreviation for "Bringy Nylon."

Bright nylon. Nylon fiber that has had no delusterant applied to it. It is a very lustrous fiber.

Bulky yarn. Class D yarn. See page 000.

Cabled yarn. Yarn that is spun in such a way that it appears to have been knitted into a cable. It looks rather funny on the skein, but it works up beautifully.

cm. An abbreviation for centimeter.

Comfort 12. A certification mark for a DuPont acrylic fiber that has aesthetics similar to cotton.

Cone. A way in which large amounts of yarn are "put-up" for sale, often weighing a pound or more.

Courtelle. A trade mark of fiber made by Cortaulds, an English manufacturing company.

Dye lot and **dye lot number.** Terms that are used to denote a quantity of yarn that was all dyed the same color at the same time. Color may vary from one dye lot to another.

Felt. A process (on purpose or by accident) of applying steam, heat, or pressure to woolen fibers which causes them to mat together and become stiff and firm, as in a felt hat.

Filament silk. A very long, continuous strand of silk that has been carefully unwound from a cocoon without breakage.

Fingering yarn. Class A yarn. A light weight yarn often used to make socks. See page 000.

Fisherman. Wool that is "unscoured" or unwashed, leaving the natural lanolin in it to make it water repellent.

Flax. The fiber of the flax plant. The finished thread of fabric is called "linen."

Gauge. The number of stitches and rows there are in a measured square of fabric. Gauge is sometimes given for 1 inch, 2 inches, or 4 inches (which is 10 centimeters). Usually written something like "6 st = 1" or "22 m = 10 cm."

gm(s). An abbreviation for "gram(s)."

gr(s). An abbreviation for "grain(s)." 15.43 grains = 1 gram.

Hand. A term used to describe the way a yarn feels as it runs through your fingers. Yarn with a "good hand" will fairly float through your fingers and feel smooth and fluid. Yarn with a "poor hand" will be stiff and will feel hard. Also refers to tactile aesthetics of completed knit garments.

Hank. A term manufacturers use to denote how yarn is "put-up" for retail sale. Hanked yarn must be wound into a ball before it can be used. Also sometimes refered to as a "skein."

Heather. Yarn containing a combination of colored fibers, spun and dyed in such a way as to give it a lovely glowing and soft spectrum of color shadings.

Heavy weight yarn. Class C. See page 000.

Homespun. Can mean yarn that is spun by hand, or yarn that looks as if it were. Yarn that has alternate thick and thin places in it at more or less regular intervals.

Kid. Yarn made from the first shearing of an animal that is less than one year old. It is soft like baby hair.

Linen. Thread or fabric made from fibers from the flax plant.

Loft. The amount of trapped air in a yarn. Good loft means high bulk and springiness.

m. An abbreviation for a French word meaning stitch. Also an abbreviation for "meter(s)."

Mercerized. Yarn that has been treated by a chemical process to make it both stronger and glossy.

Merino. A breed of sheep that produces soft, fine yarn.

Nap. Refers to the direction in which the individual hairs are laid in the spinning of the yarn. Knitters and crocheters will want to work with, rather than against the nap of the yarn.

Nub. Blobs or nebs of material in a yarn that give it an interesting textured effect.

Nylon. The generic term for man-made fibers composed of long chain synthetic polyamides derived from coal and petroleum. It is noted for its high strength, elasticity and abrasion resistance.

Olefin. A generic term for both polyethylene and polypropoline fibers.

Ombré. A term used to describe yarns which are dyed in multicolored or multishaded hues and tones.

Orlon ®. A registered trademark for acrylic fiber manufactured by DuPont.

oz. An abbreviation for ounce.

Perle. A loosely twisted Mercerized cotton thread. It has a high gloss and good wearing characteristics.

Perlon. A private trademark of nylon fiber.

Ply. A verb meaning to twist strands together. Also means the number of threads that are twisted together to form a single strand of yarn. An example might be 4-Ply or 12-Ply yarn. In today's world the term is meaningless in trying to figure out how thick a yarn is.

Polyester. A generic term for man-made fibers made of ethylene glycol and terepthalic acid. It is noted for crease-resistance, minimum care, quick-drying and good shape retention in garment form.

Quality. Synonymous with "name". A European term that is used to differentiate the various "names of yarn" that a manufacturer makes.

Ramie. A natural fiber that comes from the outer layers of the flax plant. A type of linen.

Rayon. A generic term for man-made fibers composed of regenerated cellulose derived from cotton linters and/or wood pulp. Thread or yarn made from "viscose."

Resilience. The ability of a yarn to stretch and snap back to the original length and shape.

Roving. Untwisted yarn. Yarn made by laying down strands of fiber without twisting them together.

"Sayelle." A certification mark of Orlon bicomponent fiber manufactured by DuPont.

Shetland. A breed of sheep. The wool is strong and warm, but somewhat scratchy.

Skein. A term used by manufacturers to describe the way yarn is "put-up" for retail sale. Many skeins are intended to be used from the inside out.

Slubbed. A marvelous kind of novelty yarn that has blobs in it. Often the blobs are of different colors or textures than the strand.

Solana. Monsanto's trademark for producer colored acrylic fiber.

Sport weight. Class B yarn. See page 000.

Super yarn or **super bulky.** Class D yarn. See page 000.

Targhee. A breed of sheep developed in the United States noted for it's fine quality wool. Wool from a targhee sheep.

Tension. A term that has two meanings. Tension is synonymous for "gauge" in many European instruction books. The word also means "flow" or "finished appearance," as in: "It has an uneven and irregular tension."

Tubular yarn. Yarn that has been made by knitting a number of strands into a hollow tube—as a round, flat ribbon.

Tussah. Thread from wild silkworms.

Tweed. A course, rugged and often nubby yarn used to make sportswear. Frequently multicolored.

Unscoured. Yarn from which the lanolin has not been removed. It is water repellant and smells like wet sheep. Also, man-made yarns, i.e. acrylic, which have not had the finish removed.

Vinyon. Man-made fiber produced from polyethelene.

Virgin. Thread that has never been used for any other purpose before. Not reclaimed.

Viscose. One of the processes used to manufacture rayon. Fiber made from cellulose which has been treated with a caustic alkali solution and carbon disulfide.

Waxed yarn. Yarn that has been specially treated to cause it to have better flow when worked on a knitting machine.

Wintuk ®. Registered certification mark of DuPont for acrylic yarns and fabrics made of monocomponent and bicomponent acrylic fibers of Orlon.

Wool. Technically the term *could* mean fiber from any fur bearing animal. Usually it means only the fiber from sheep, and that is the way it is used in the "Fiber Content" column.

Worsted. Twisted. "Worsted yarn" is a smooth classic yarn that has been twisted in the spinning process. Worsted yarns are prepared from fibers of longer length compared to cotton yarns.

Zephyr yarn. A light weight yarn that is soft as a gentle breeze.

Coats + Clark   Luster Sheen (100% creslan [acrylic fiber])
23. skeins   #5 needles in stockinette   6 st = 1"; 8 rows = 1"

Bedspread-weight cotton thread such as:
    J&P Coats "Knit-Cro-Sheen" / American Thread Giant / Grandma's Best
    Susan Bates "Fashion-Tone Mercerized Cotton / Bucilla Wondersheen
    DMC "Cebelia Size 10" / DMC Baroque, Article 158 / South Maid

J&P Coats   Best 6 Cord – Big Ball Crochet
    size 20 – 300 yds.

Clarks 3 cord Big Ball
    size 30 – 500 yds.

Perle Cotton Crochet #8   OR   Crochet Cotton #40
Pearl Cotton Crochet #5   OR   Crochet Cotton #10
Pearl Cotton Crochet #12 OR   possibly size 80